ROYAL CITY™

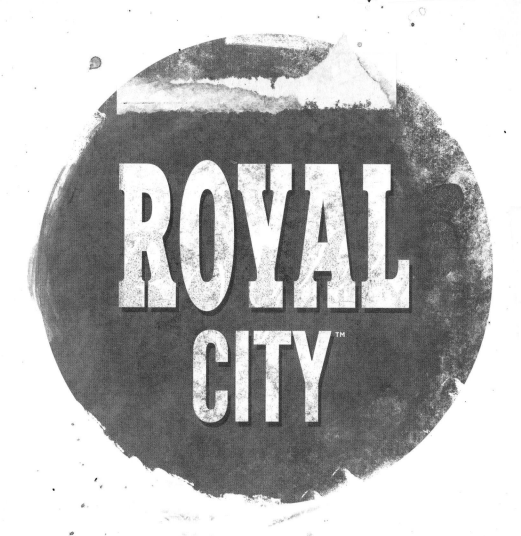

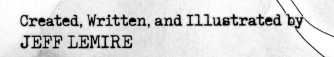

Created, Written, and Illustrated by
JEFF LEMIRE

Lettered by STEVE WANDS

Special Thanks to
RYAN BREWER,
WILL DENNIS

ROYAL CITY, VOL. 3: WE ALL FLOAT ON. First printing. October 2018. Published by Image Comics, Inc. Office of publication: 2701 NW Vaughn St., Suite 780, Portland, OR 97210. Copyright © 2018 171 Studios, Inc. All rights reserved. Contains material originally published in single magazine form as ROYAL CITY #11-14. "Royal City," its logos, and the likenesses of all characters herein are trademarks of 171 Studios, Inc., unless otherwise noted. "Image" and the Image Comics logos are registered trademarks of Image Comics, Inc. No part of this publication may be reproduced or transmitted, in any form or by any means (except for short excerpts for journalistic or review purposes), without the express written permission of 171 Studios, Inc. or Image Comics, Inc. All names, characters, events, and locales in this publication are entirely fictional. Any resemblance to actual persons (living or dead), events, or places, without satiric intent, is coincidental. Printed in the USA. For information regarding the CPSIA on this printed material call: 203-595-3636 and provide reference #RICH-815923. For international rights, contact: foreignlicensing@imagecomics.com. ISBN: 978-1-5343-0849-7.

IMAGE COMICS, INC. • Robert Kirkman—Chief Operating Officer • Erik Larsen—Chief Financial Officer • Todd McFarlane—President • Marc Silvestri—Chief Executive Officer • Jim Valentino—Vice President • Eric Stephenson—Publisher / Chief Creative Officer • Corey Hart—Director of Sales • Jeff Boison—Director of Publishing Planning & Book Trade Sales • Chris Ross—Director of Digital Sales • Jeff Stang—Director of Specialty Sales • Kat Salazar—Director of PR & Marketing • Drew Gill—Art Director • Heather Doornink—Production Director • Nicole Lapalme—Controller • **IMAGECOMICS.COM**

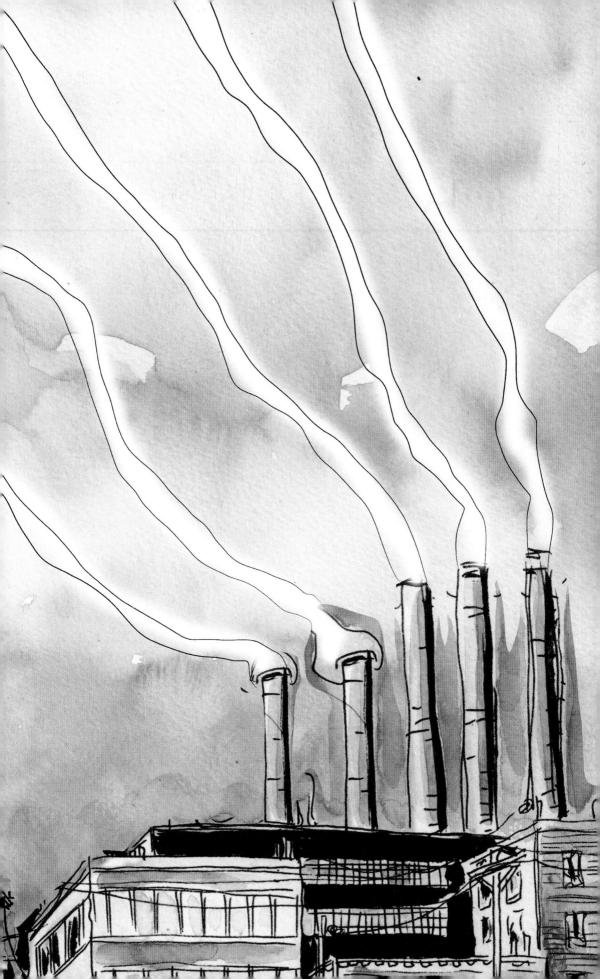

CHAPTER ELEVEN

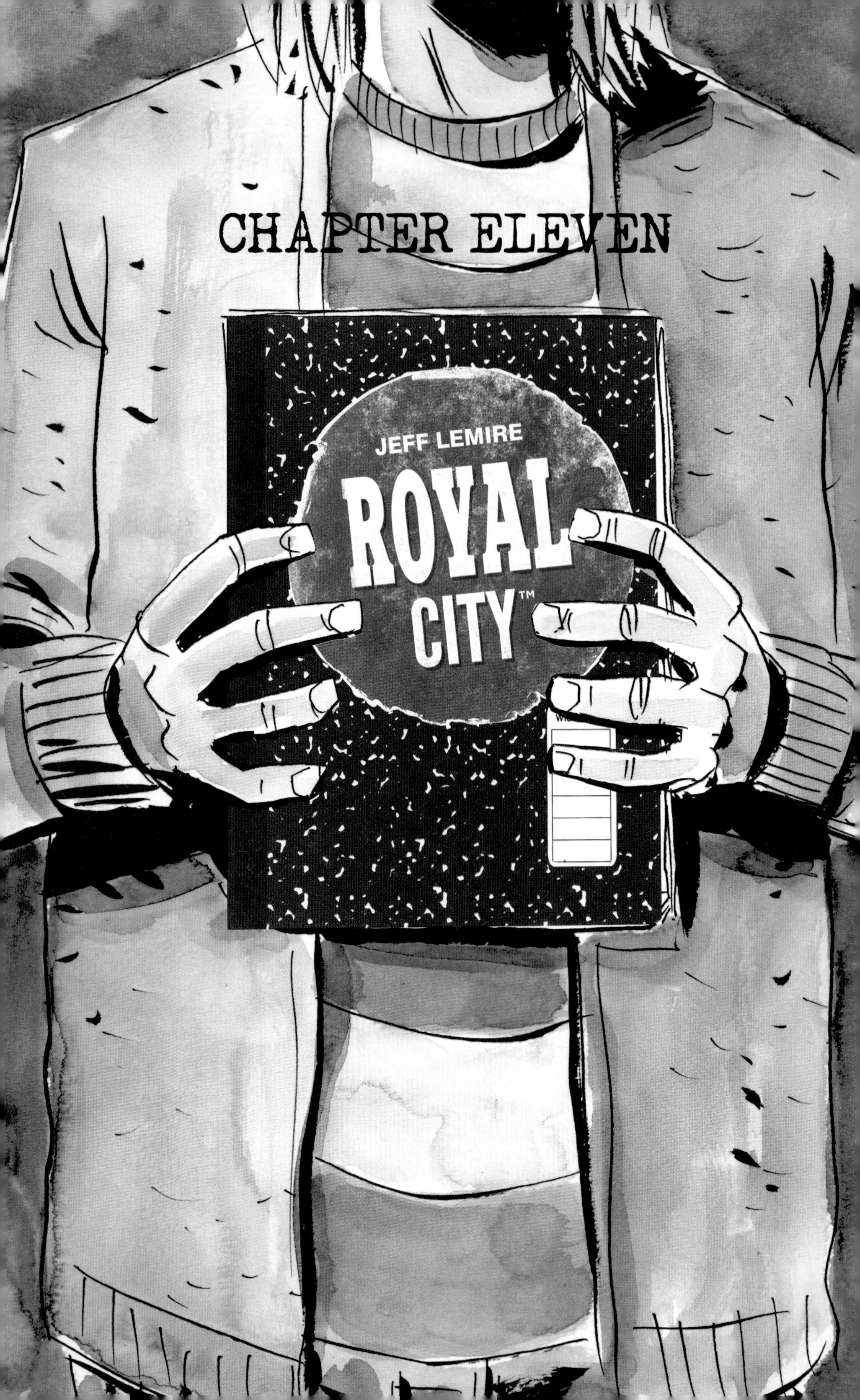
JEFF LEMIRE
ROYAL CITY™

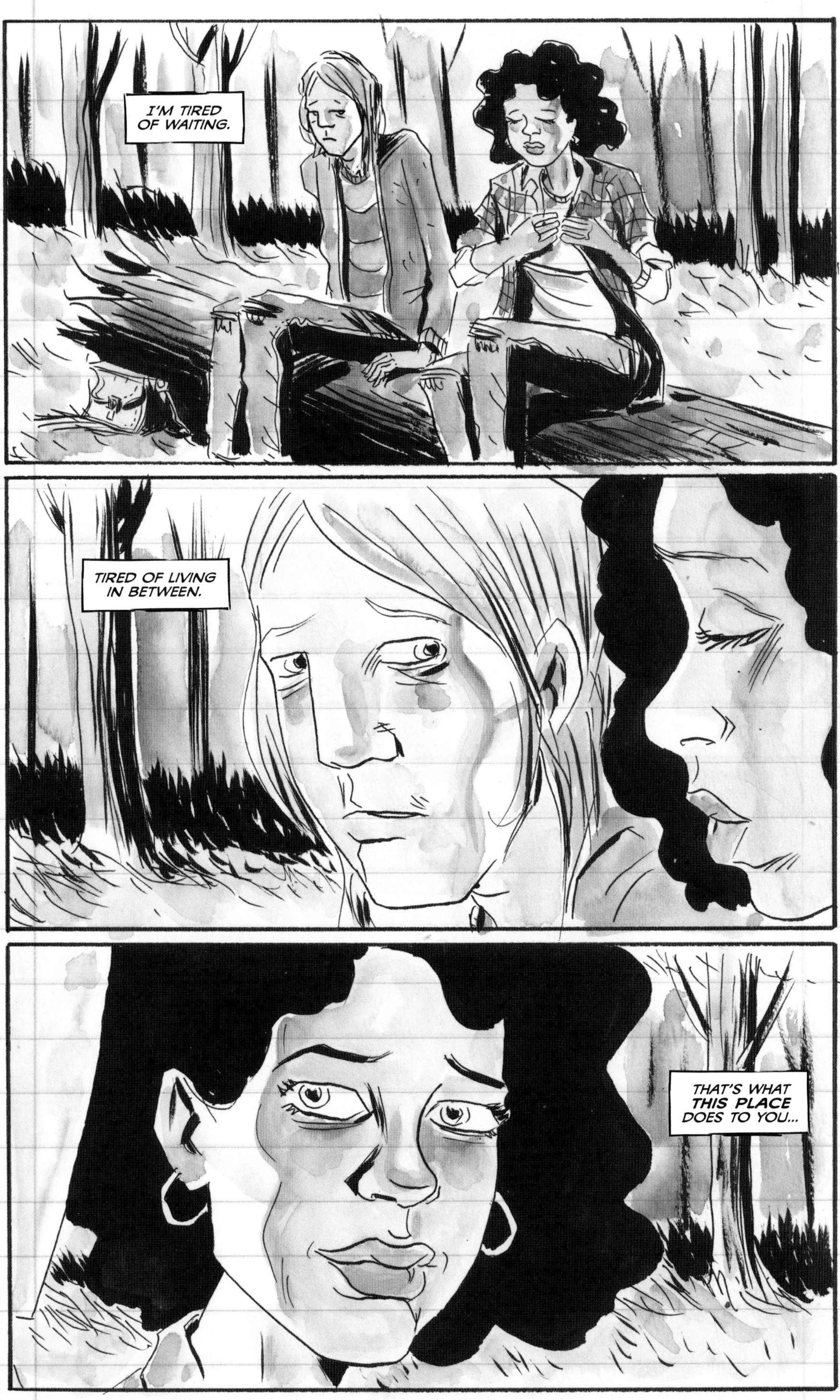
I'M TIRED OF WAITING.
TIRED OF LIVING IN BETWEEN.
THAT'S WHAT THIS PLACE DOES TO YOU...

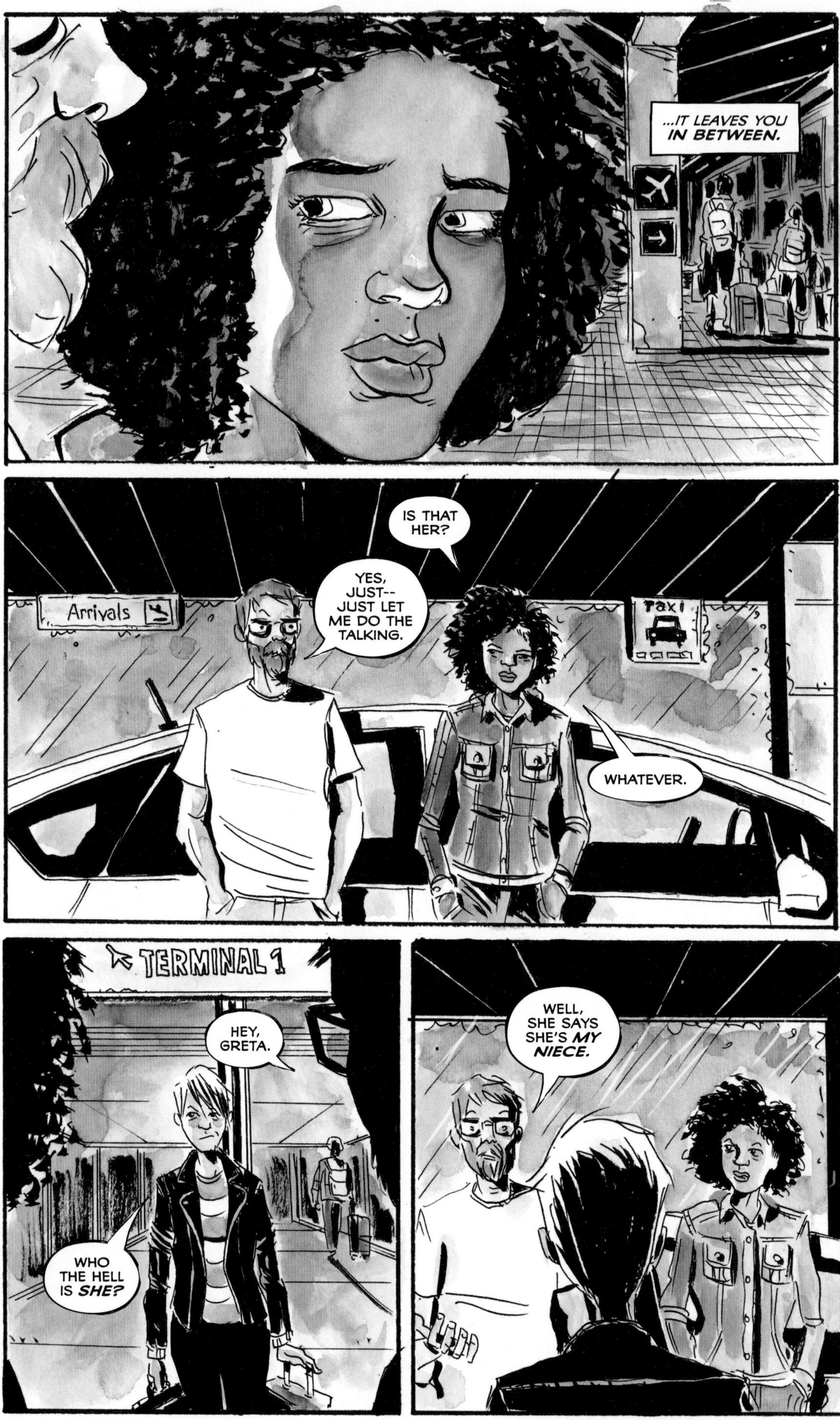
...IT LEAVES YOU IN BETWEEN.
IS THAT HER?
YES, JUST-- JUST LET ME DO THE TALKING.
Arrivals
Taxi
WHATEVER.
TERMINAL 1
HEY, GRETA.
WHO THE HELL IS SHE?
WELL, SHE SAYS SHE'S MY NIECE.

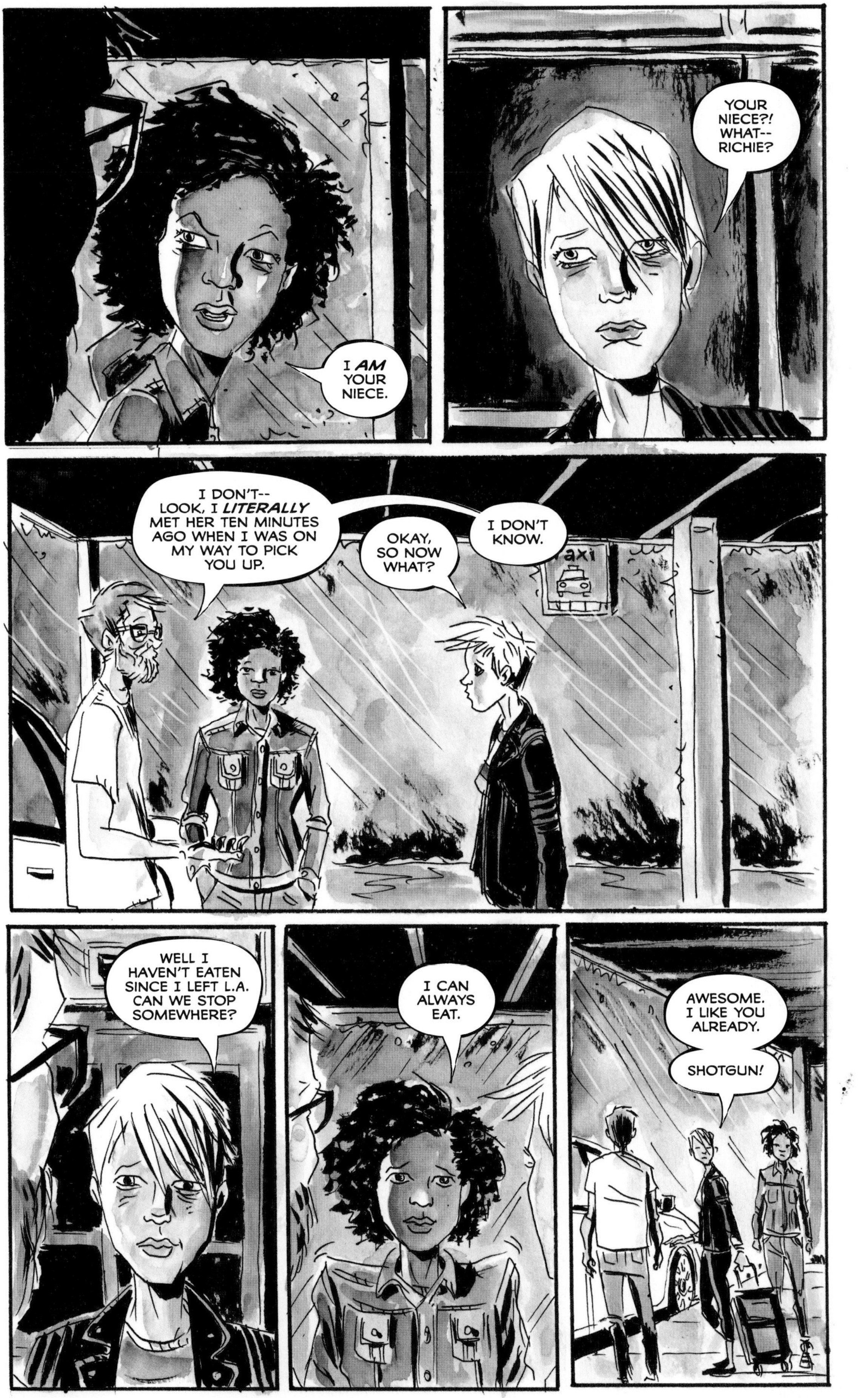
I AM YOUR NIECE.
YOUR NIECE?! WHAT-- RICHIE?
I DON'T-- LOOK, I LITERALLY MET HER TEN MINUTES AGO WHEN I WAS ON MY WAY TO PICK YOU UP.
OKAY, SO NOW WHAT?
I DON'T KNOW.
TAXI
WELL I HAVEN'T EATEN SINCE I LEFT L.A. CAN WE STOP SOMEWHERE?
I CAN ALWAYS EAT.
AWESOME. I LIKE YOU ALREADY.
SHOTGUN!

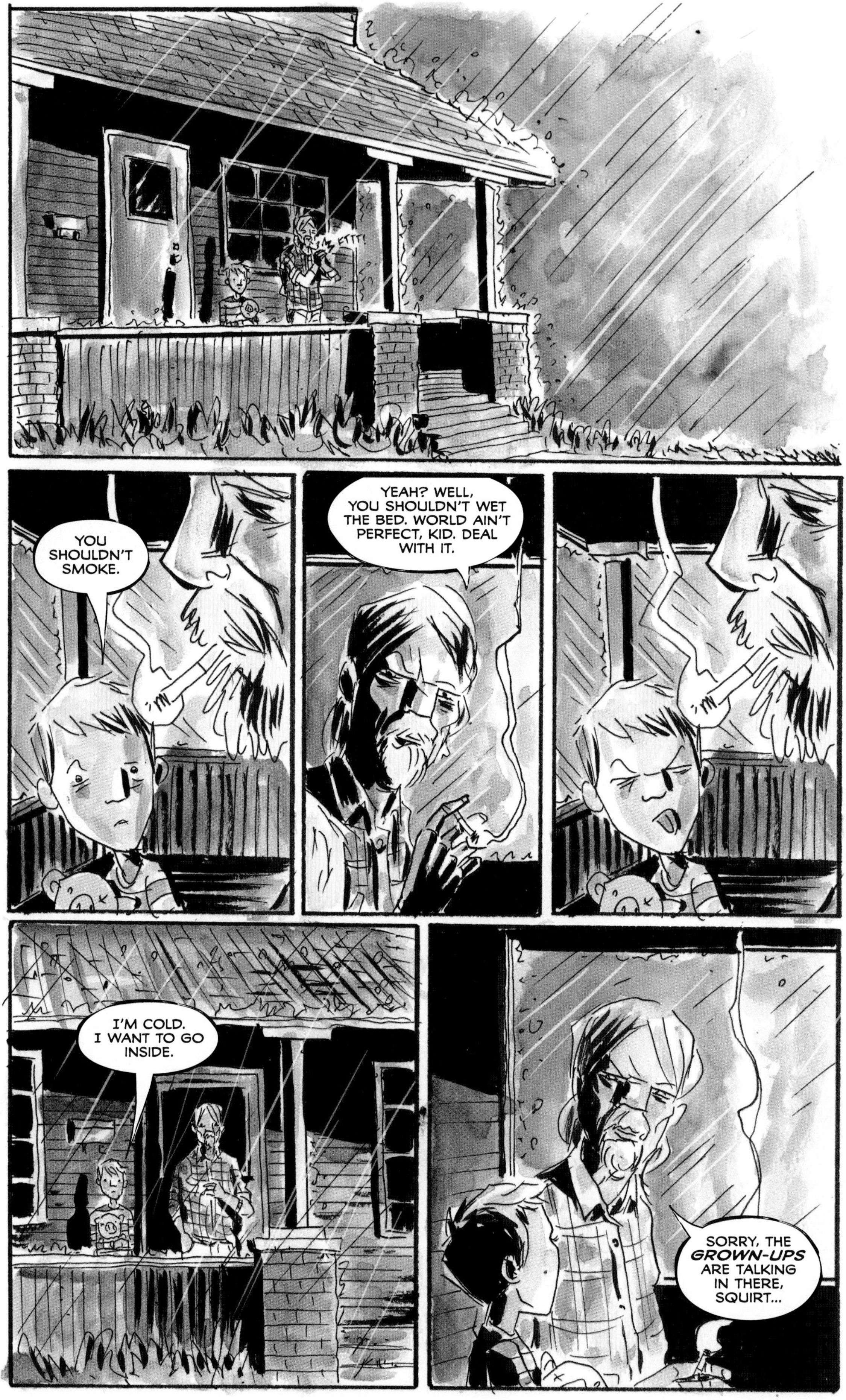
YOU SHOULDN'T SMOKE.
YEAH? WELL, YOU SHOULDN'T WET THE BED. WORLD AIN'T PERFECT, KID. DEAL WITH IT.
I'M COLD. I WANT TO GO INSIDE.
SORRY, THE *GROWN-UPS* ARE TALKING IN THERE, SQUIRT...

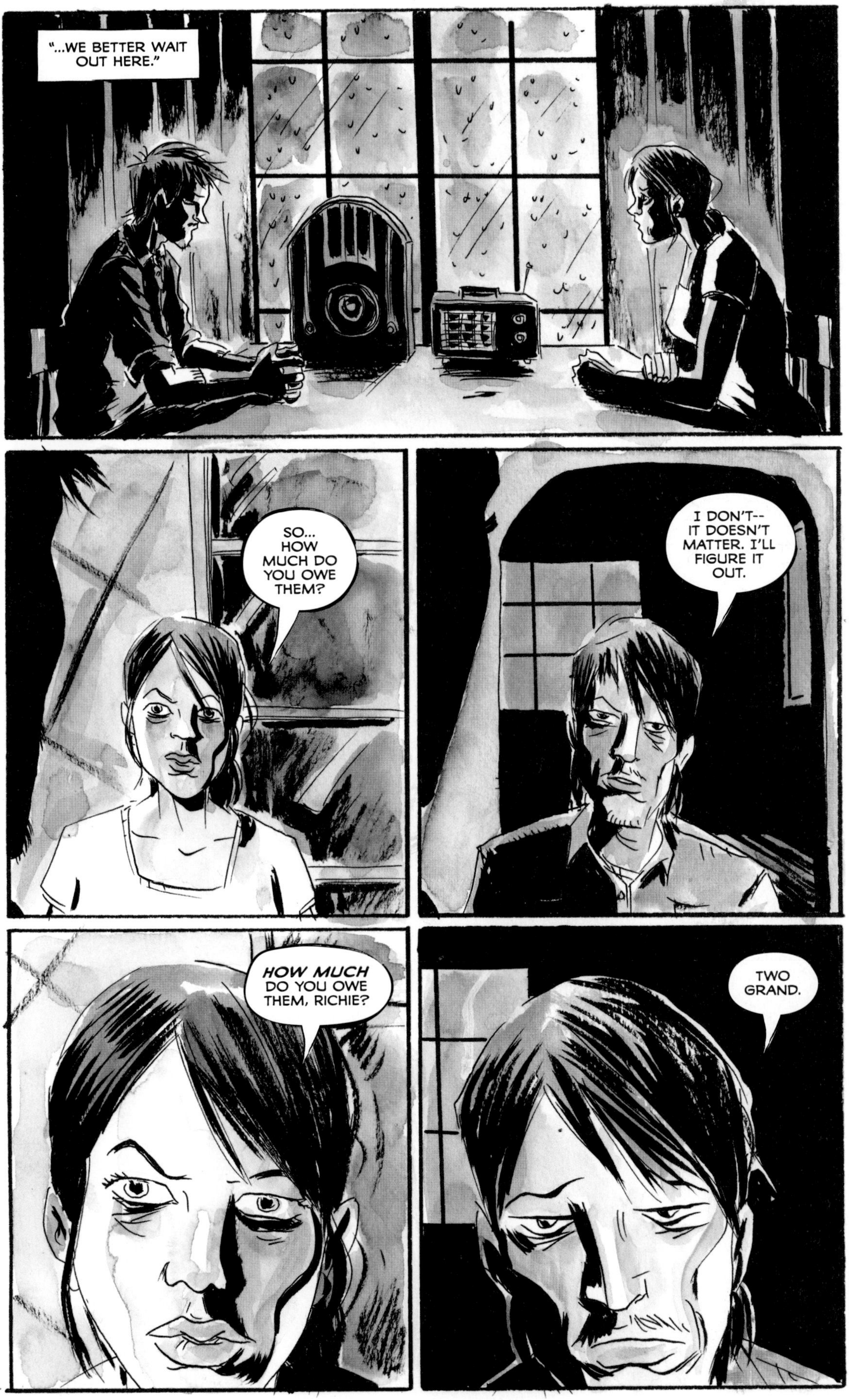
"...WE BETTER WAIT OUT HERE."
SO... HOW MUCH DO YOU OWE THEM?
I DON'T-- IT DOESN'T MATTER. I'LL FIGURE IT OUT.
HOW MUCH DO YOU OWE THEM, RICHIE?
TWO GRAND.

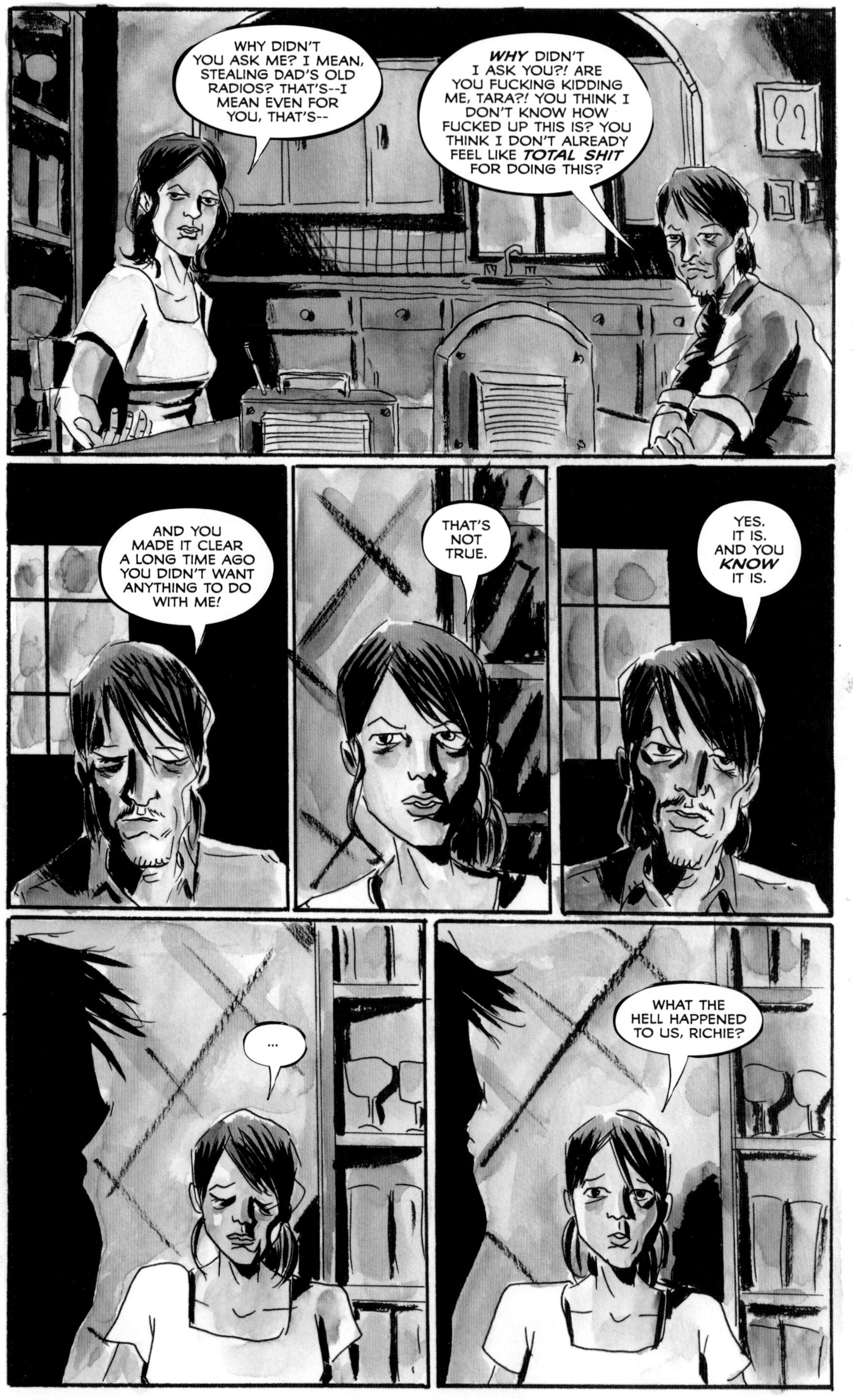
WHY DIDN'T YOU ASK ME? I MEAN, STEALING DAD'S OLD RADIOS? THAT'S--I MEAN EVEN FOR YOU, THAT'S--
WHY DIDN'T I ASK YOU?! ARE YOU FUCKING KIDDING ME, TARA?! YOU THINK I DON'T KNOW HOW FUCKED UP THIS IS? YOU THINK I DON'T ALREADY FEEL LIKE TOTAL SHIT FOR DOING THIS?
AND YOU MADE IT CLEAR A LONG TIME AGO YOU DIDN'T WANT ANYTHING TO DO WITH ME!
THAT'S NOT TRUE.
YES. IT IS. AND YOU KNOW IT IS.
...
WHAT THE HELL HAPPENED TO US, RICHIE?

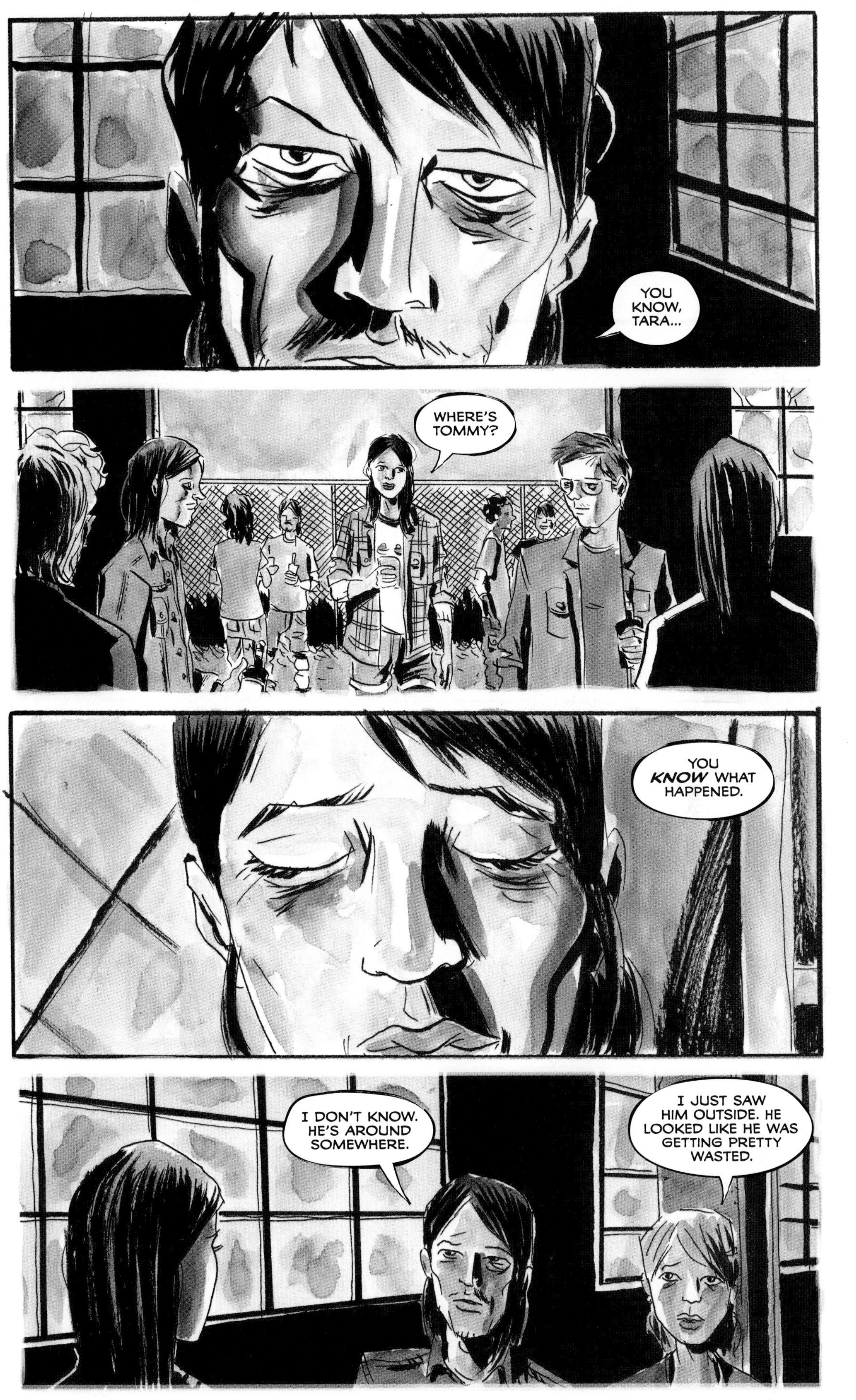
YOU KNOW, TARA...
WHERE'S TOMMY?
YOU *KNOW* WHAT HAPPENED.
I DON'T KNOW. HE'S AROUND SOMEWHERE.
I JUST SAW HIM OUTSIDE. HE LOOKED LIKE HE WAS GETTING PRETTY WASTED.

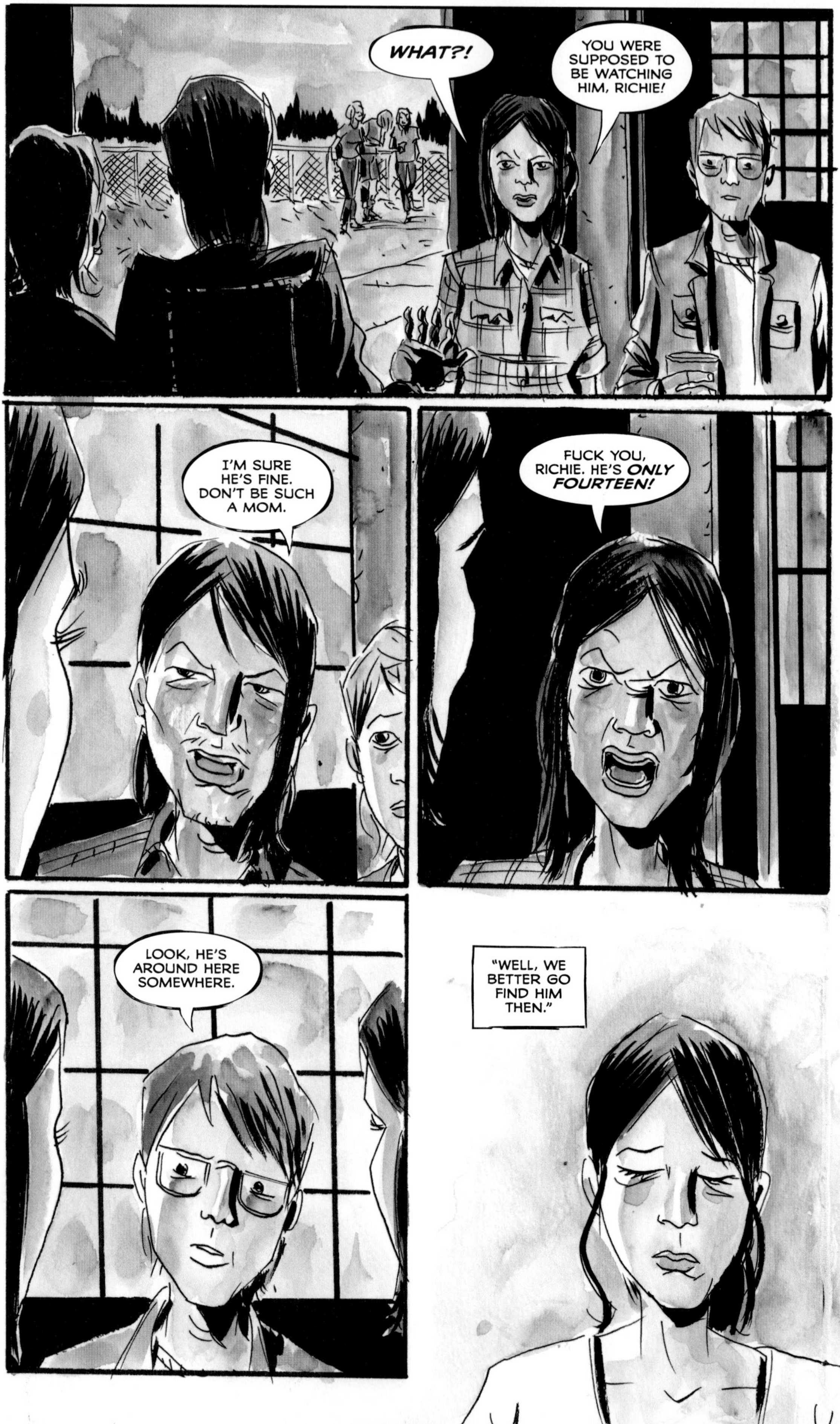
WHAT?!
YOU WERE SUPPOSED TO BE WATCHING HIM, RICHIE!
I'M SURE HE'S FINE. DON'T BE SUCH A MOM.
FUCK YOU, RICHIE. HE'S ONLY FOURTEEN!
LOOK, HE'S AROUND HERE SOMEWHERE.
"WELL, WE BETTER GO FIND HIM THEN."

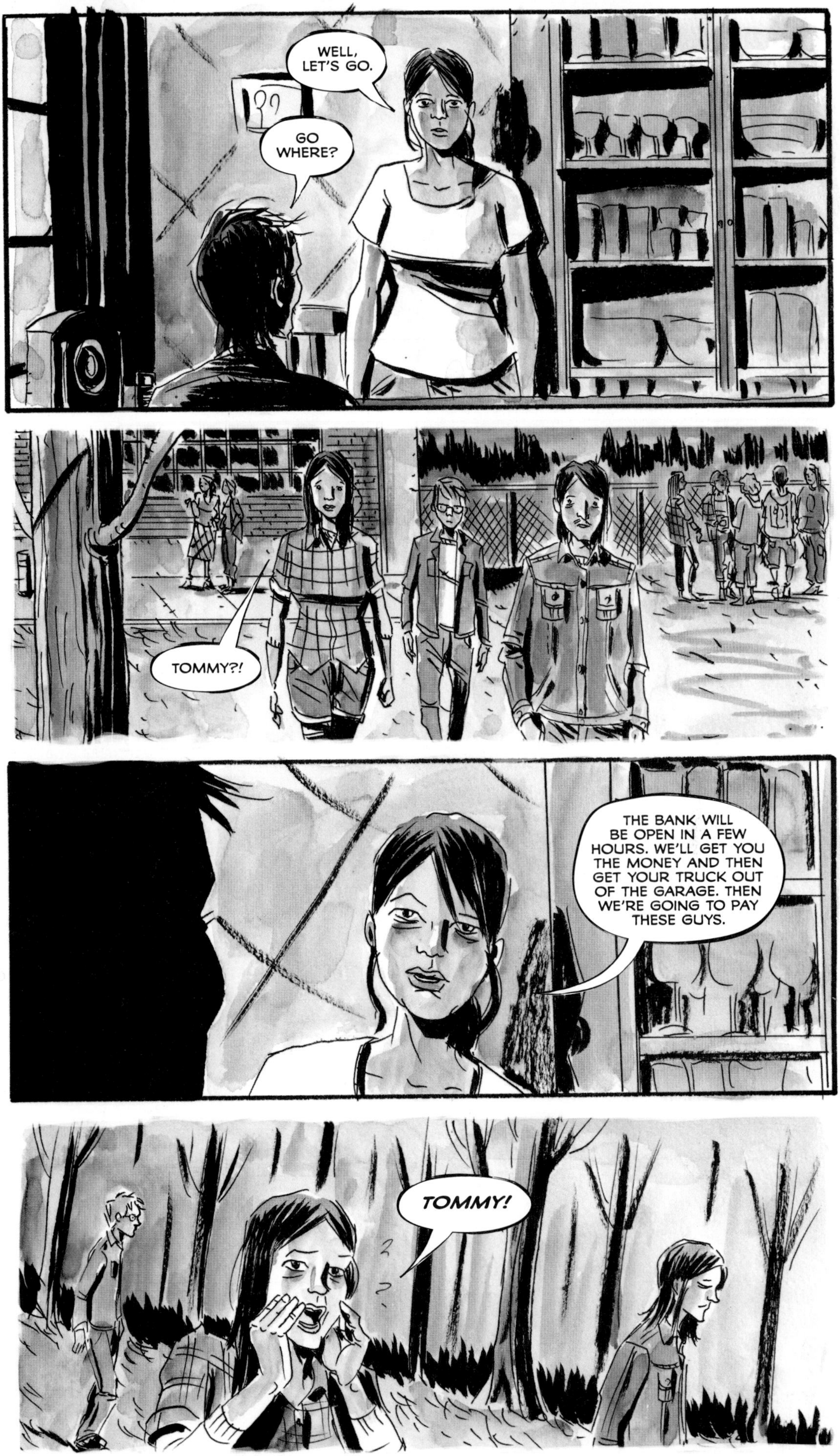
WELL, LET'S GO.
GO WHERE?
TOMMY?!
THE BANK WILL BE OPEN IN A FEW HOURS. WE'LL GET YOU THE MONEY AND THEN GET YOUR TRUCK OUT OF THE GARAGE. THEN WE'RE GOING TO PAY THESE GUYS.
TOMMY!

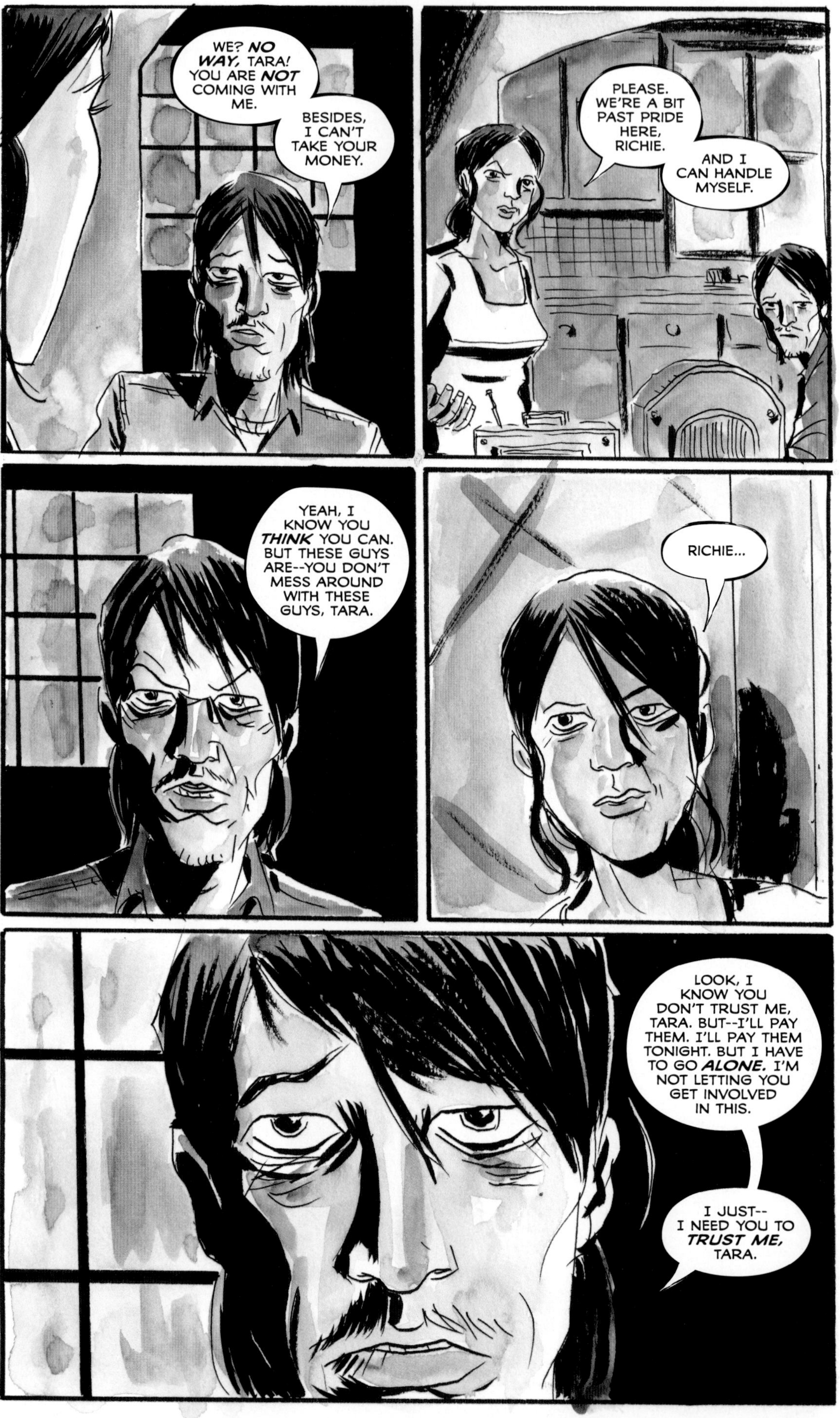
WE? NO WAY, TARA! YOU ARE NOT COMING WITH ME.
BESIDES, I CAN'T TAKE YOUR MONEY.
PLEASE. WE'RE A BIT PAST PRIDE HERE, RICHIE.
AND I CAN HANDLE MYSELF.
YEAH, I KNOW YOU THINK YOU CAN. BUT THESE GUYS ARE--YOU DON'T MESS AROUND WITH THESE GUYS, TARA.
RICHIE...
LOOK, I KNOW YOU DON'T TRUST ME, TARA. BUT--I'LL PAY THEM. I'LL PAY THEM TONIGHT. BUT I HAVE TO GO ALONE. I'M NOT LETTING YOU GET INVOLVED IN THIS.
I JUST-- I NEED YOU TO TRUST ME, TARA.

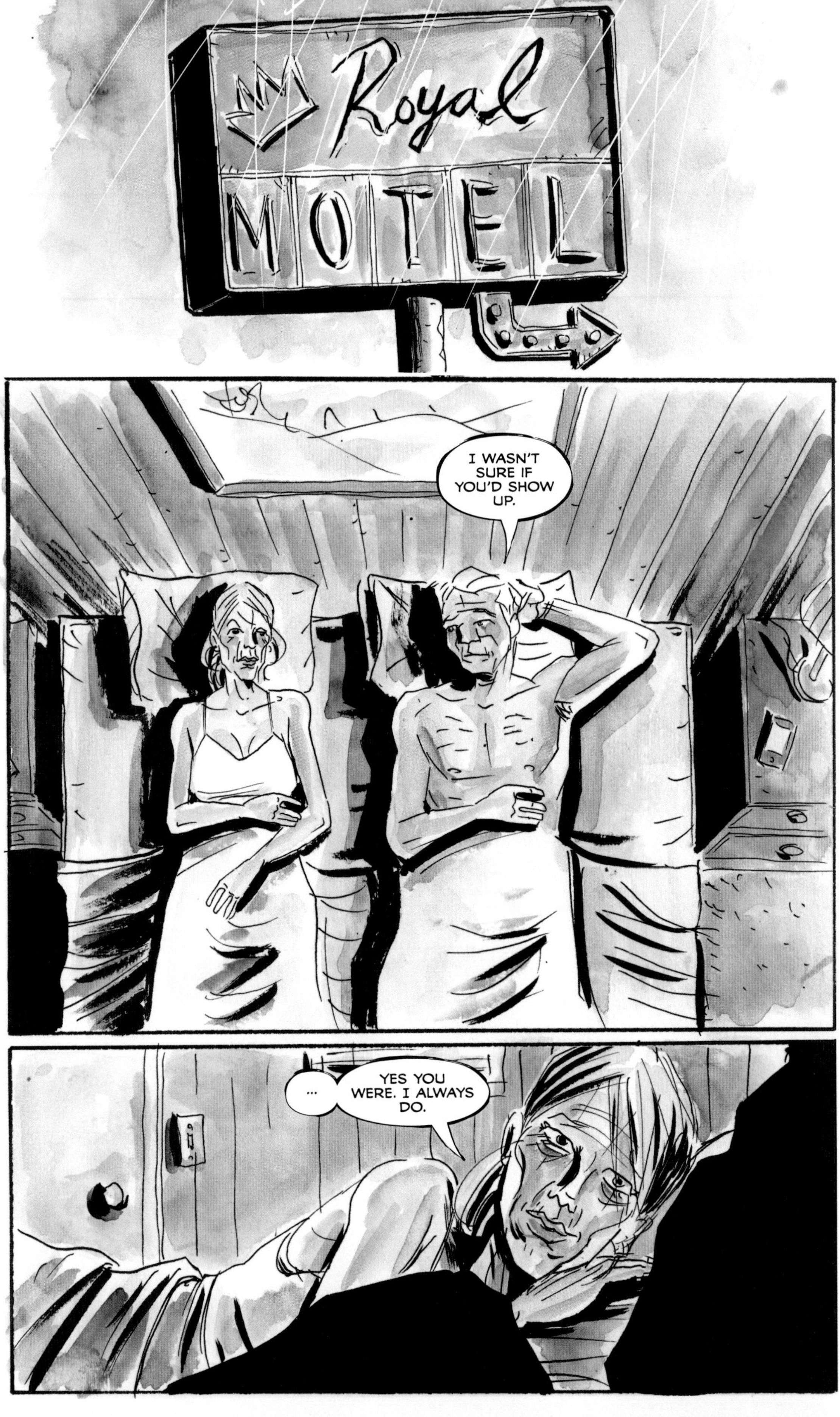
Royal
MOTEL
I WASN'T SURE IF YOU'D SHOW UP.
...
YES YOU WERE. I ALWAYS DO.

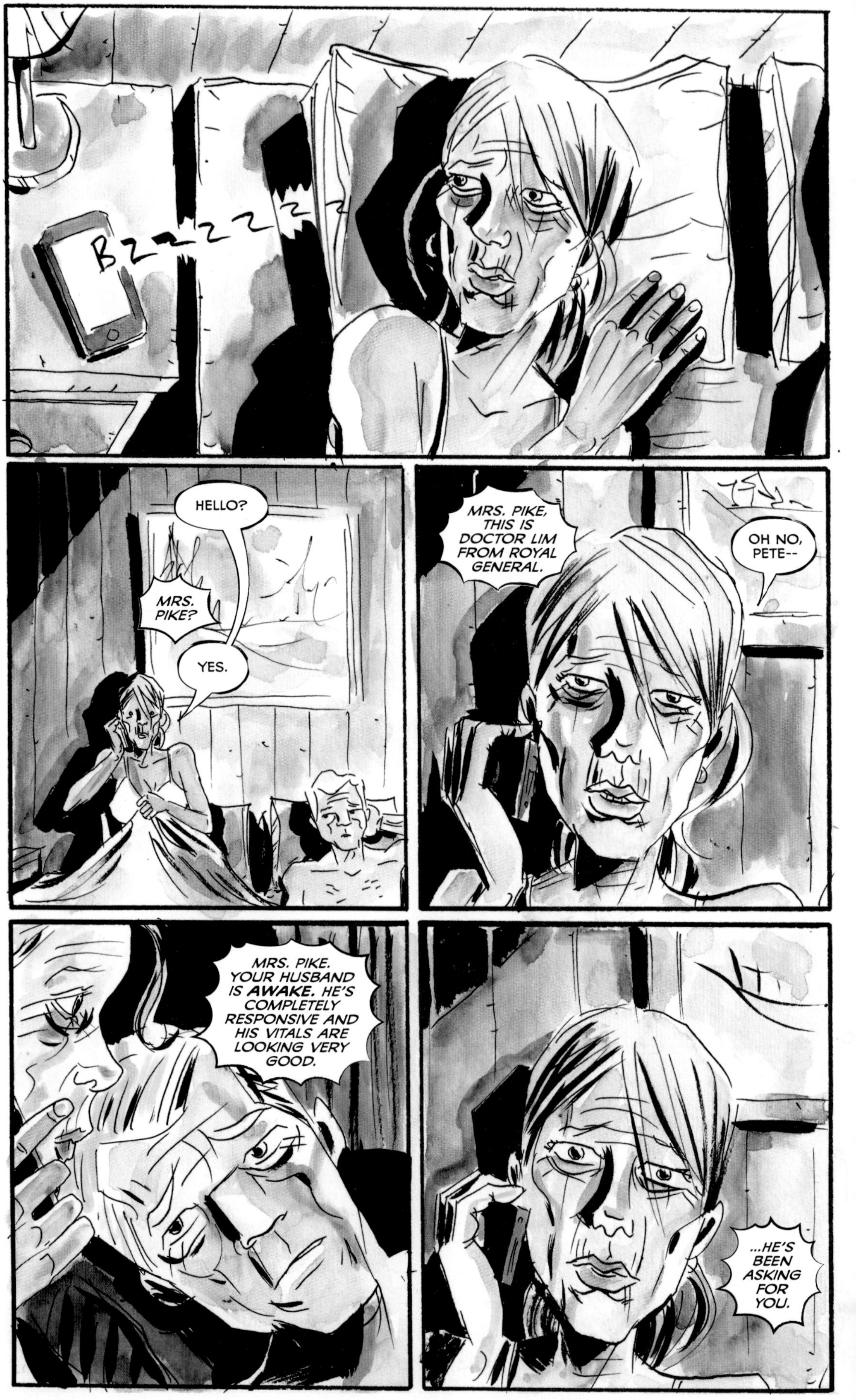
BZZZZZZ
HELLO?
MRS. PIKE?
YES.
MRS. PIKE, THIS IS DOCTOR LIM FROM ROYAL GENERAL.
OH NO, PETE--
MRS. PIKE. YOUR HUSBAND IS AWAKE. HE'S COMPLETELY RESPONSIVE AND HIS VITALS ARE LOOKING VERY GOOD.
...HE'S BEEN ASKING FOR YOU.

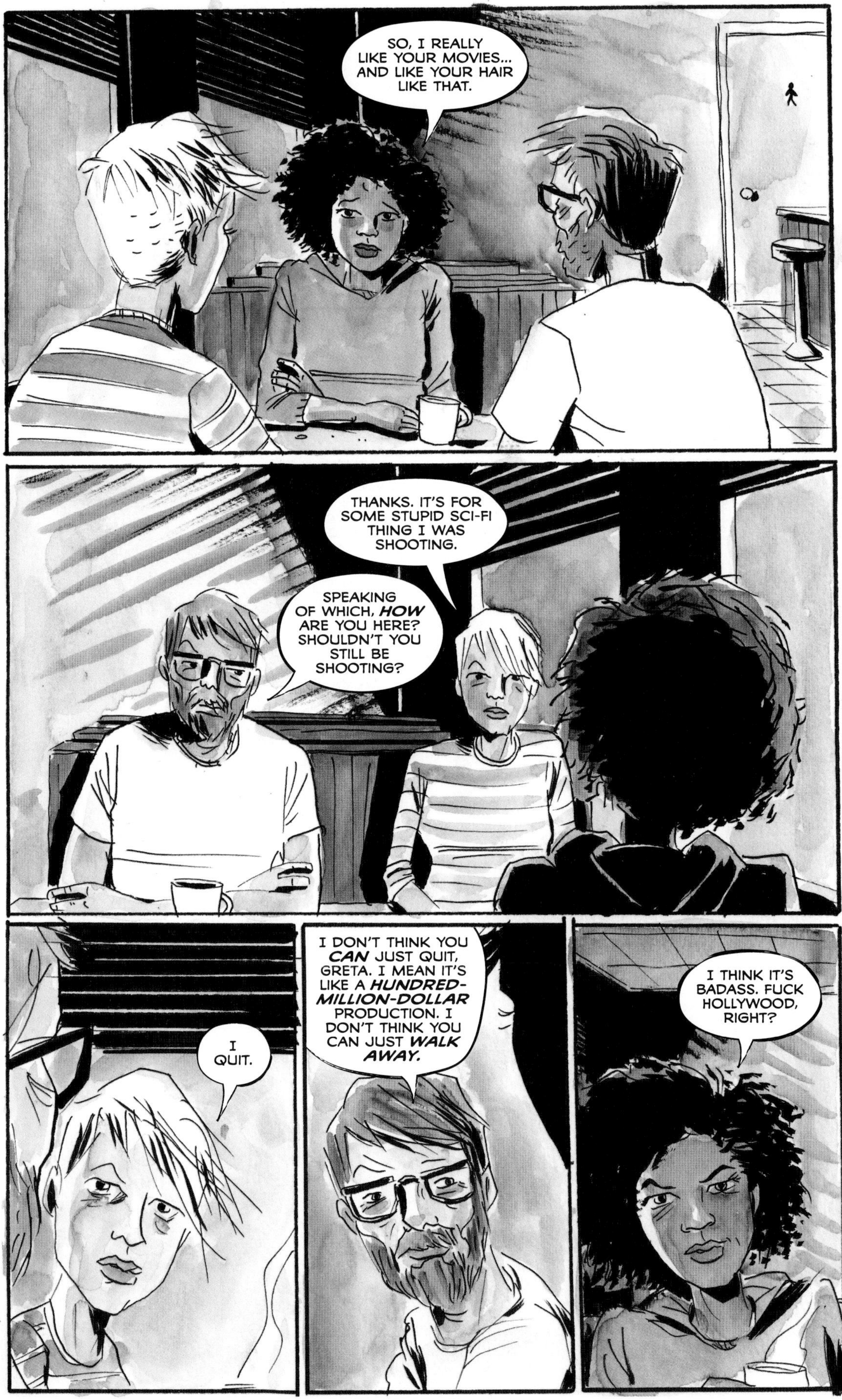
SO, I REALLY LIKE YOUR MOVIES... AND LIKE YOUR HAIR LIKE THAT.
THANKS. IT'S FOR SOME STUPID SCI-FI THING I WAS SHOOTING.
SPEAKING OF WHICH, ***HOW*** ARE YOU HERE? SHOULDN'T YOU STILL BE SHOOTING?
I QUIT.
I DON'T THINK YOU ***CAN*** JUST QUIT, GRETA. I MEAN IT'S LIKE A ***HUNDRED-MILLION-DOLLAR*** PRODUCTION. I DON'T THINK YOU CAN JUST ***WALK AWAY.***
I THINK IT'S BADASS. FUCK HOLLYWOOD, RIGHT?

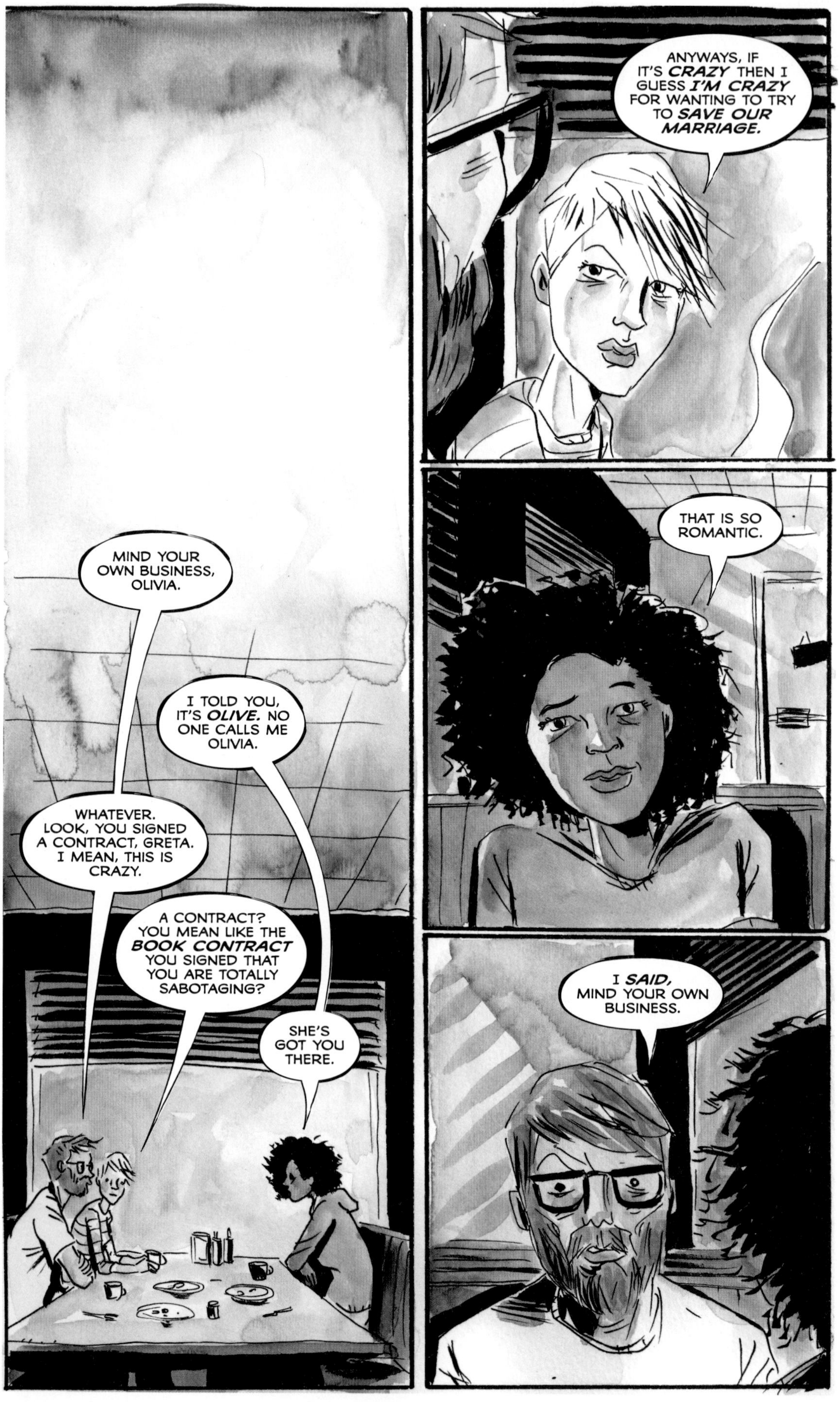
MIND YOUR OWN BUSINESS, OLIVIA.
I TOLD YOU, IT'S *OLIVE.* NO ONE CALLS ME OLIVIA.
WHATEVER. LOOK, YOU SIGNED A CONTRACT, GRETA. I MEAN, THIS IS CRAZY.
A CONTRACT? YOU MEAN LIKE THE *BOOK CONTRACT* YOU SIGNED THAT YOU ARE TOTALLY SABOTAGING?
SHE'S GOT YOU THERE.
ANYWAYS, IF IT'S *CRAZY* THEN I GUESS *I'M CRAZY* FOR WANTING TO TRY TO *SAVE OUR MARRIAGE.*
THAT IS SO ROMANTIC.
I *SAID,* MIND YOUR OWN BUSINESS.

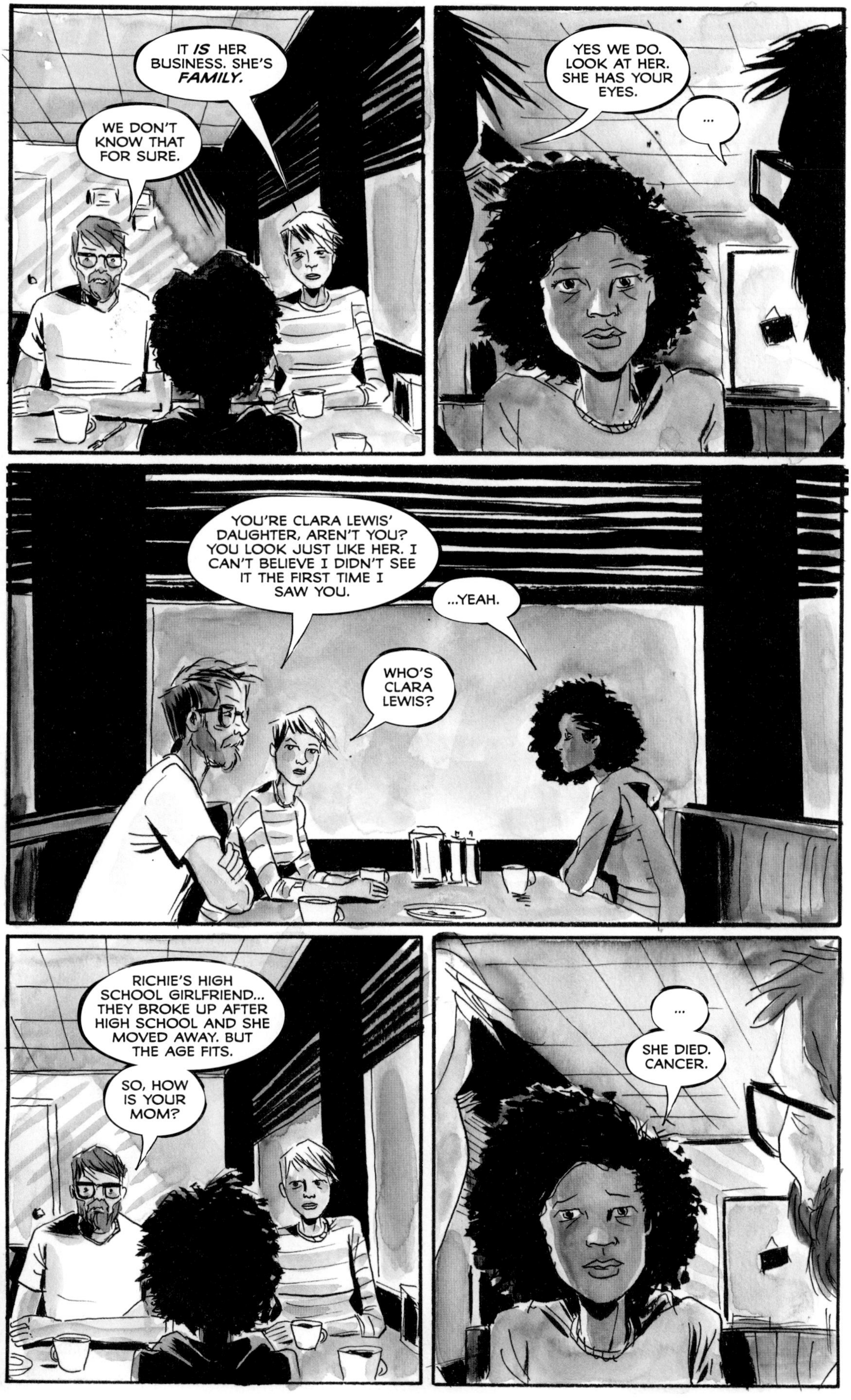
WE DON'T KNOW THAT FOR SURE.
IT *IS* HER BUSINESS. SHE'S *FAMILY.*
YES WE DO. LOOK AT HER. SHE HAS YOUR EYES.
...
YOU'RE CLARA LEWIS' DAUGHTER, AREN'T YOU? YOU LOOK JUST LIKE HER. I CAN'T BELIEVE I DIDN'T SEE IT THE FIRST TIME I SAW YOU.
WHO'S CLARA LEWIS?
...YEAH.
RICHIE'S HIGH SCHOOL GIRLFRIEND... THEY BROKE UP AFTER HIGH SCHOOL AND SHE MOVED AWAY. BUT THE AGE FITS.
SO, HOW IS YOUR MOM?
...
SHE DIED. CANCER.

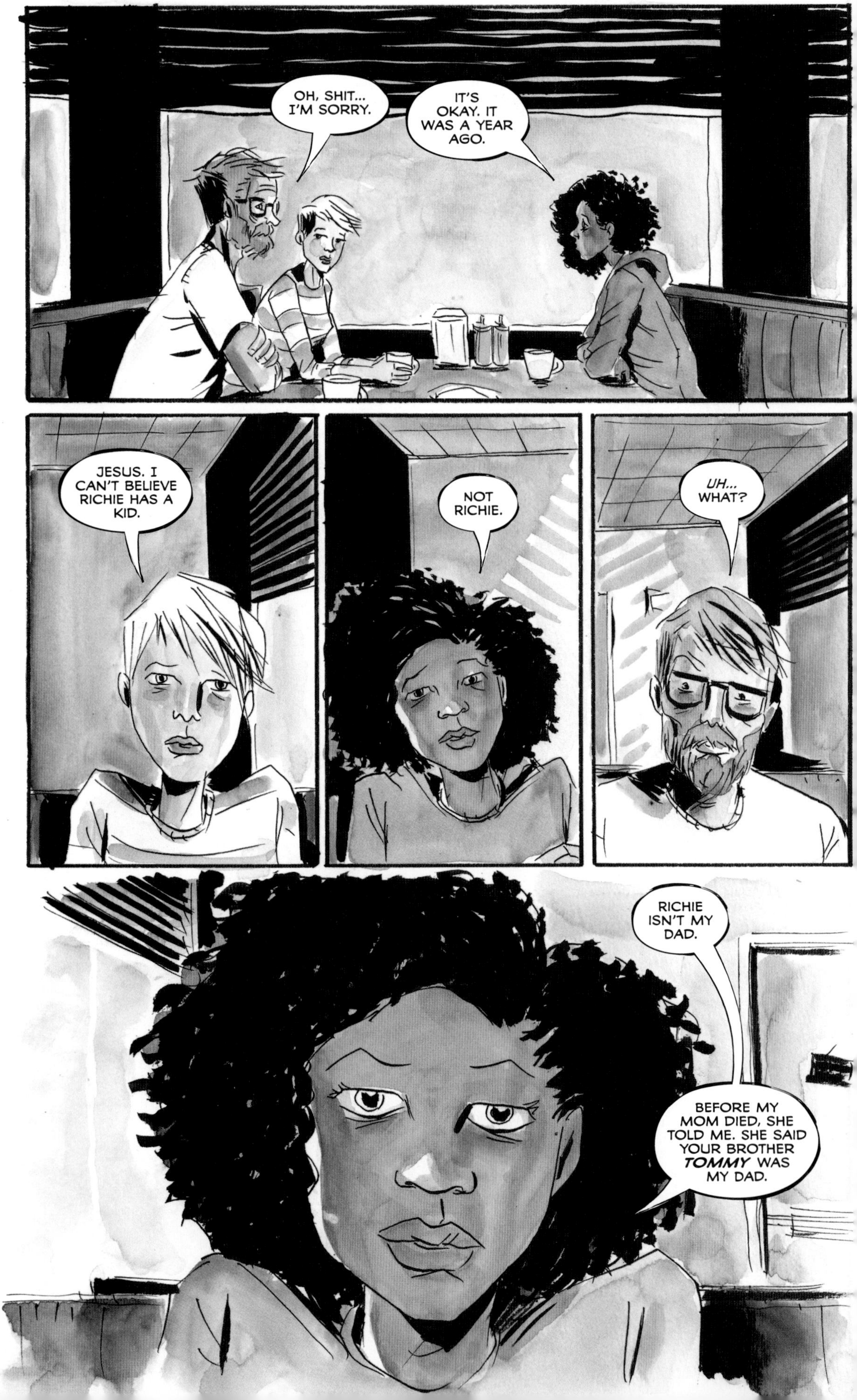
OH, SHIT... I'M SORRY.
IT'S OKAY. IT WAS A YEAR AGO.
JESUS. I CAN'T BELIEVE RICHIE HAS A KID.
NOT RICHIE.
UH... WHAT?
RICHIE ISN'T MY DAD.
BEFORE MY MOM DIED, SHE TOLD ME. SHE SAID YOUR BROTHER TOMMY WAS MY DAD.

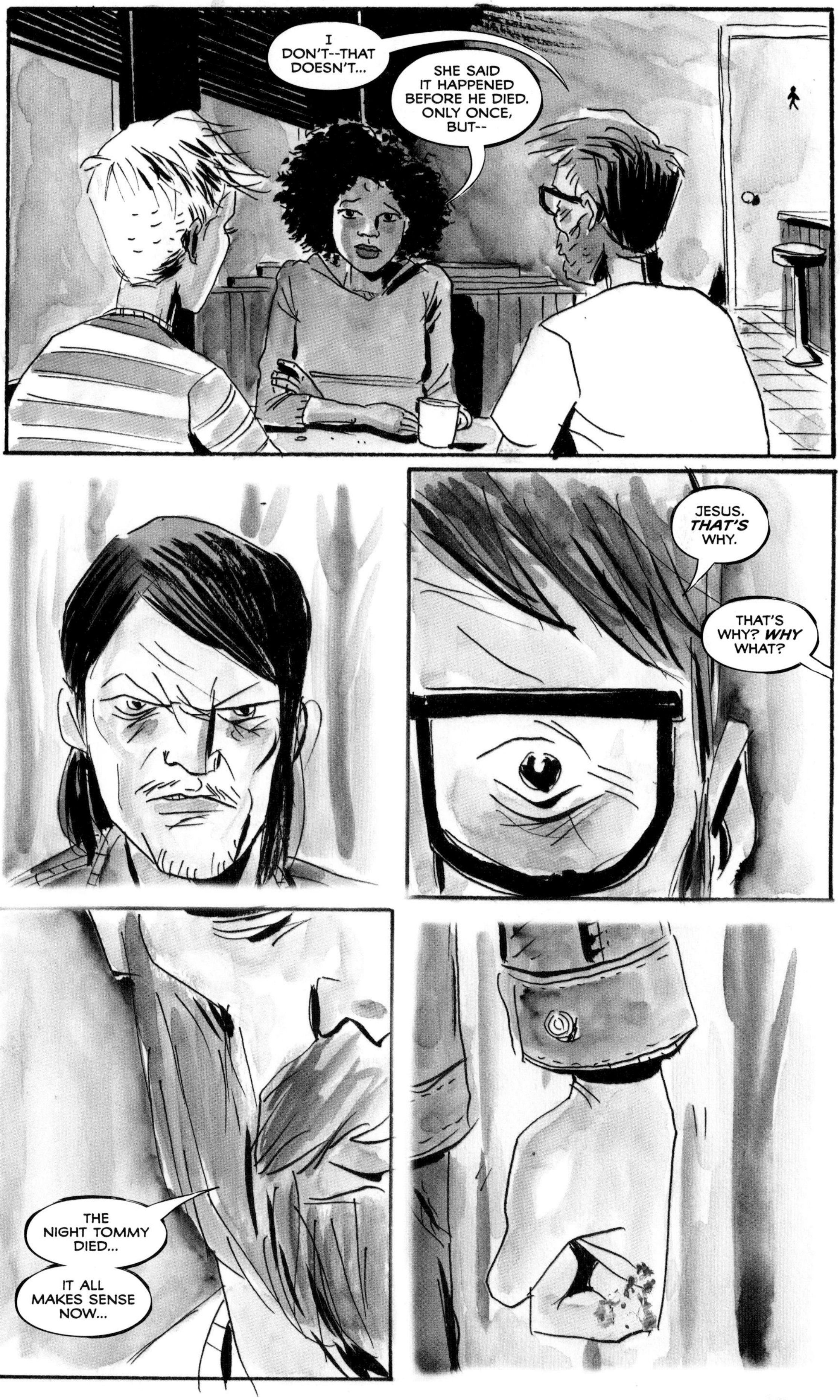

I DON'T--THAT DOESN'T...
SHE SAID IT HAPPENED BEFORE HE DIED. ONLY ONCE, BUT--
JESUS. THAT'S WHY.
THAT'S WHY? WHY WHAT?
THE NIGHT TOMMY DIED...
IT ALL MAKES SENSE NOW...

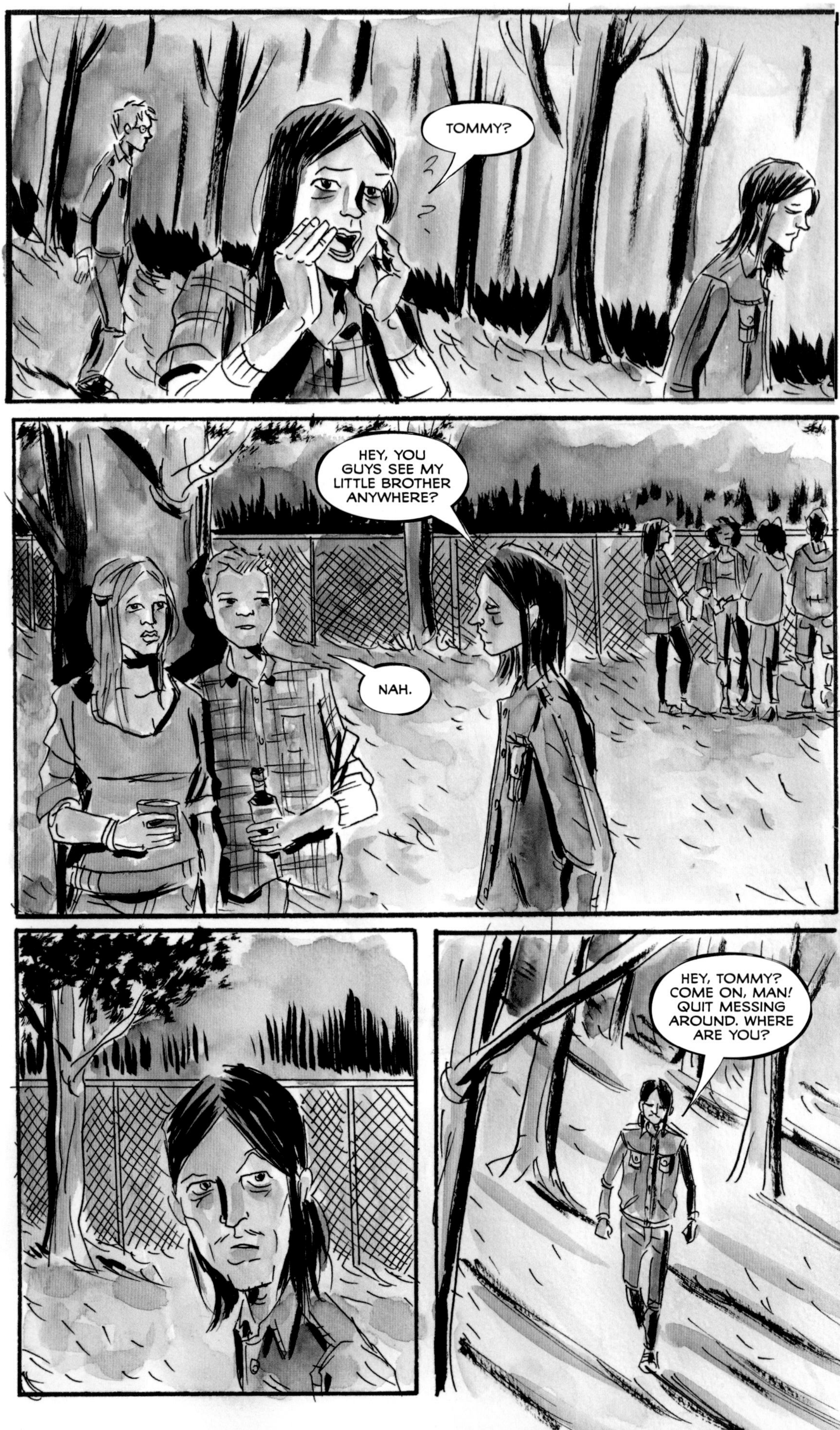
TOMMY?
HEY, YOU GUYS SEE MY LITTLE BROTHER ANYWHERE?
NAH.
HEY, TOMMY? COME ON, MAN! QUIT MESSING AROUND. WHERE ARE YOU?

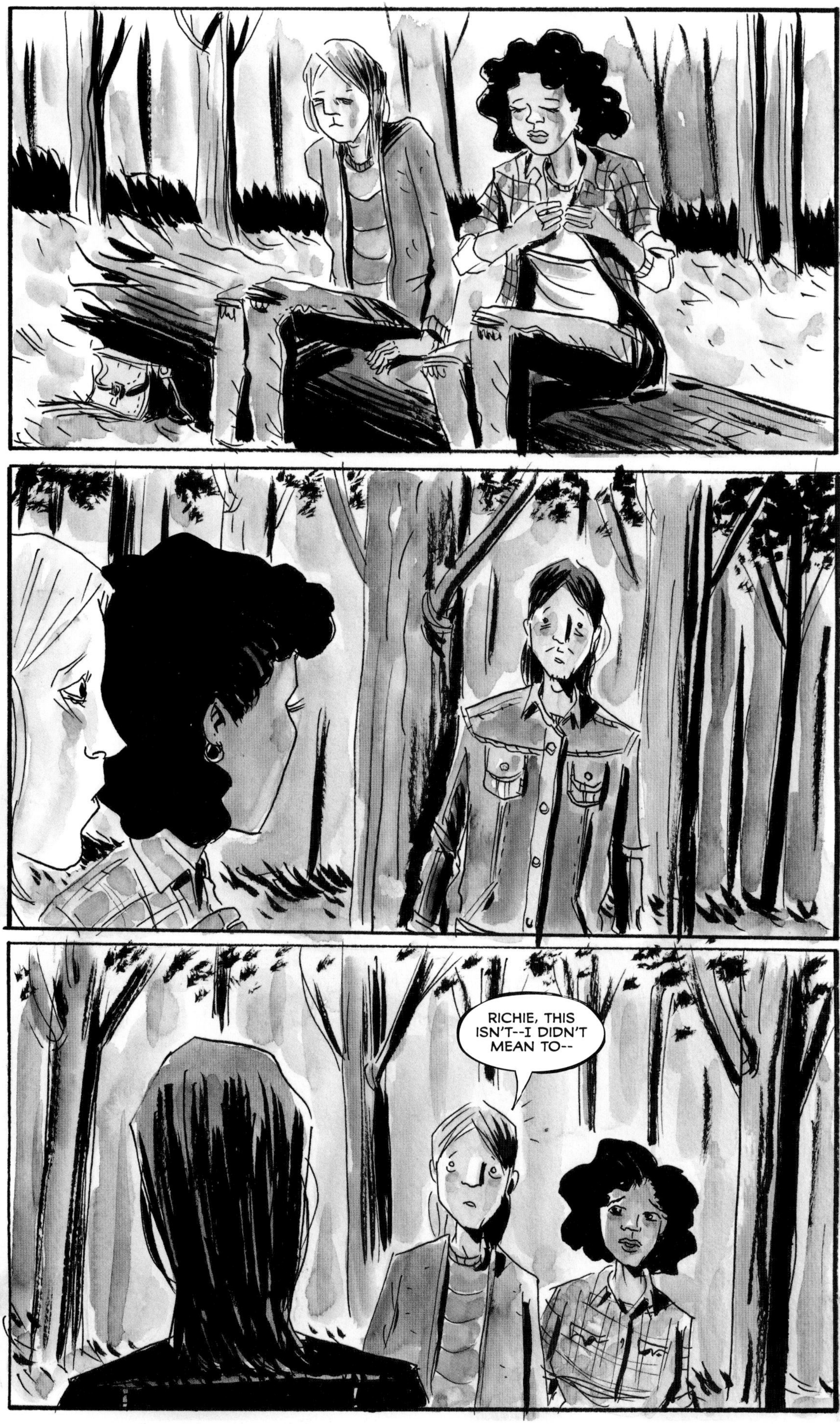
RICHIE, THIS ISN'T--I DIDN'T MEAN TO--

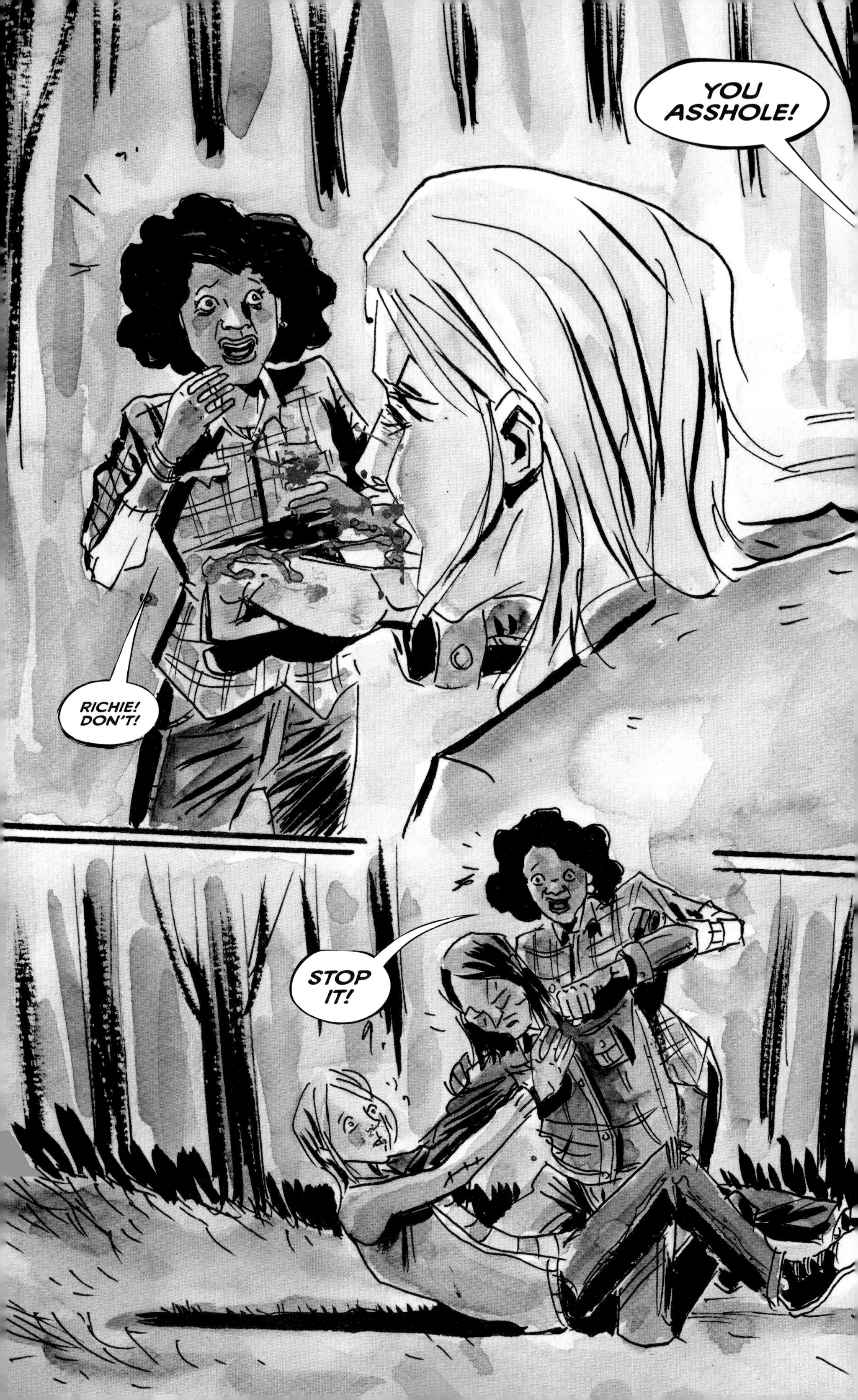
YOU ASSHOLE!
RICHIE! DON'T!
STOP IT!

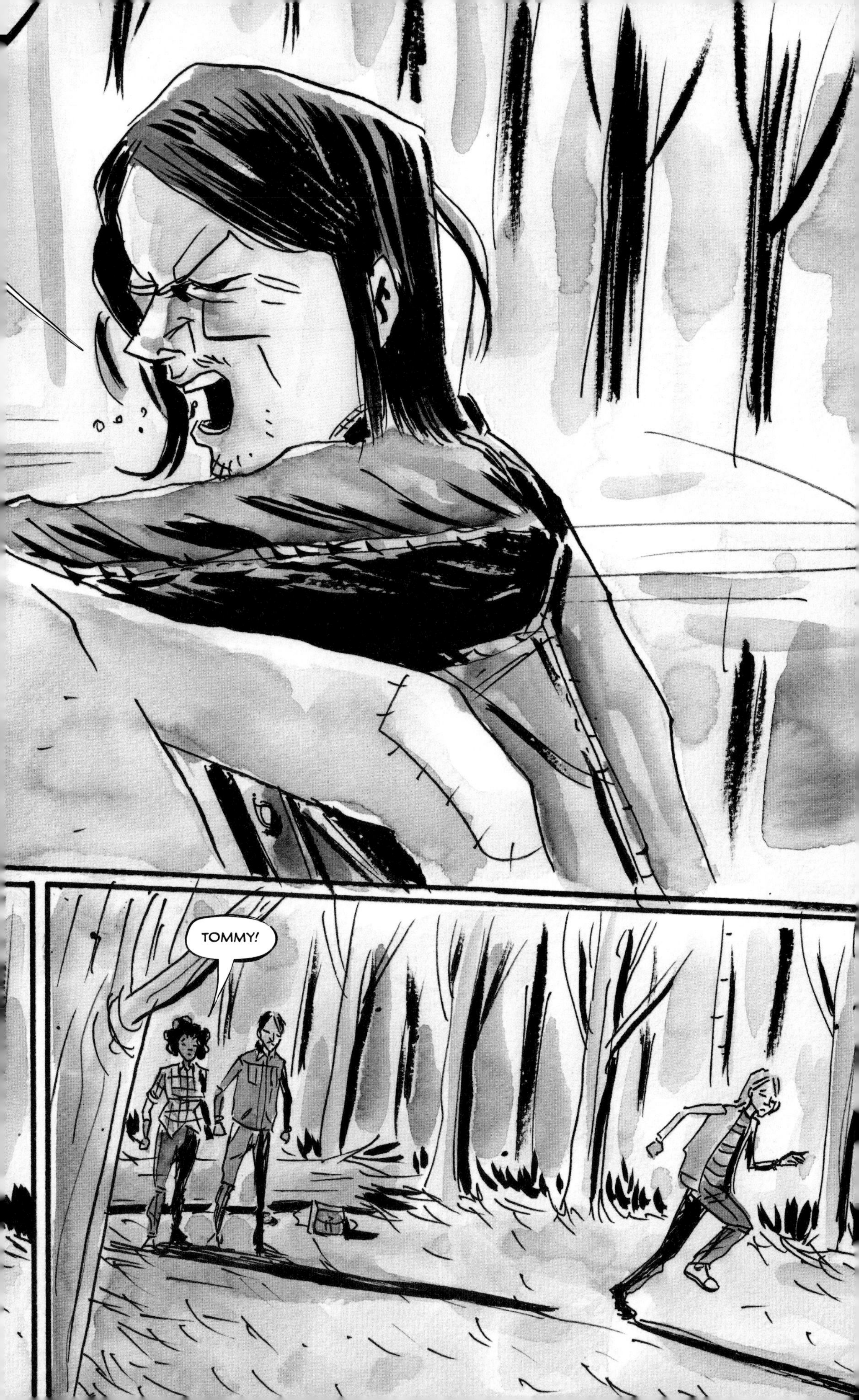
TOMMY!

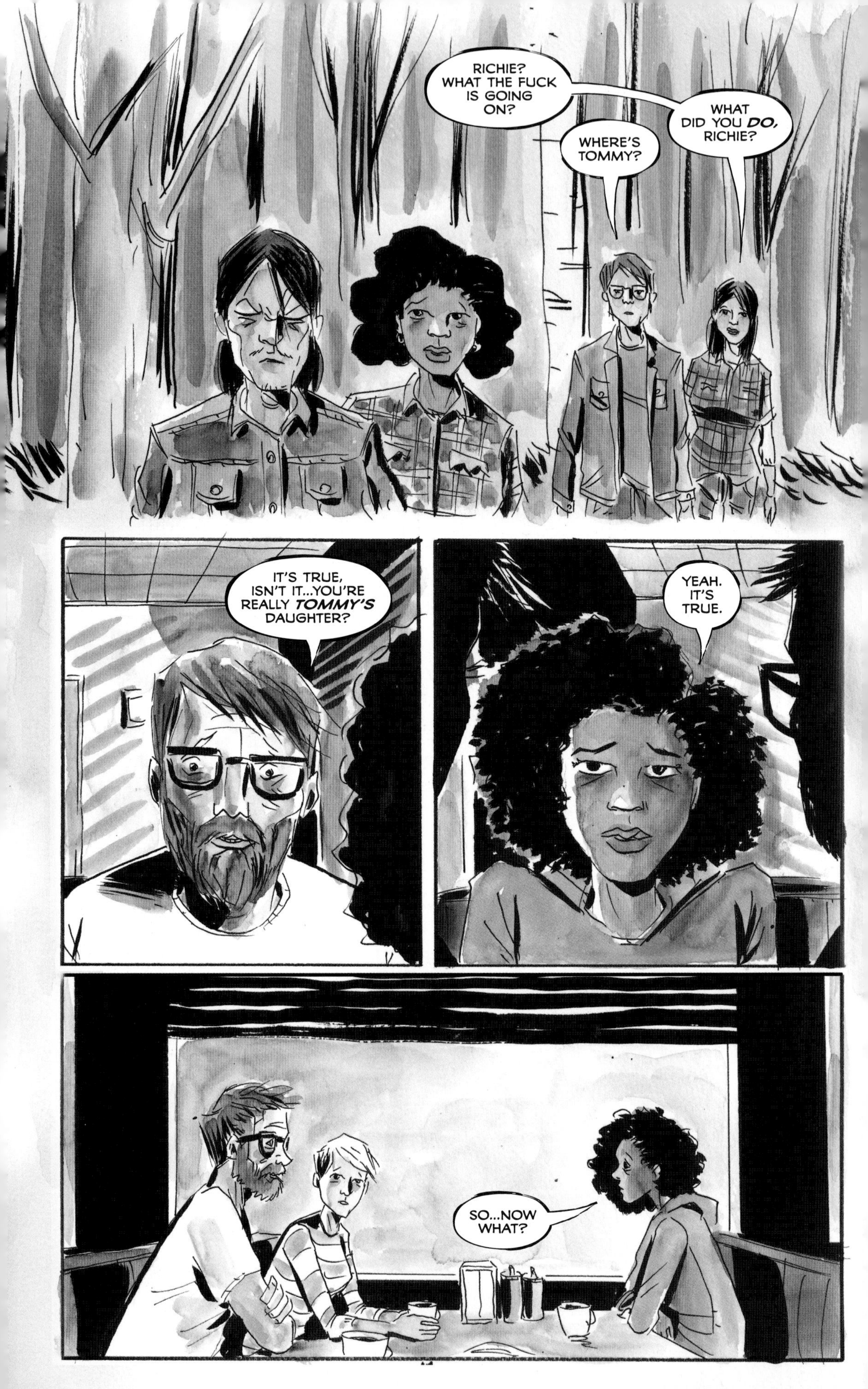
RICHIE? WHAT THE FUCK IS GOING ON?
WHERE'S TOMMY?
WHAT DID YOU *DO,* RICHIE?
IT'S TRUE, ISN'T IT...YOU'RE REALLY *TOMMY'S* DAUGHTER?
YEAH. IT'S TRUE.
SO...NOW WHAT?

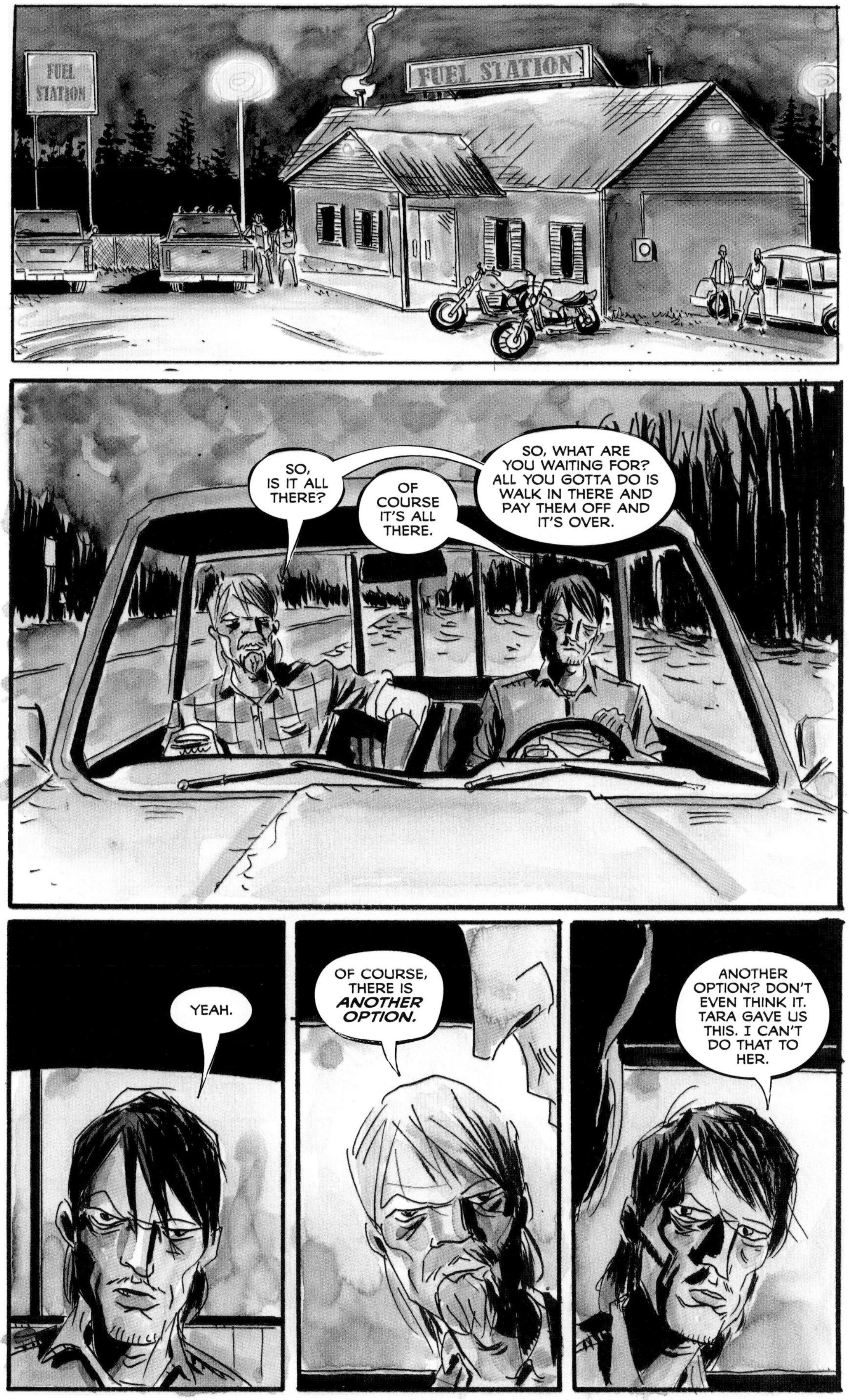
FUEL STATION
FUEL STATION
SO, IS IT ALL THERE?
OF COURSE IT'S ALL THERE.
SO, WHAT ARE YOU WAITING FOR? ALL YOU GOTTA DO IS WALK IN THERE AND PAY THEM OFF AND IT'S OVER.
YEAH.
OF COURSE, THERE IS *ANOTHER OPTION.*
ANOTHER OPTION? DON'T EVEN THINK IT. TARA GAVE US THIS. I CAN'T DO THAT TO HER.

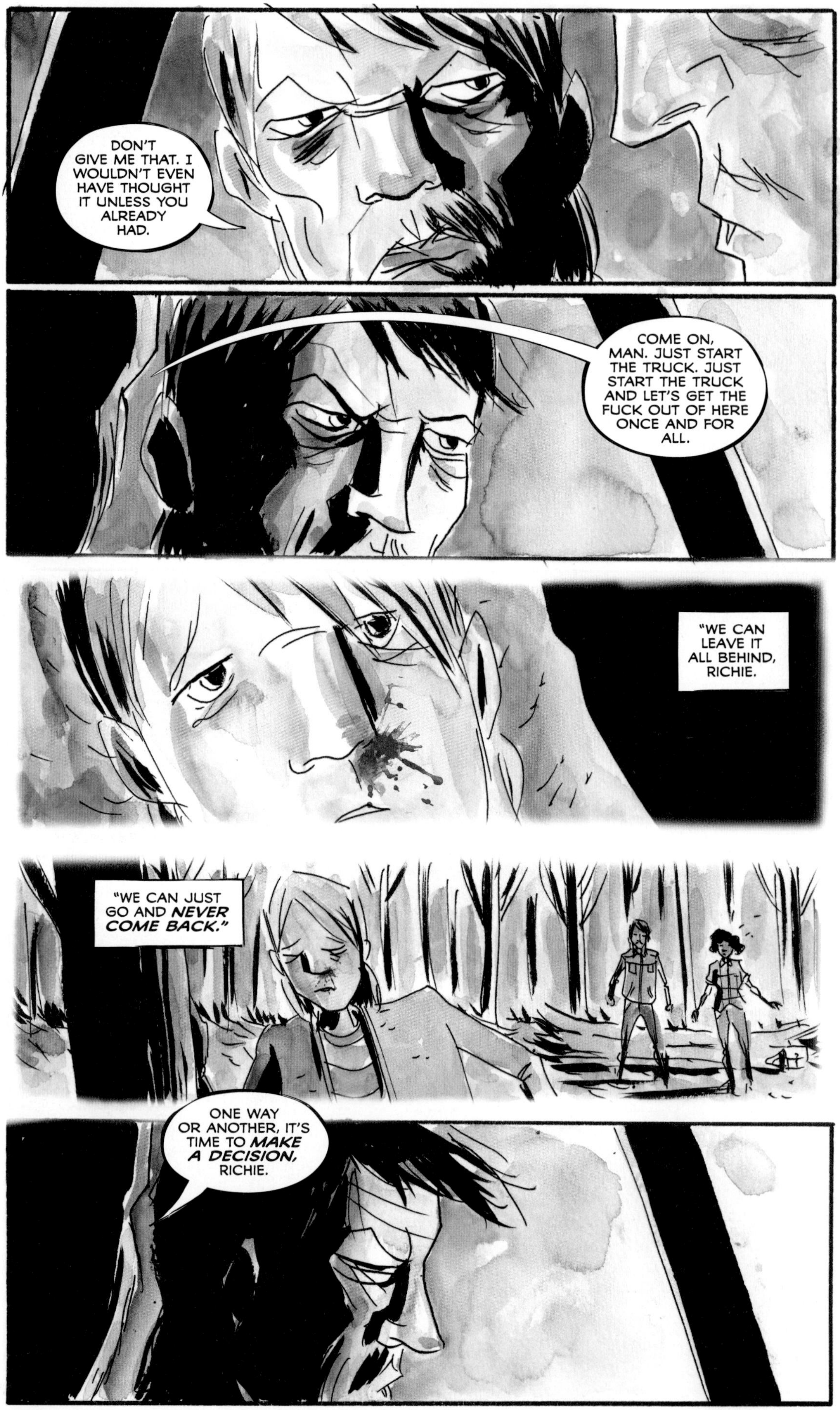

DON'T GIVE ME THAT. I WOULDN'T EVEN HAVE THOUGHT IT UNLESS YOU ALREADY HAD.
COME ON, MAN. JUST START THE TRUCK. JUST START THE TRUCK AND LET'S GET THE FUCK OUT OF HERE ONCE AND FOR ALL.
"WE CAN LEAVE IT ALL BEHIND, RICHIE.
"WE CAN JUST GO AND *NEVER COME BACK.*"
ONE WAY OR ANOTHER, IT'S TIME TO *MAKE A DECISION,* RICHIE.

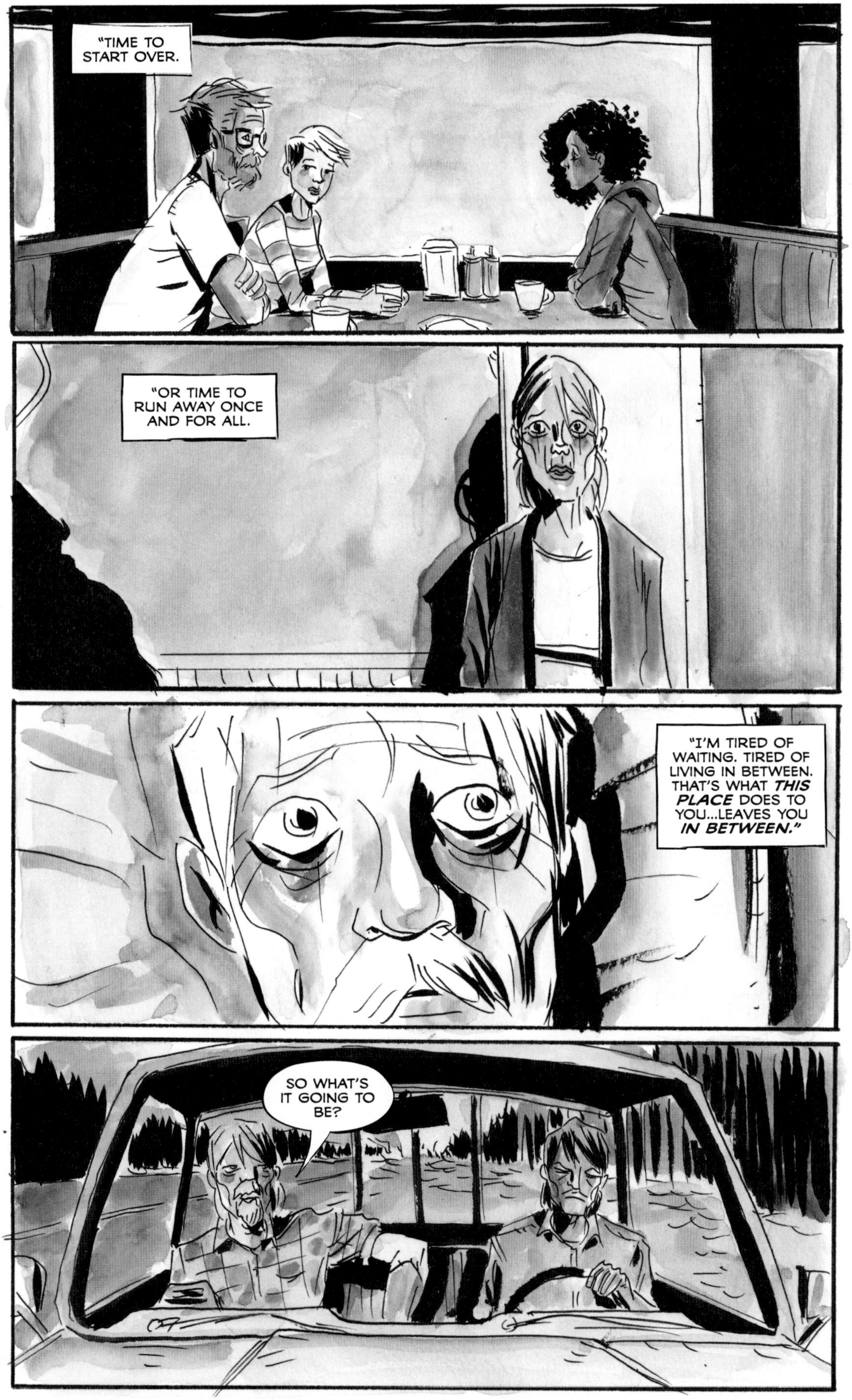
"TIME TO START OVER.
"OR TIME TO RUN AWAY ONCE AND FOR ALL.
"I'M TIRED OF WAITING. TIRED OF LIVING IN BETWEEN. THAT'S WHAT ***THIS PLACE*** DOES TO YOU...LEAVES YOU ***IN BETWEEN."***
SO WHAT'S IT GOING TO BE?

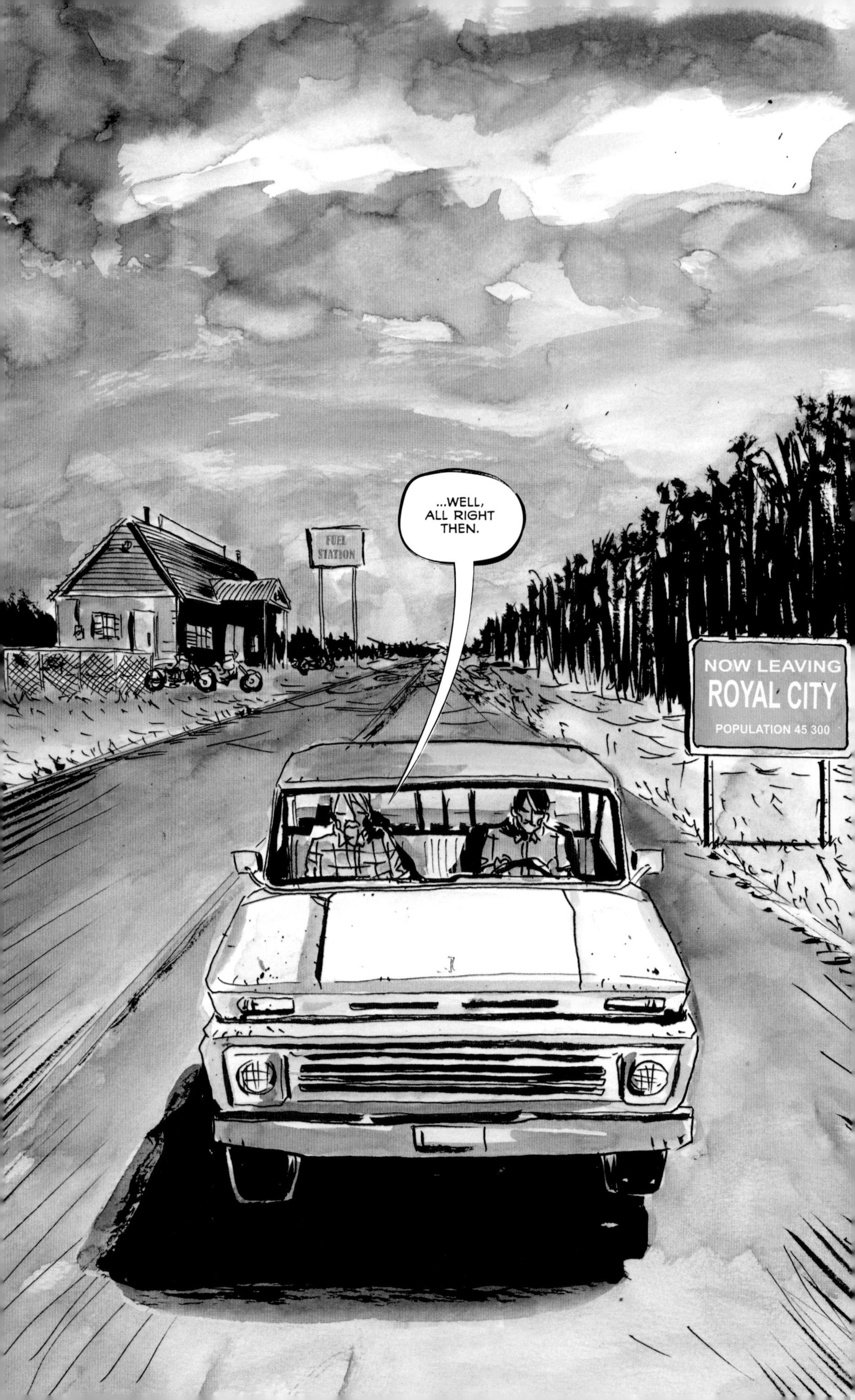
...WELL, ALL RIGHT THEN.
FUEL STATION
NOW LEAVING
ROYAL CITY
POPULATION 45 300

CHAPTER TWELVE

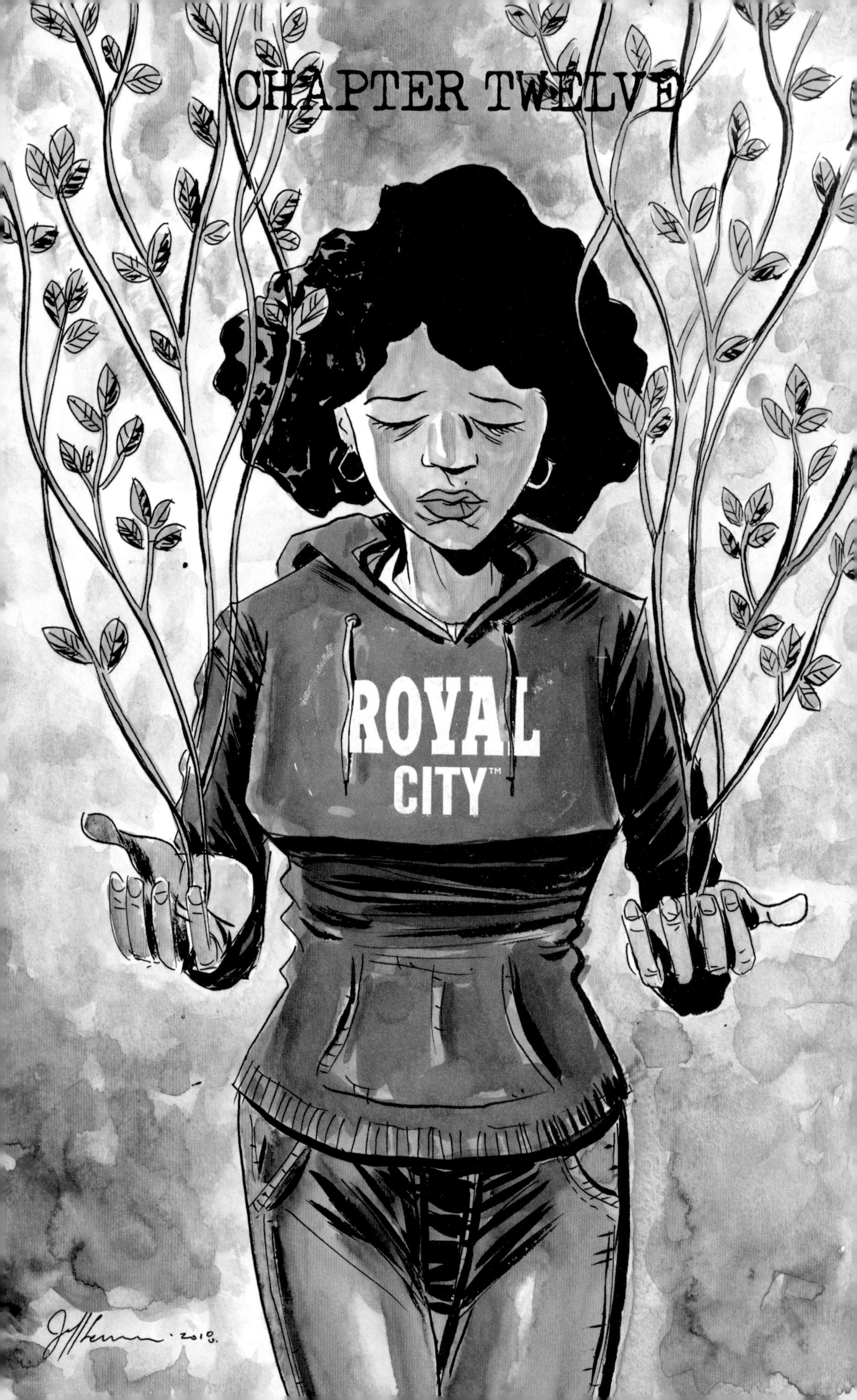
ROYAL
CITY™

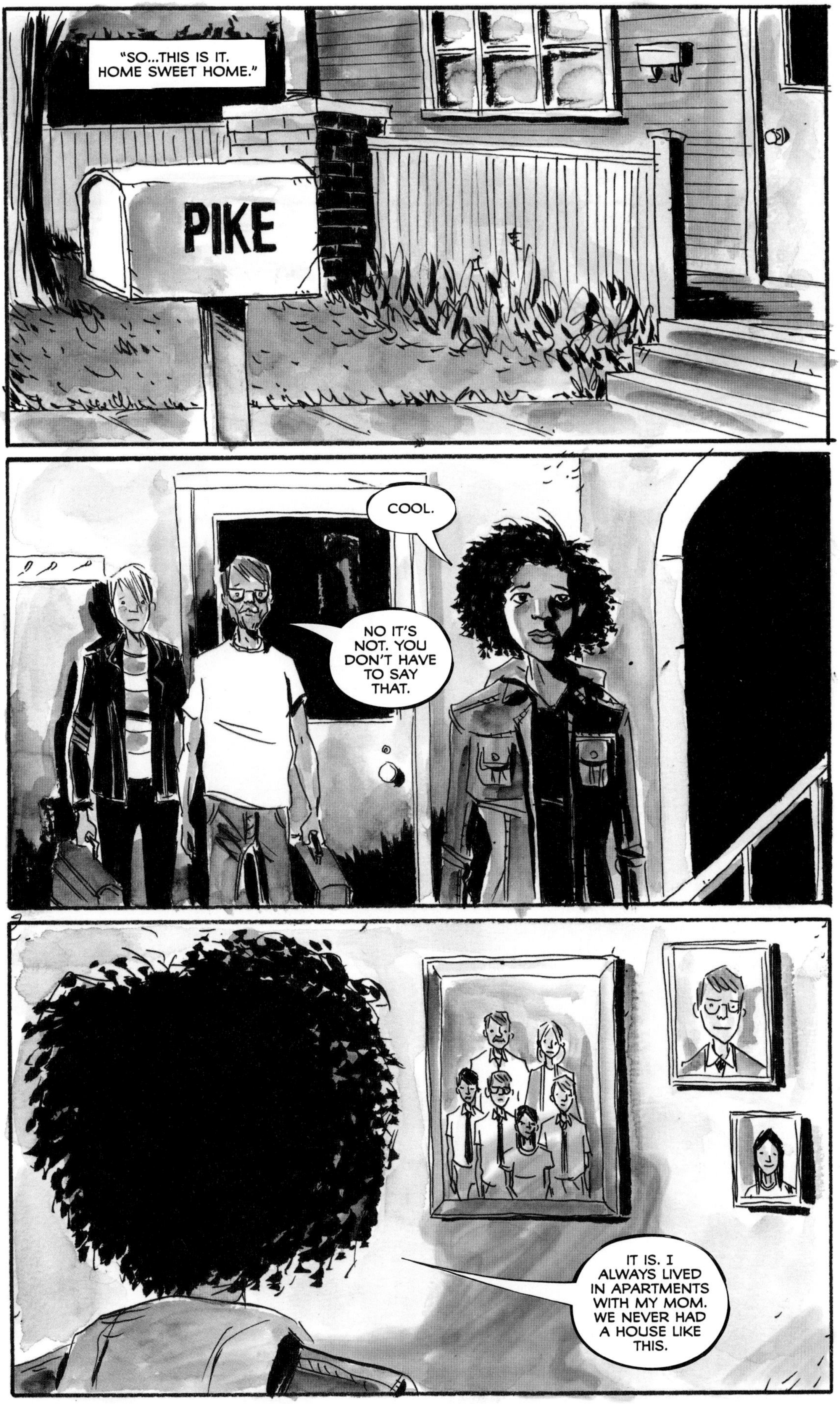
"SO...THIS IS IT. HOME SWEET HOME."
PIKE
COOL.
NO IT'S NOT. YOU DON'T HAVE TO SAY THAT.
IT IS. I ALWAYS LIVED IN APARTMENTS WITH MY MOM. WE NEVER HAD A HOUSE LIKE THIS.

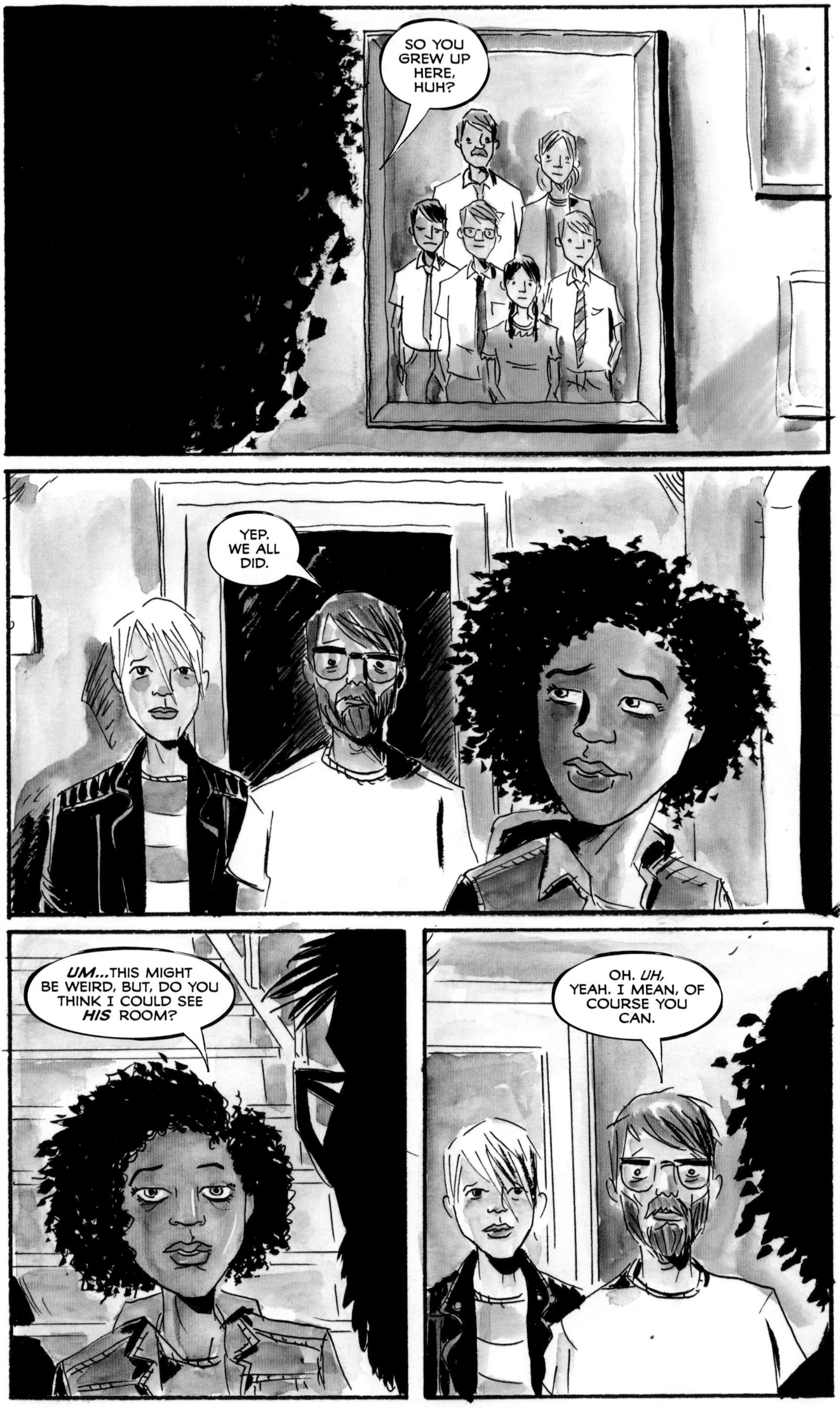
SO YOU GREW UP HERE, HUH?
YEP. WE ALL DID.
UM... THIS MIGHT BE WEIRD, BUT, DO YOU THINK I COULD SEE *HIS* ROOM?
OH. *UH,* YEAH. I MEAN, OF COURSE YOU CAN.

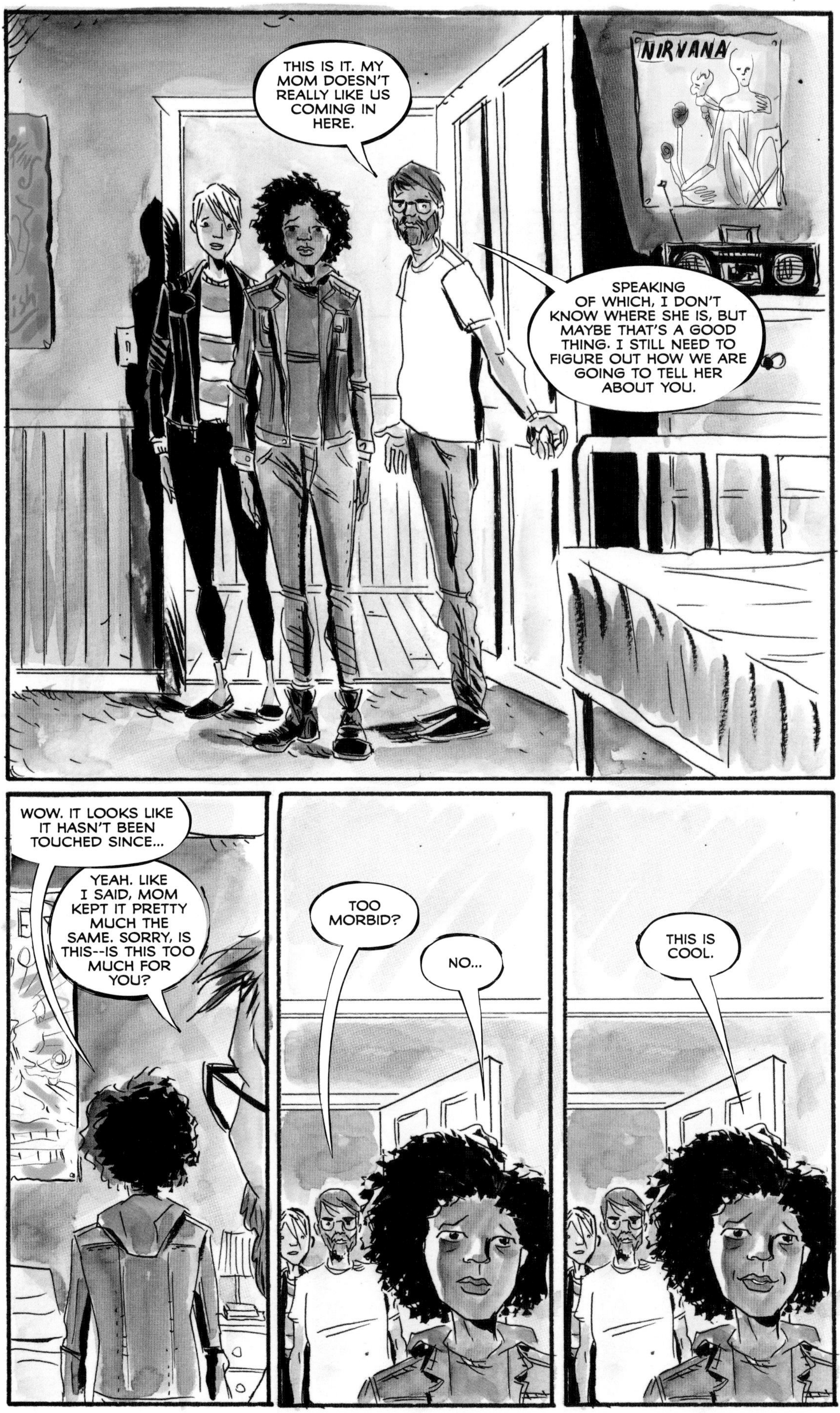
NIRVANA
THIS IS IT. MY MOM DOESN'T REALLY LIKE US COMING IN HERE.
SPEAKING OF WHICH, I DON'T KNOW WHERE SHE IS, BUT MAYBE THAT'S A GOOD THING. I STILL NEED TO FIGURE OUT HOW WE ARE GOING TO TELL HER ABOUT YOU.
WOW. IT LOOKS LIKE IT HASN'T BEEN TOUCHED SINCE...
YEAH. LIKE I SAID, MOM KEPT IT PRETTY MUCH THE SAME. SORRY, IS THIS--IS THIS TOO MUCH FOR YOU?
TOO MORBID?
NO...
THIS IS COOL.

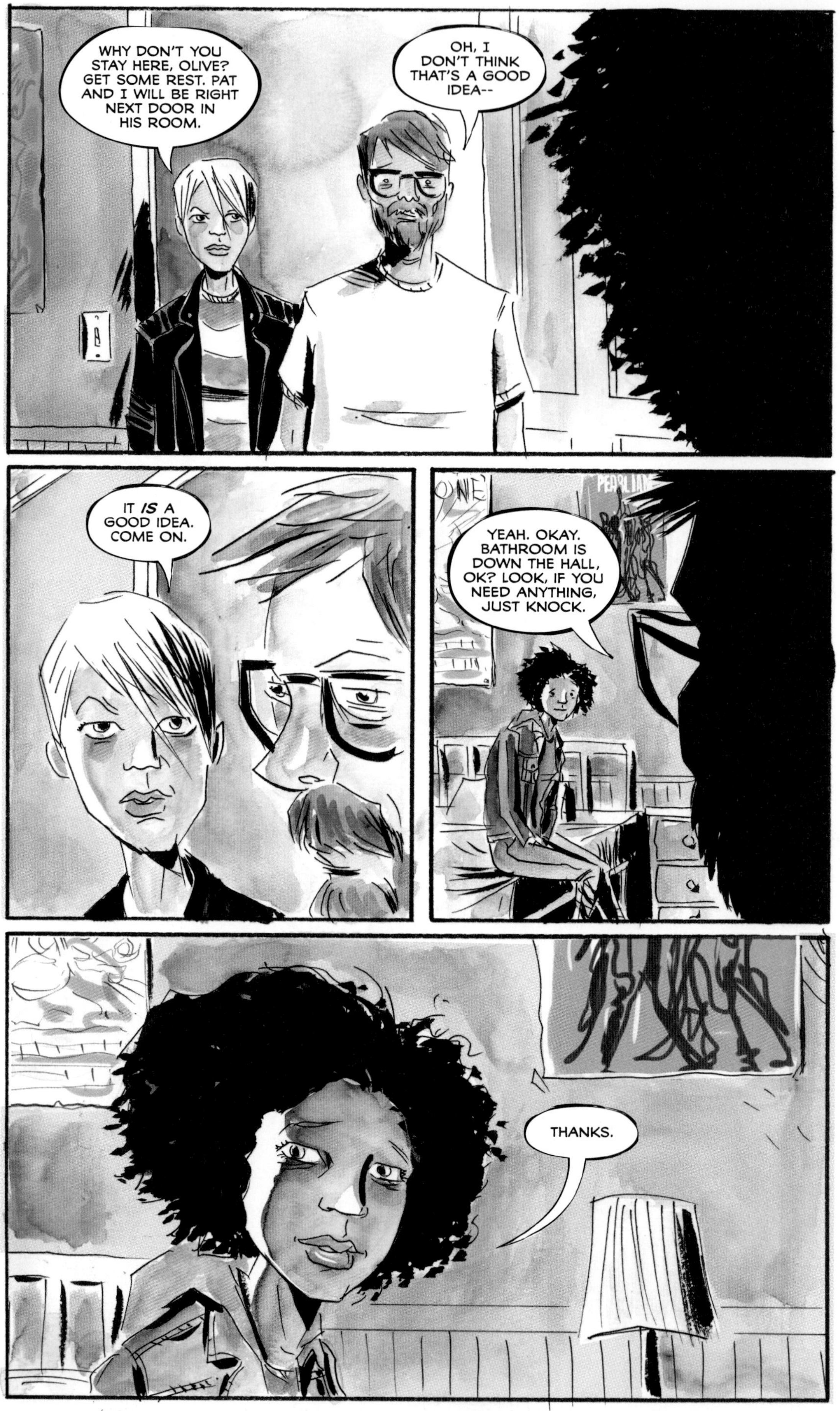
WHY DON'T YOU STAY HERE, OLIVE? GET SOME REST. PAT AND I WILL BE RIGHT NEXT DOOR IN HIS ROOM.
OH, I DON'T THINK THAT'S A GOOD IDEA--
IT *IS* A GOOD IDEA. COME ON.
YEAH. OKAY. BATHROOM IS DOWN THE HALL, OK? LOOK, IF YOU NEED ANYTHING, JUST KNOCK.
THANKS.

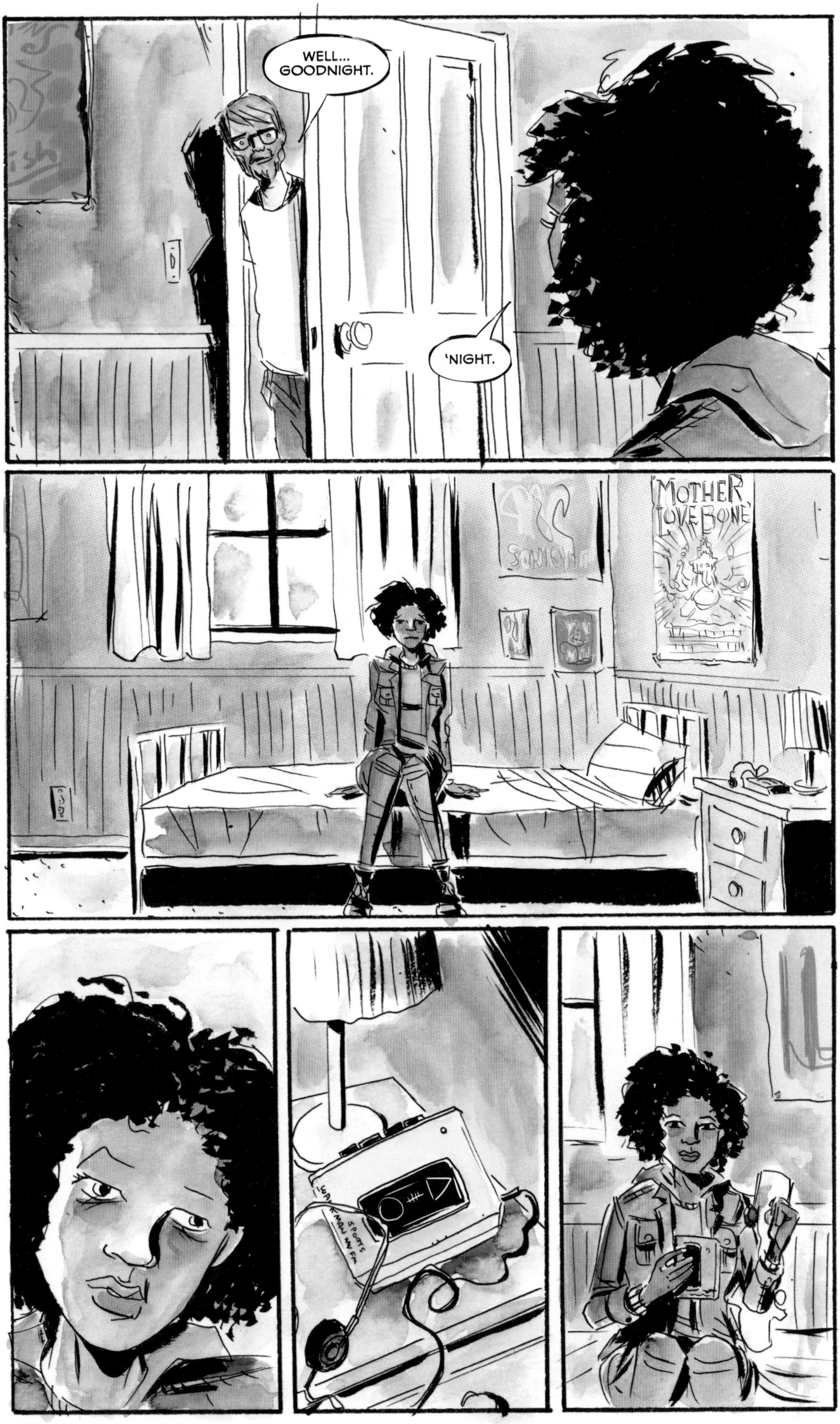
WELL... GOODNIGHT.
'NIGHT.
MOTHER LOVE BONE

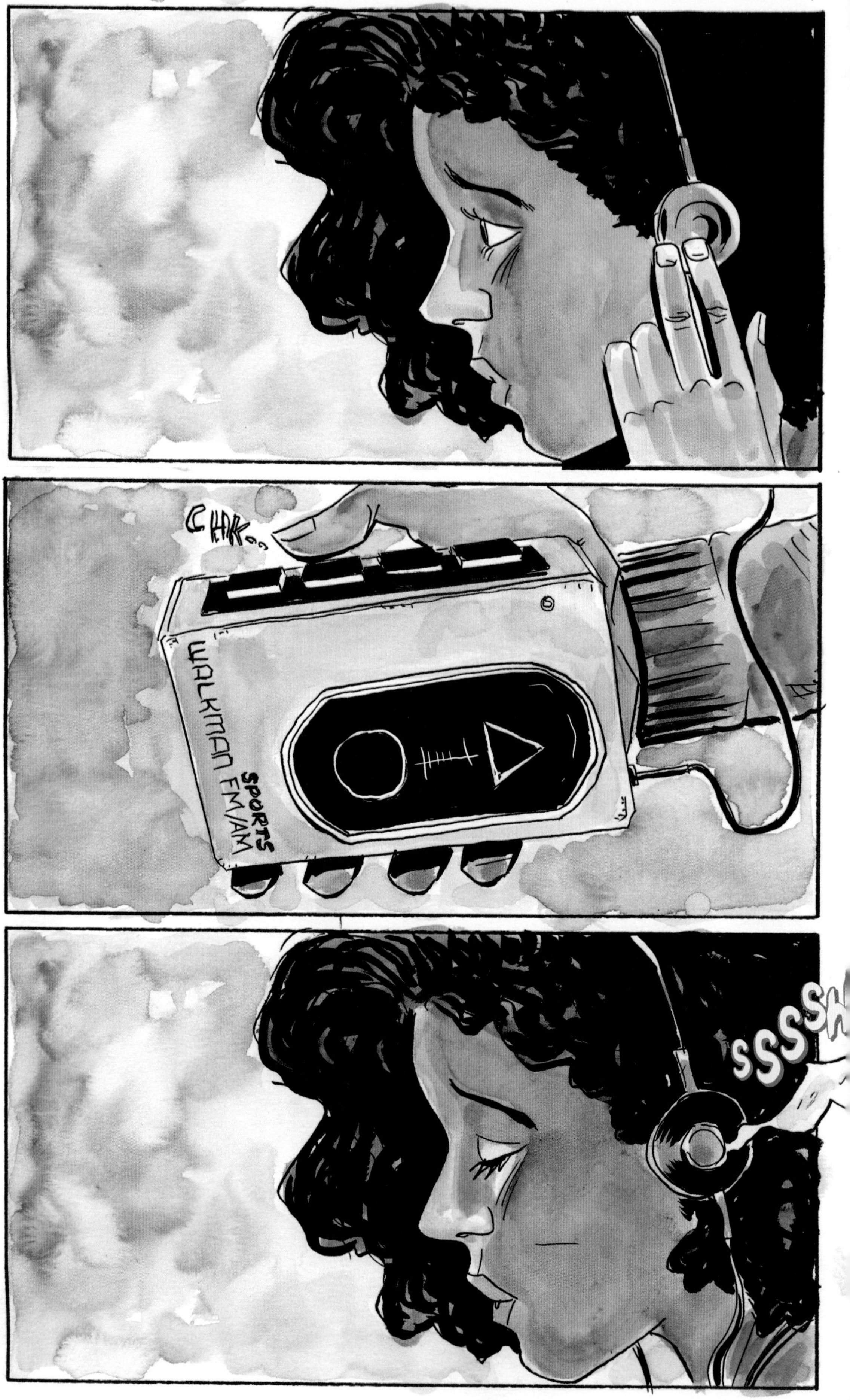
CHK..
SPORTS
WALKMAN FM/AM
SSSSH

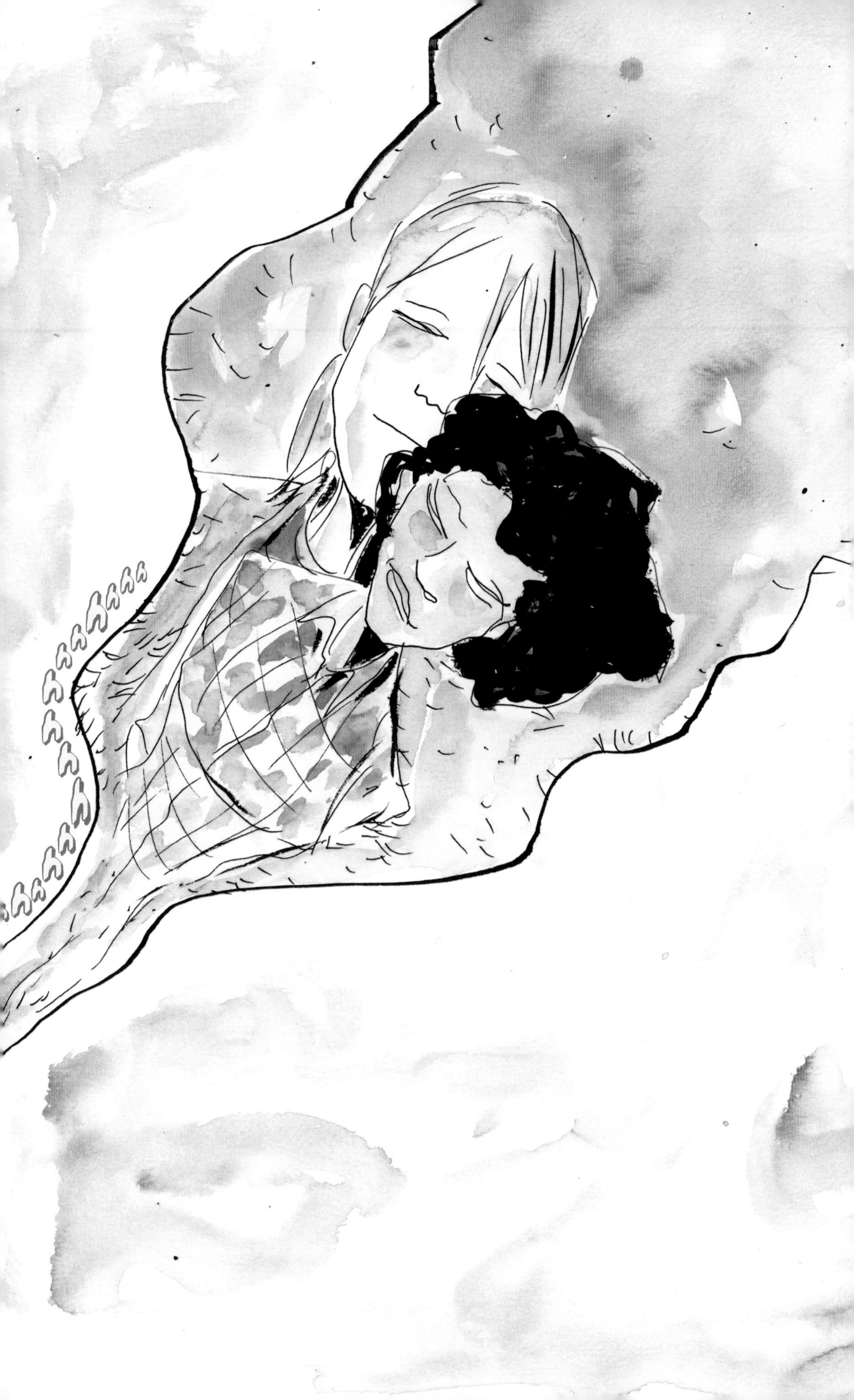

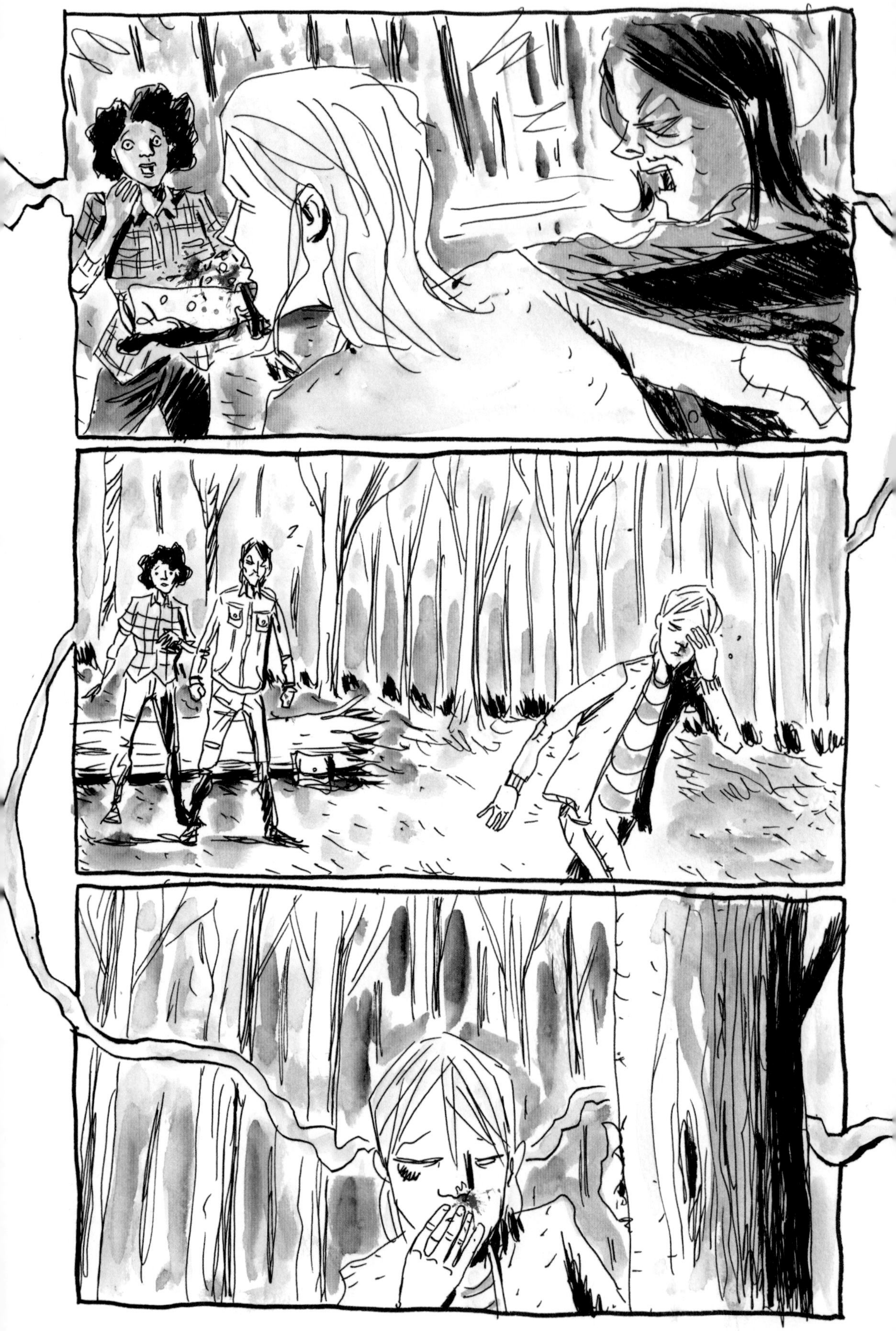

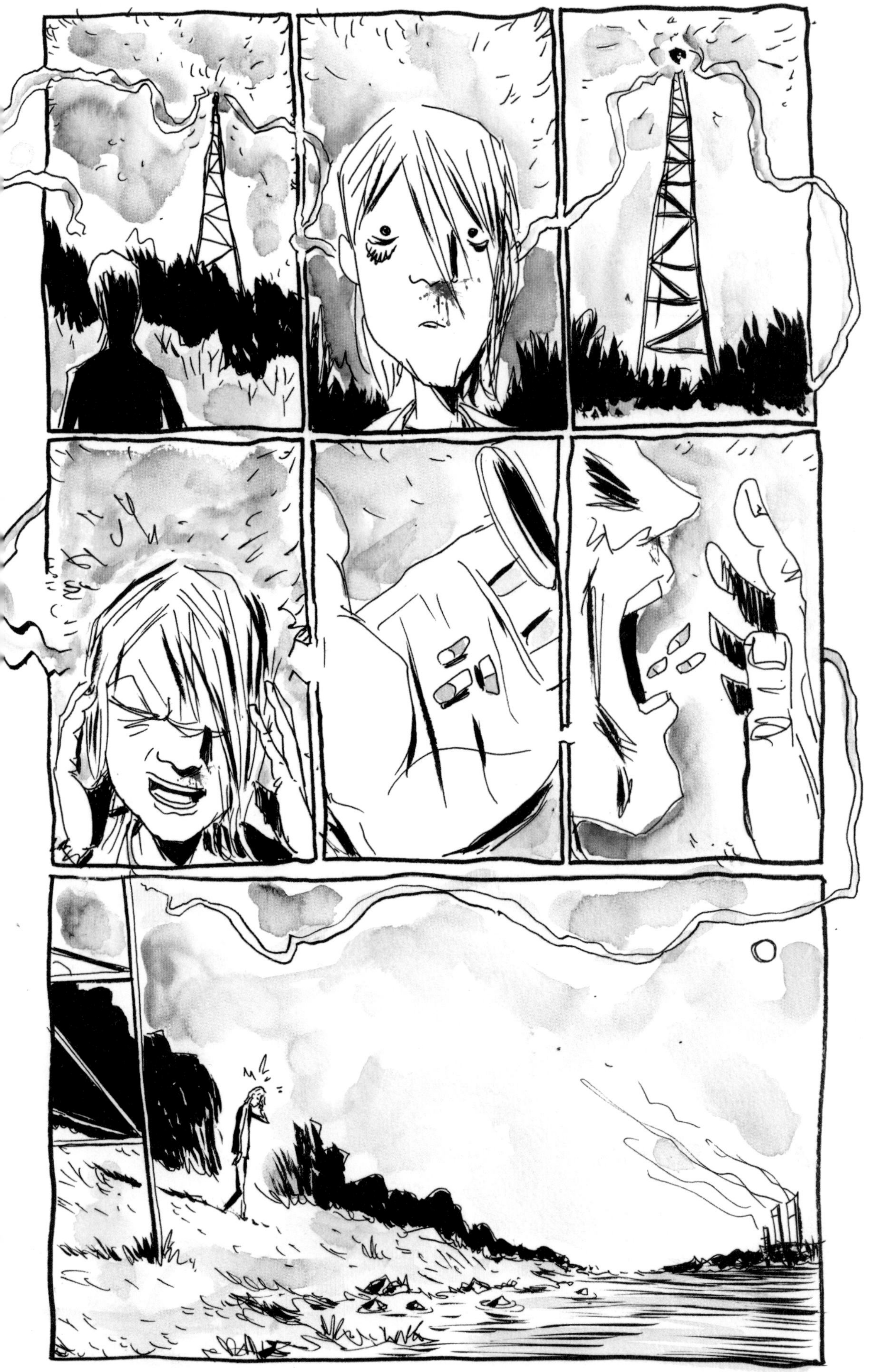

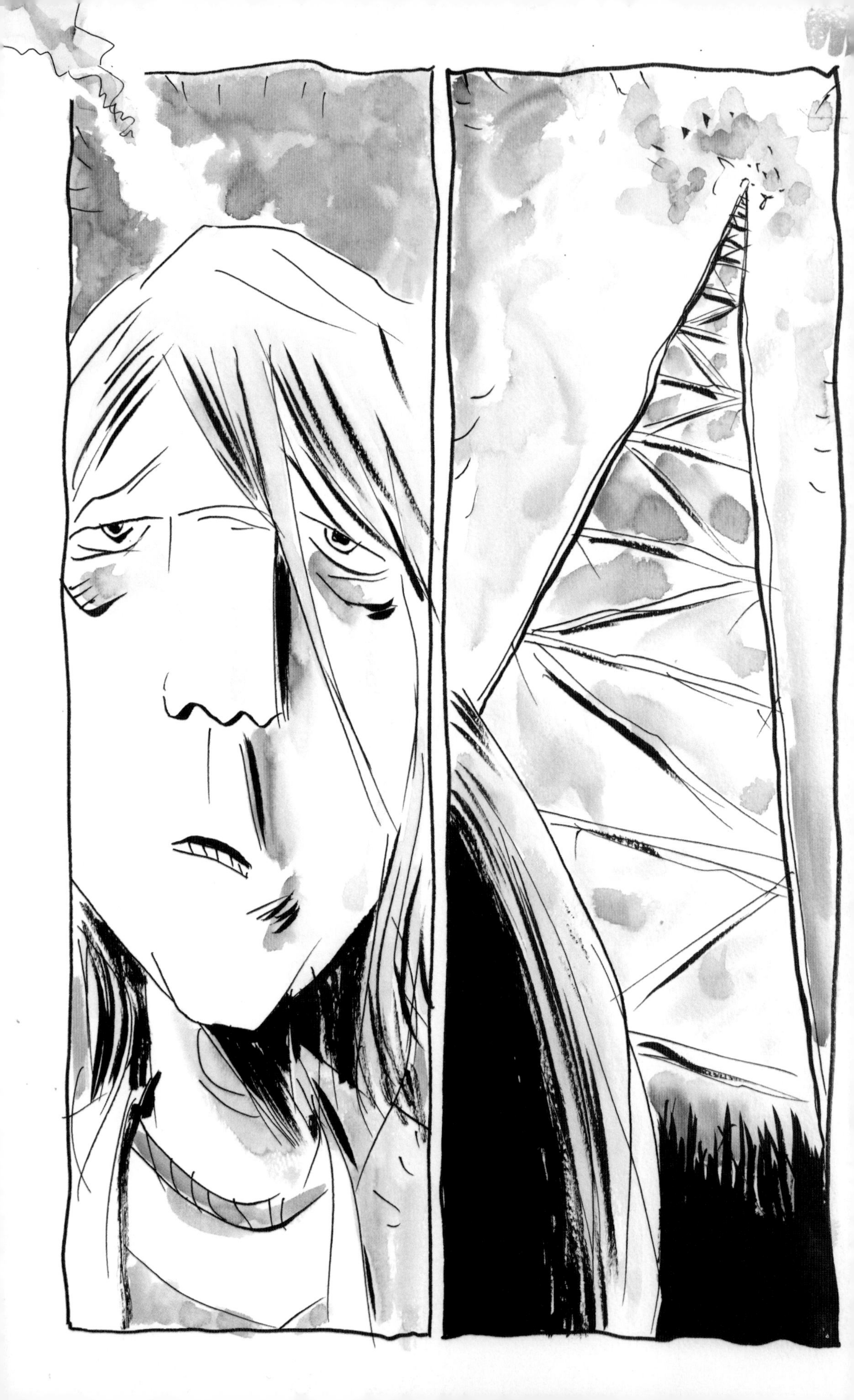

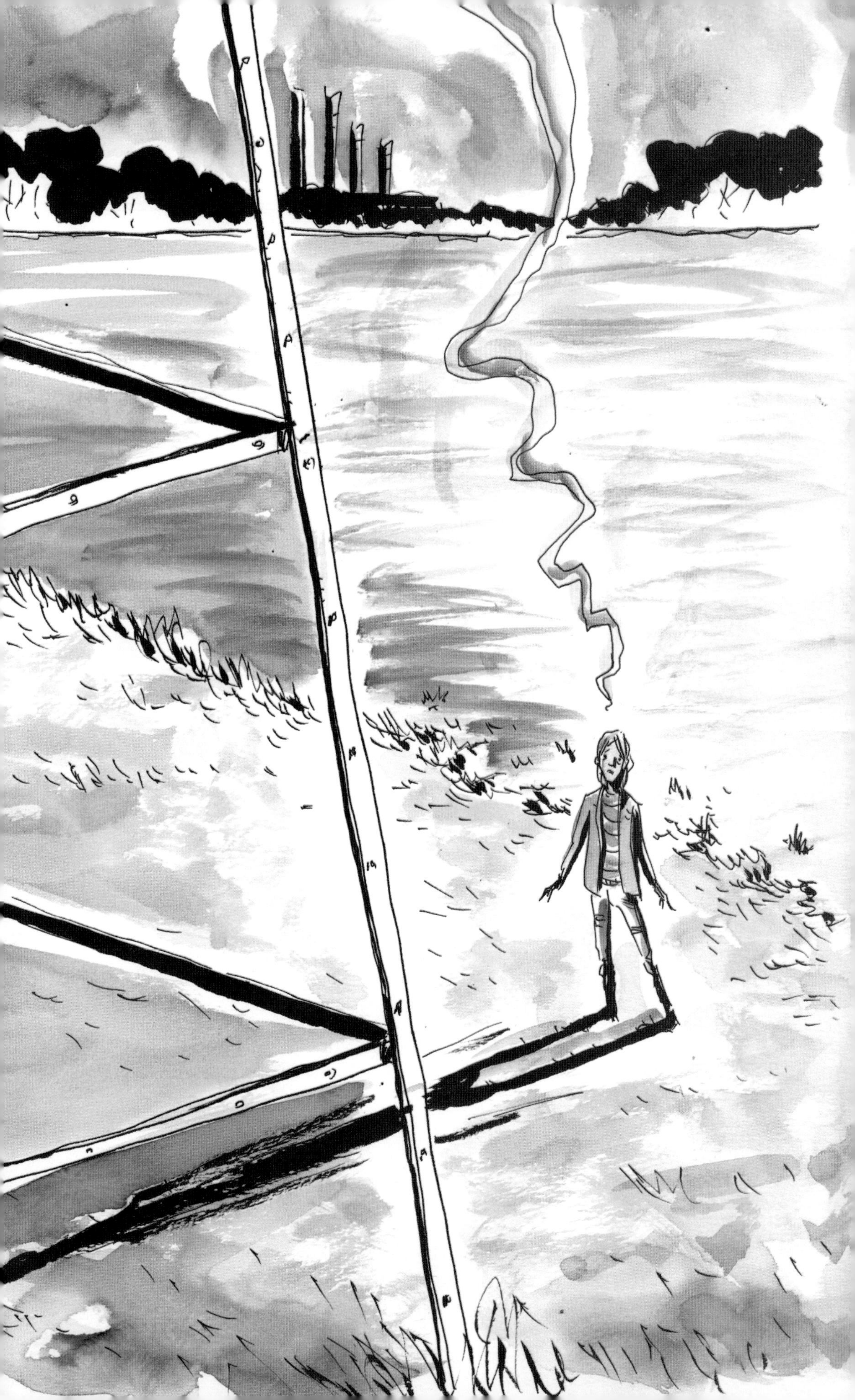

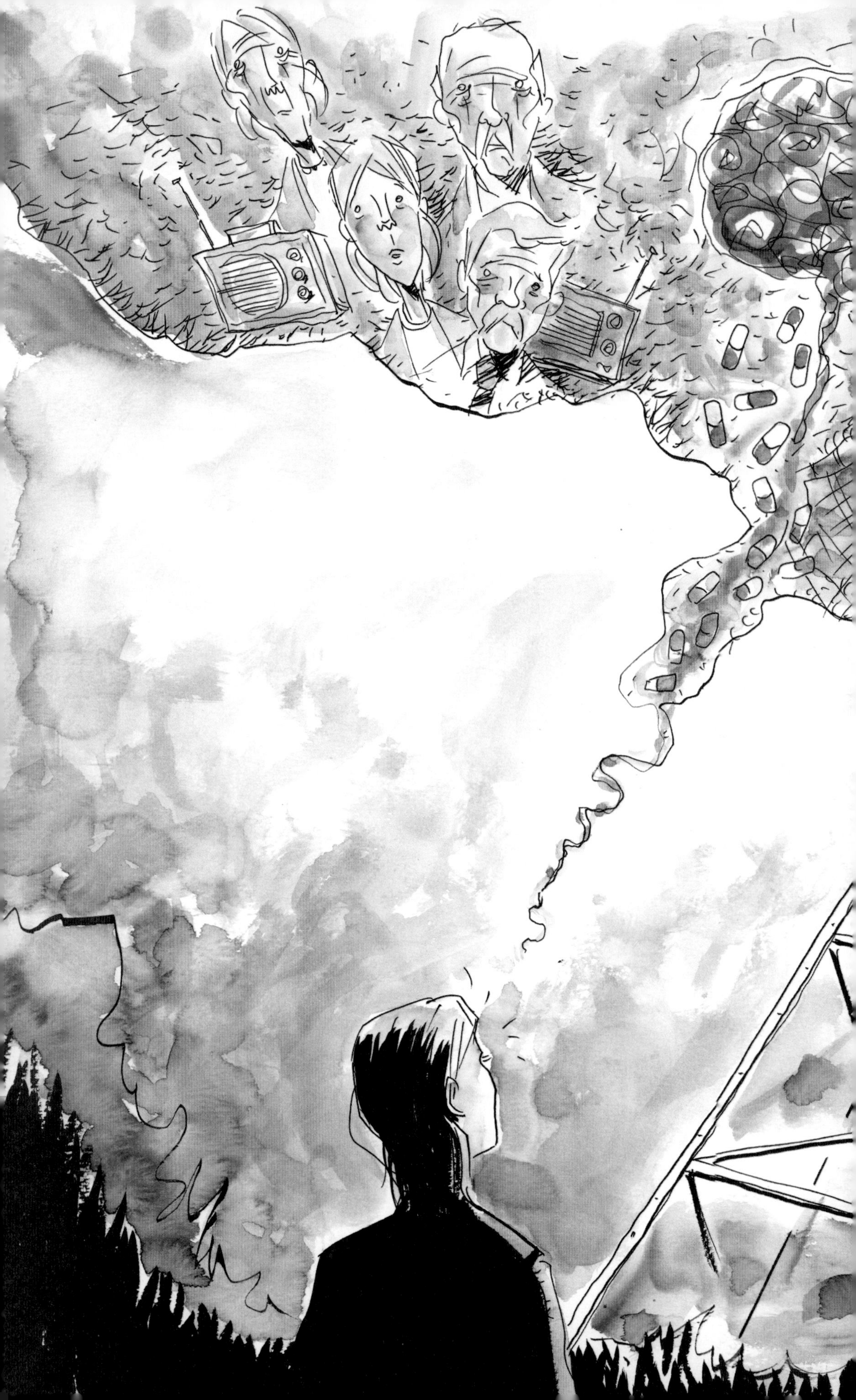

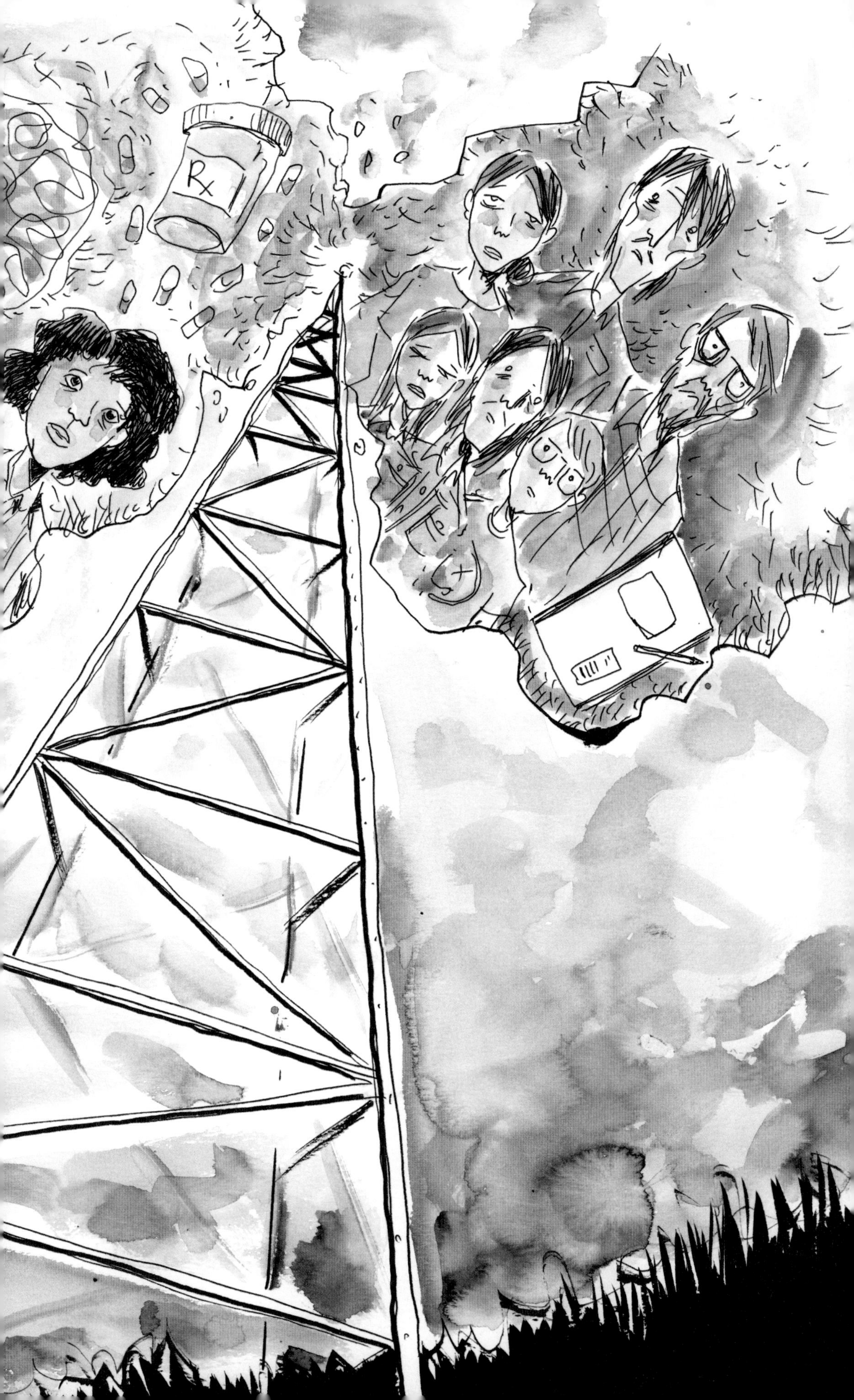
Rx

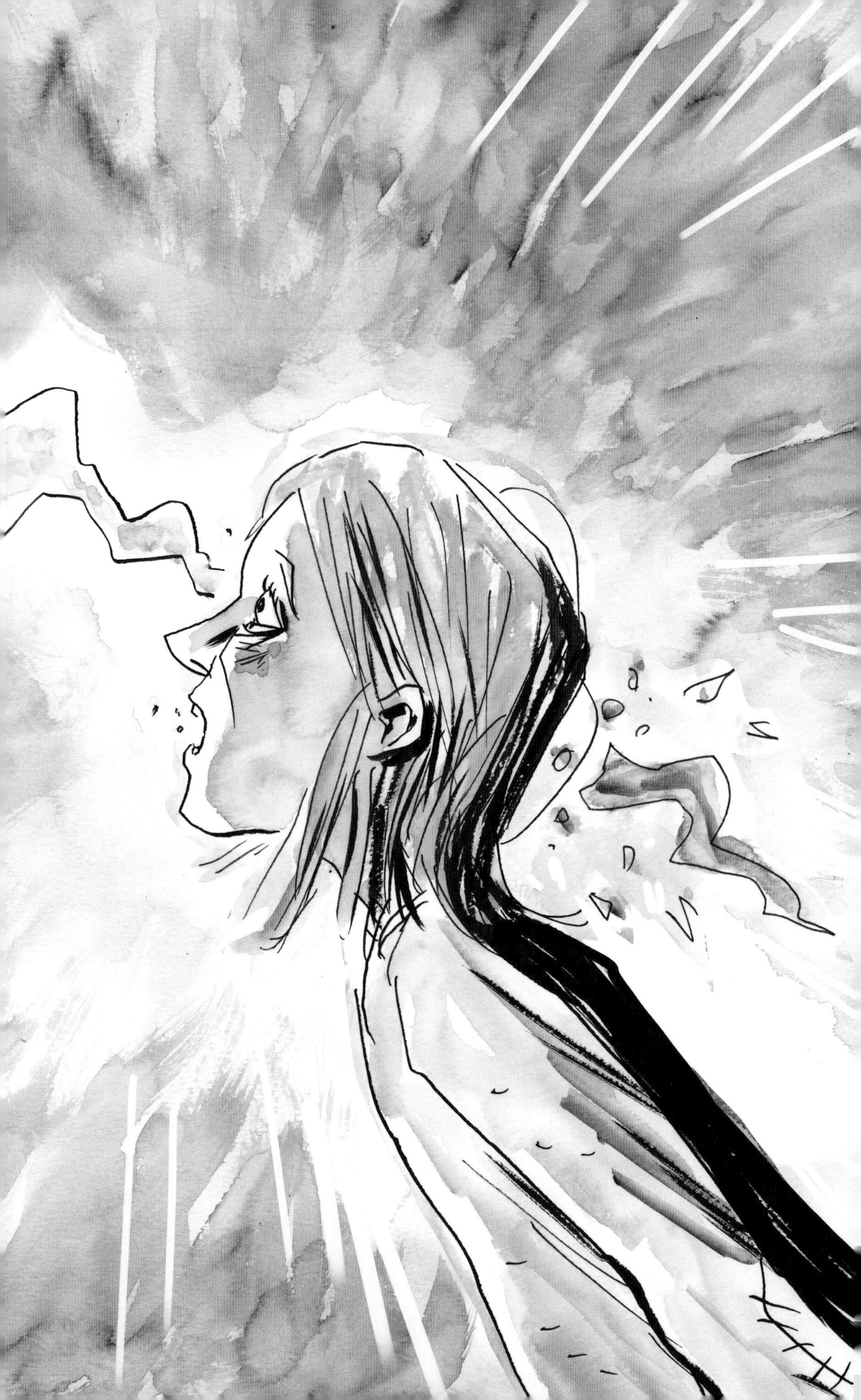

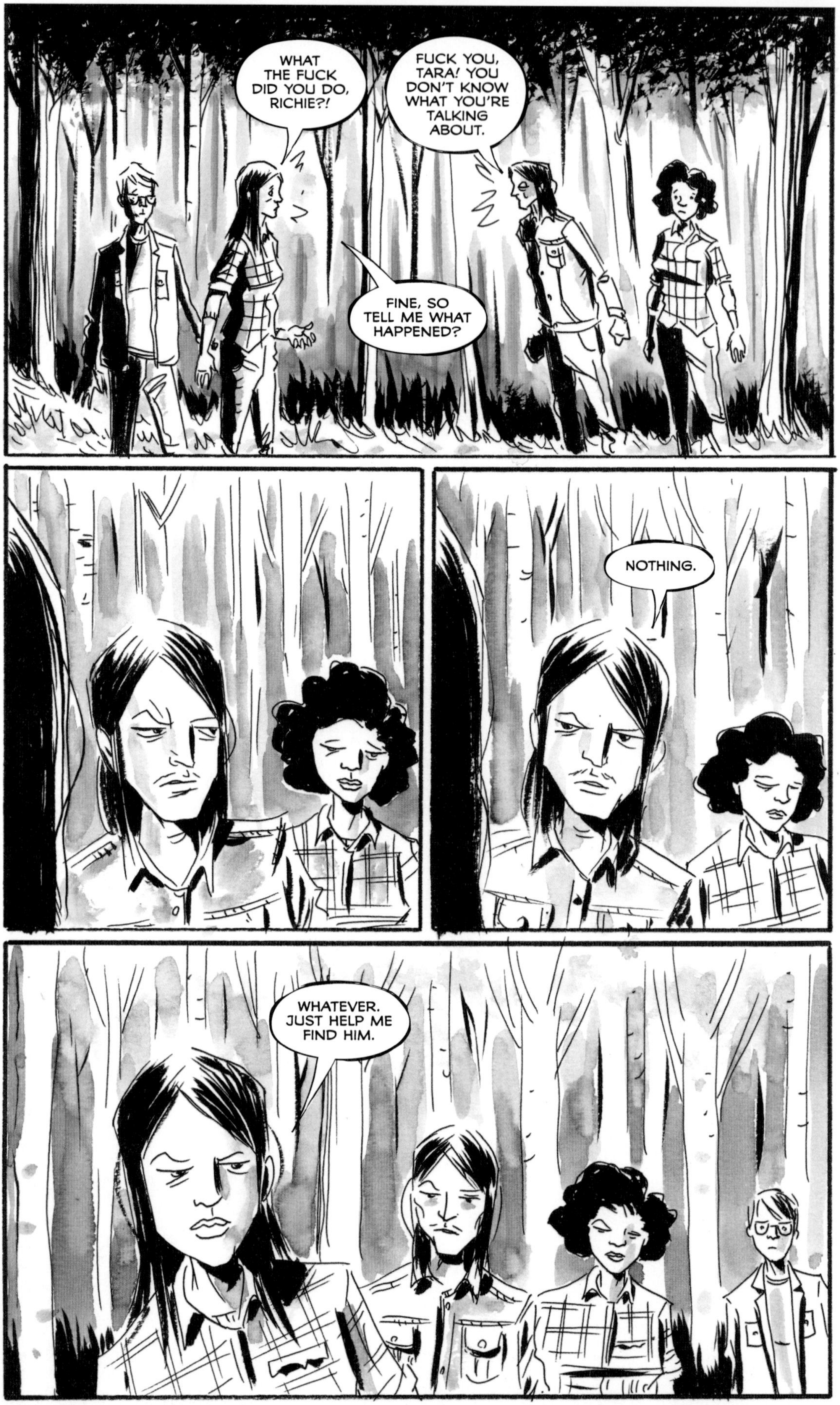
WHAT THE FUCK DID YOU DO, RICHIE?!
FUCK YOU, TARA! YOU DON'T KNOW WHAT YOU'RE TALKING ABOUT.
FINE, SO TELL ME WHAT HAPPENED?
NOTHING.
WHATEVER. JUST HELP ME FIND HIM.

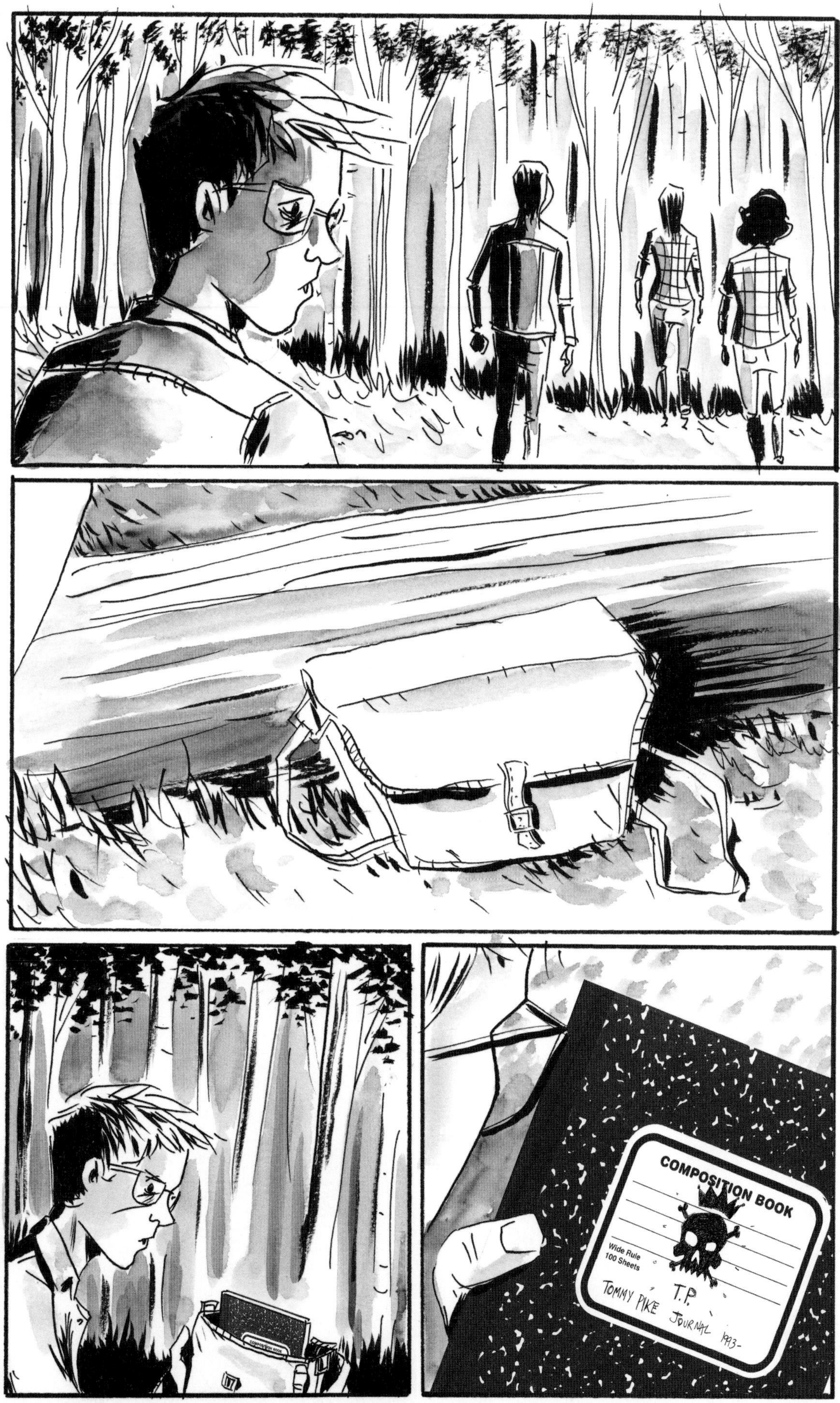
COMPOSITION BOOK
Wide Rule
100 Sheets
T.P.
TOMMY PIKE JOURNAL 1993-

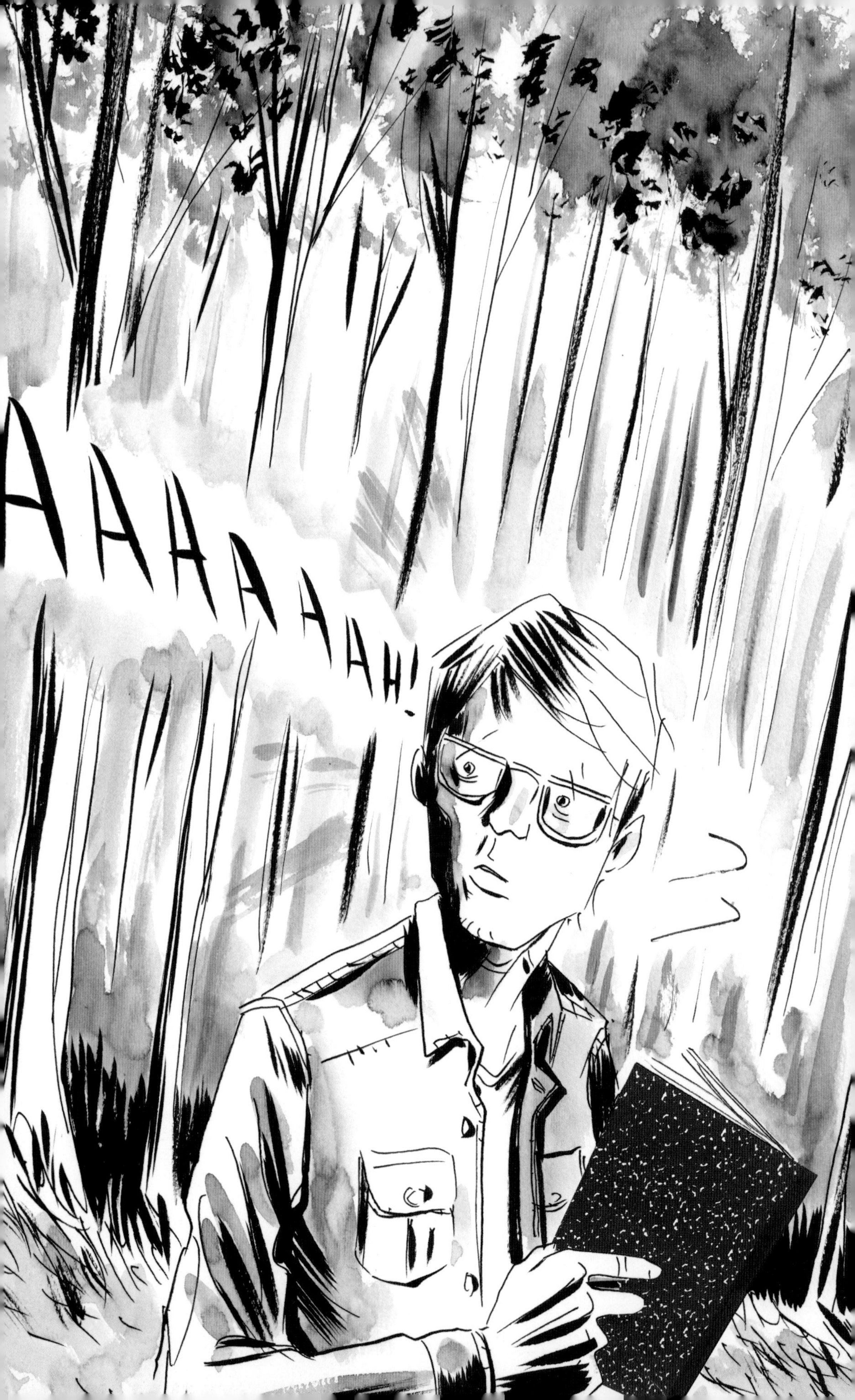
AAAAAAAAH!

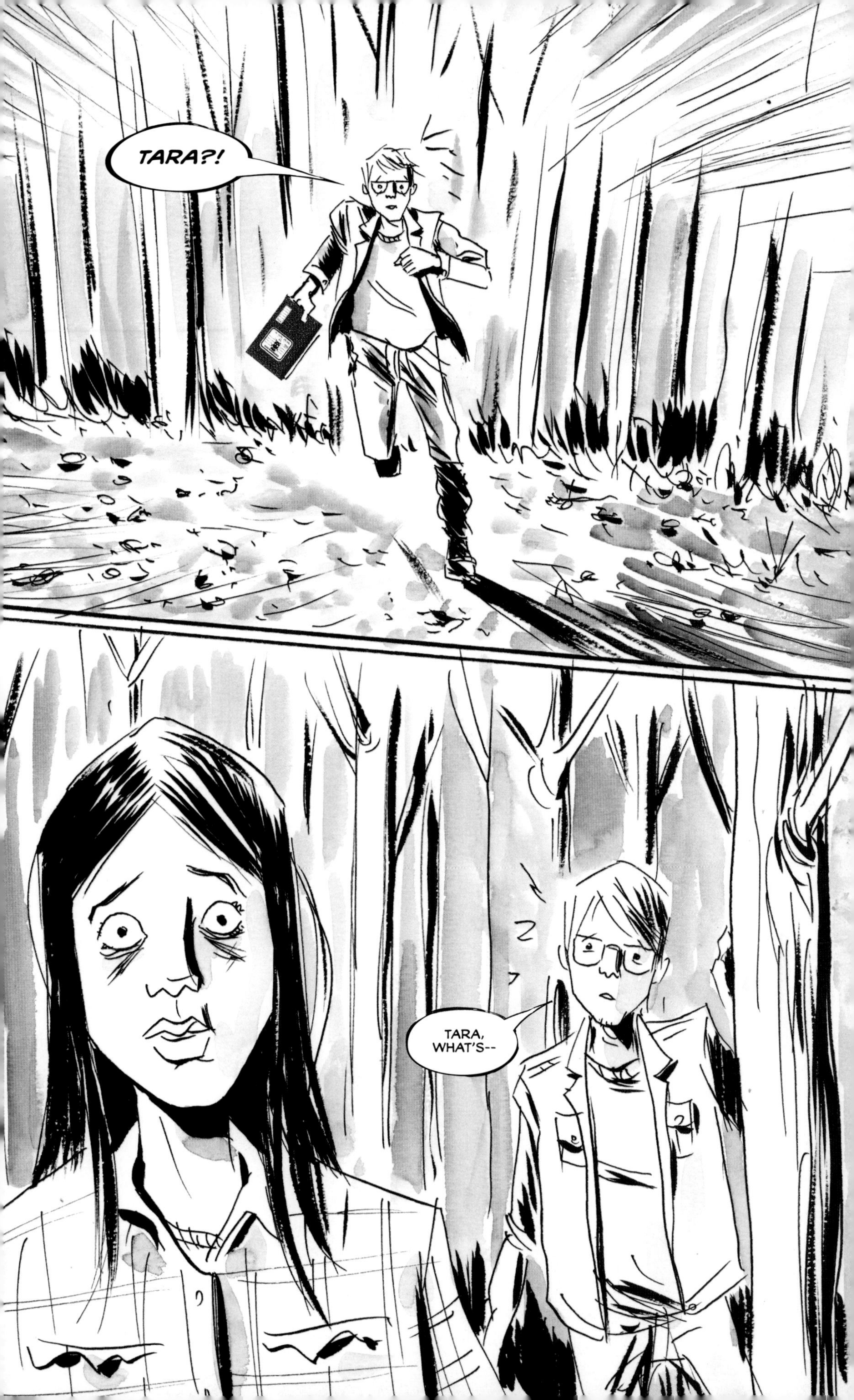
TARA?!
TARA, WHAT'S--

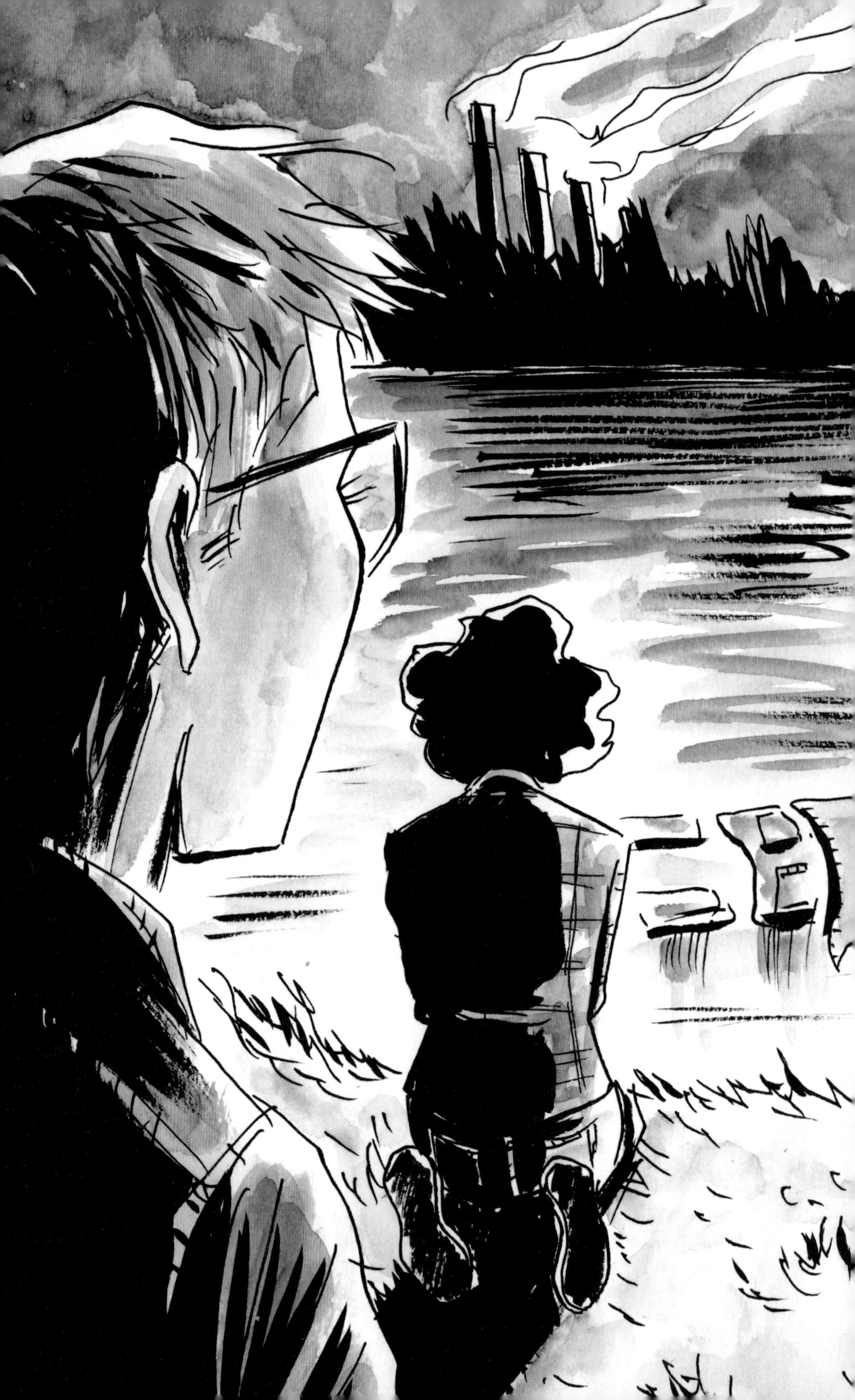

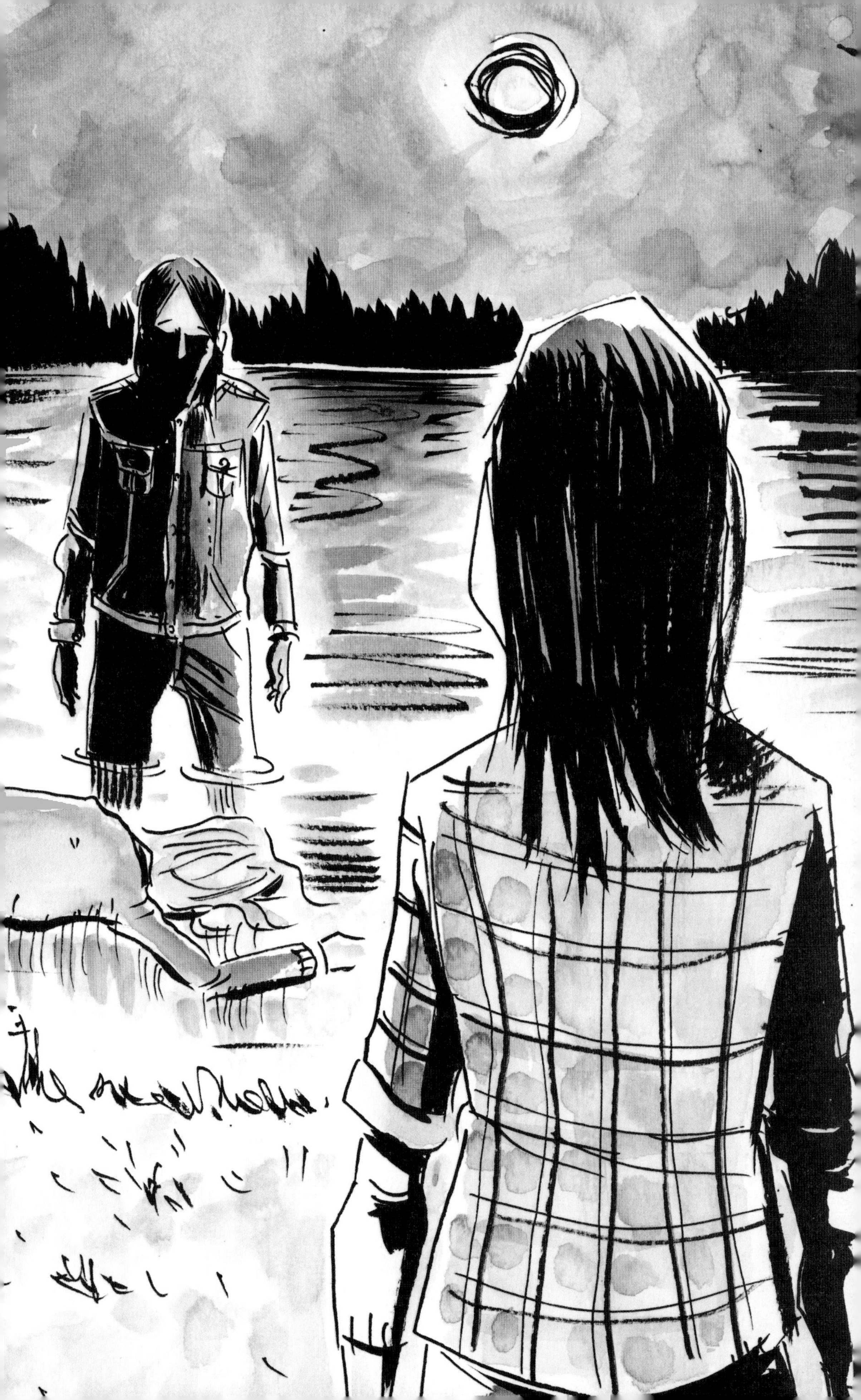

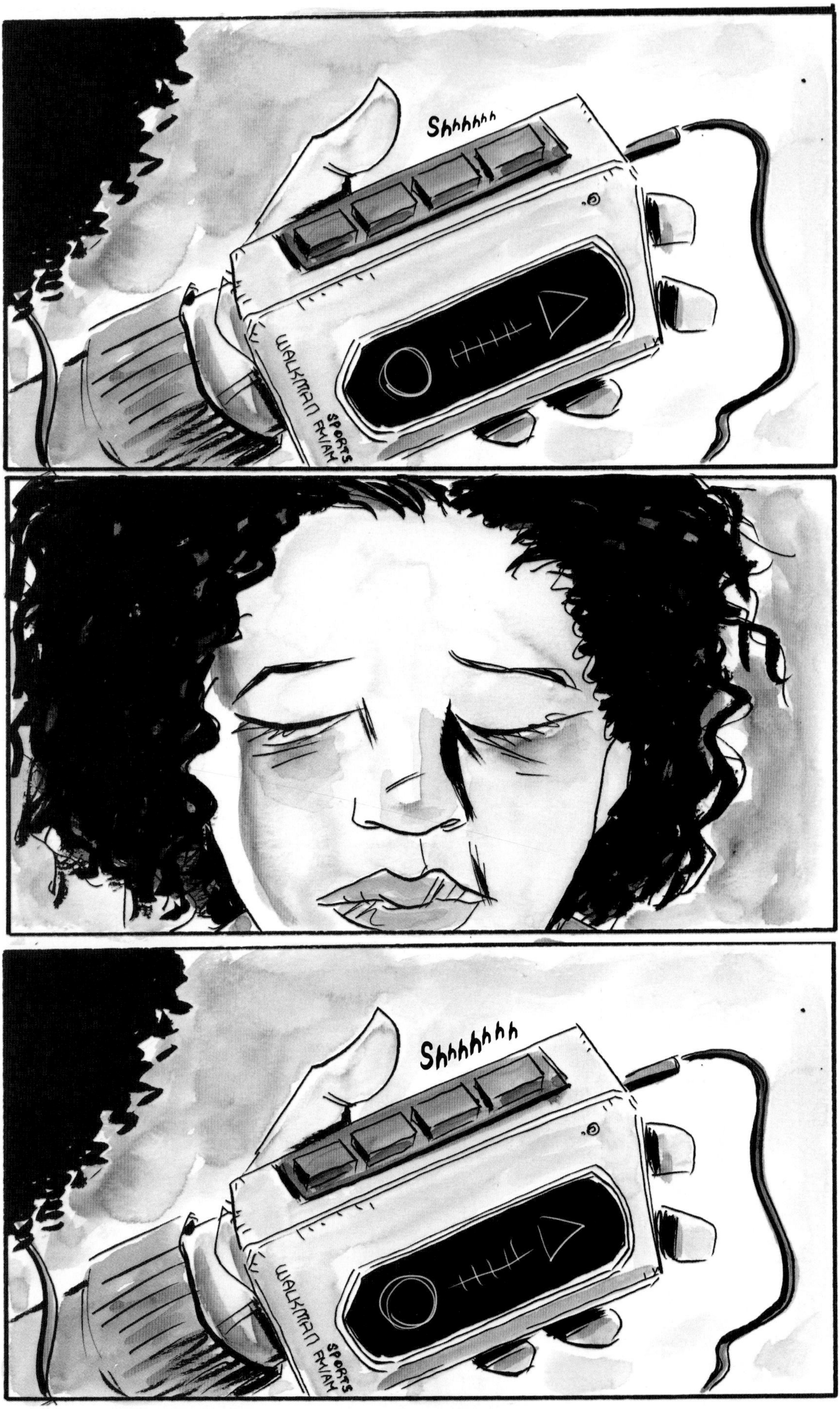
Shhhhhh
WALKMAN
SPORTS
FM/AM
Shhhhhhh
WALKMAN
SPORTS
FM/AM

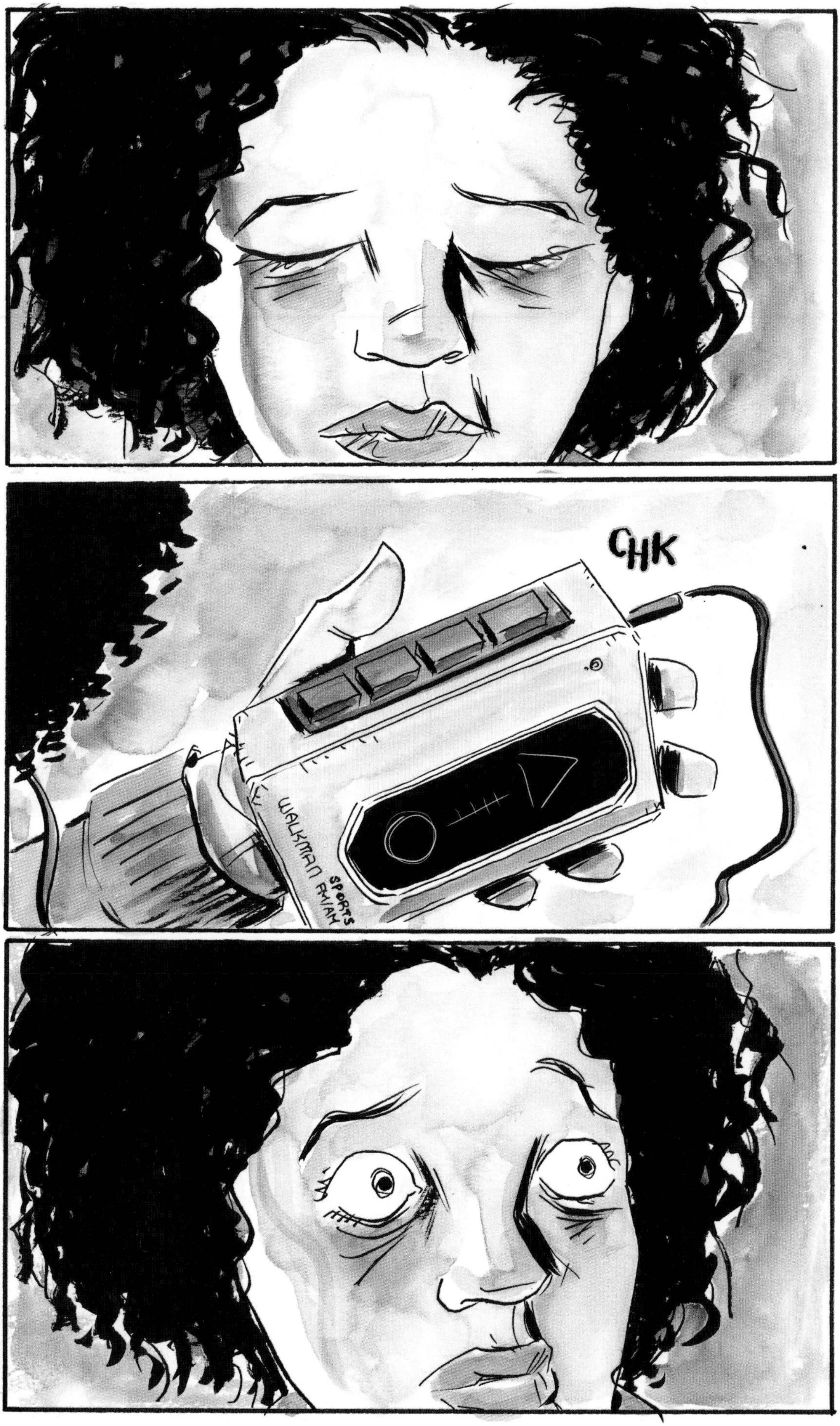
CHK
WALKMAN
SPORTS
FM/AM

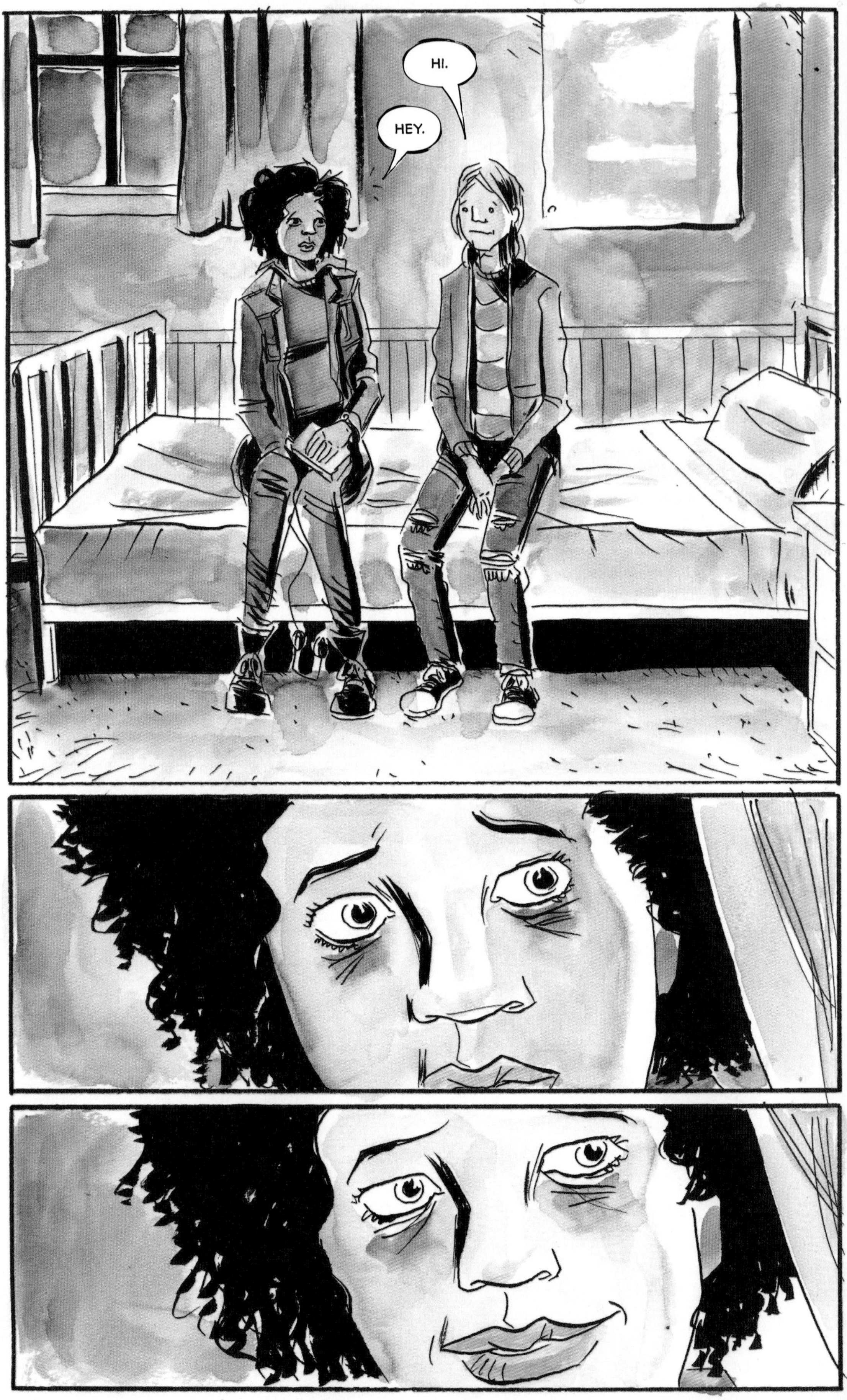
HEY.
HI.

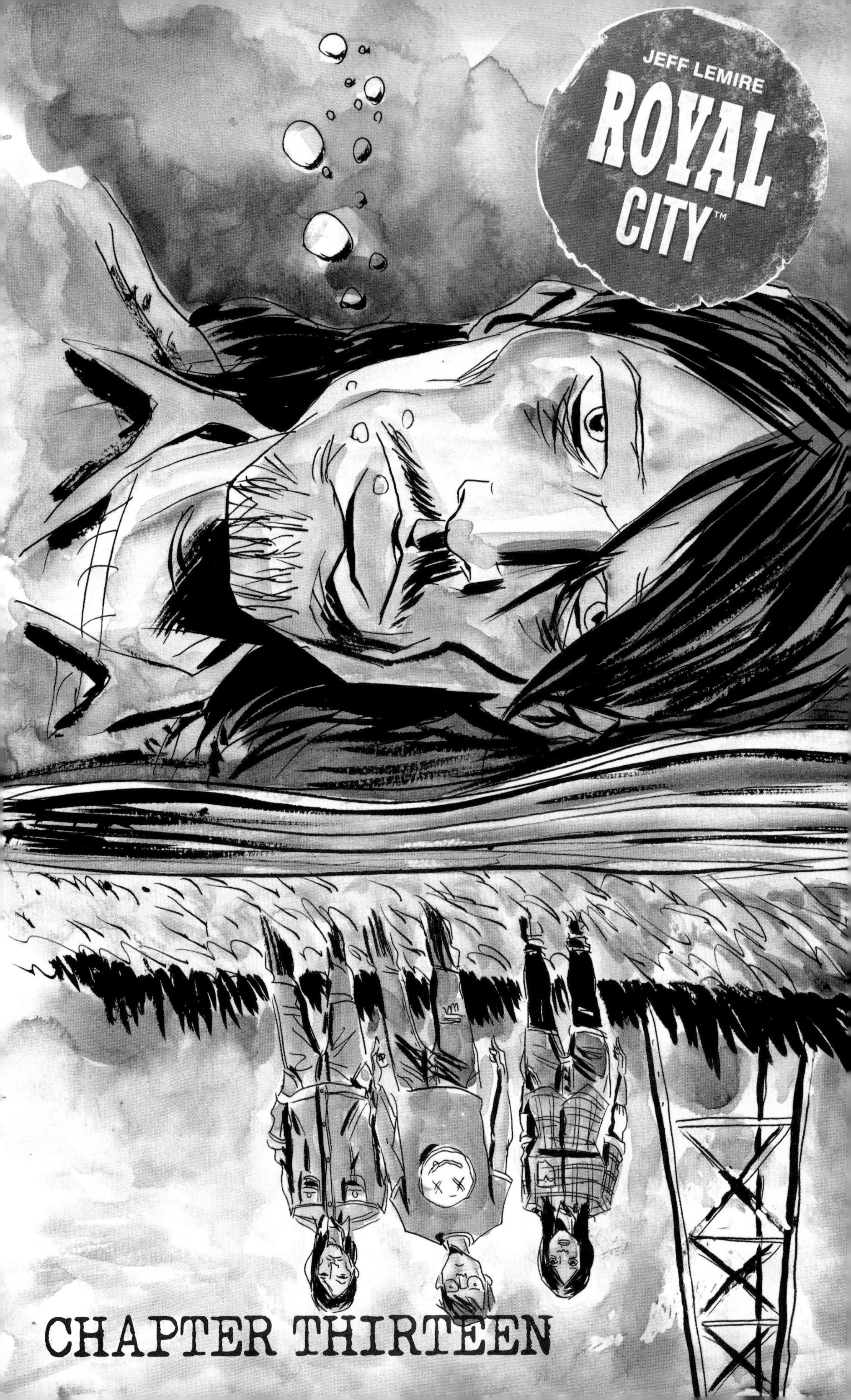
JEFF LEMIRE
ROYAL CITY™

CHAPTER THIRTEEN

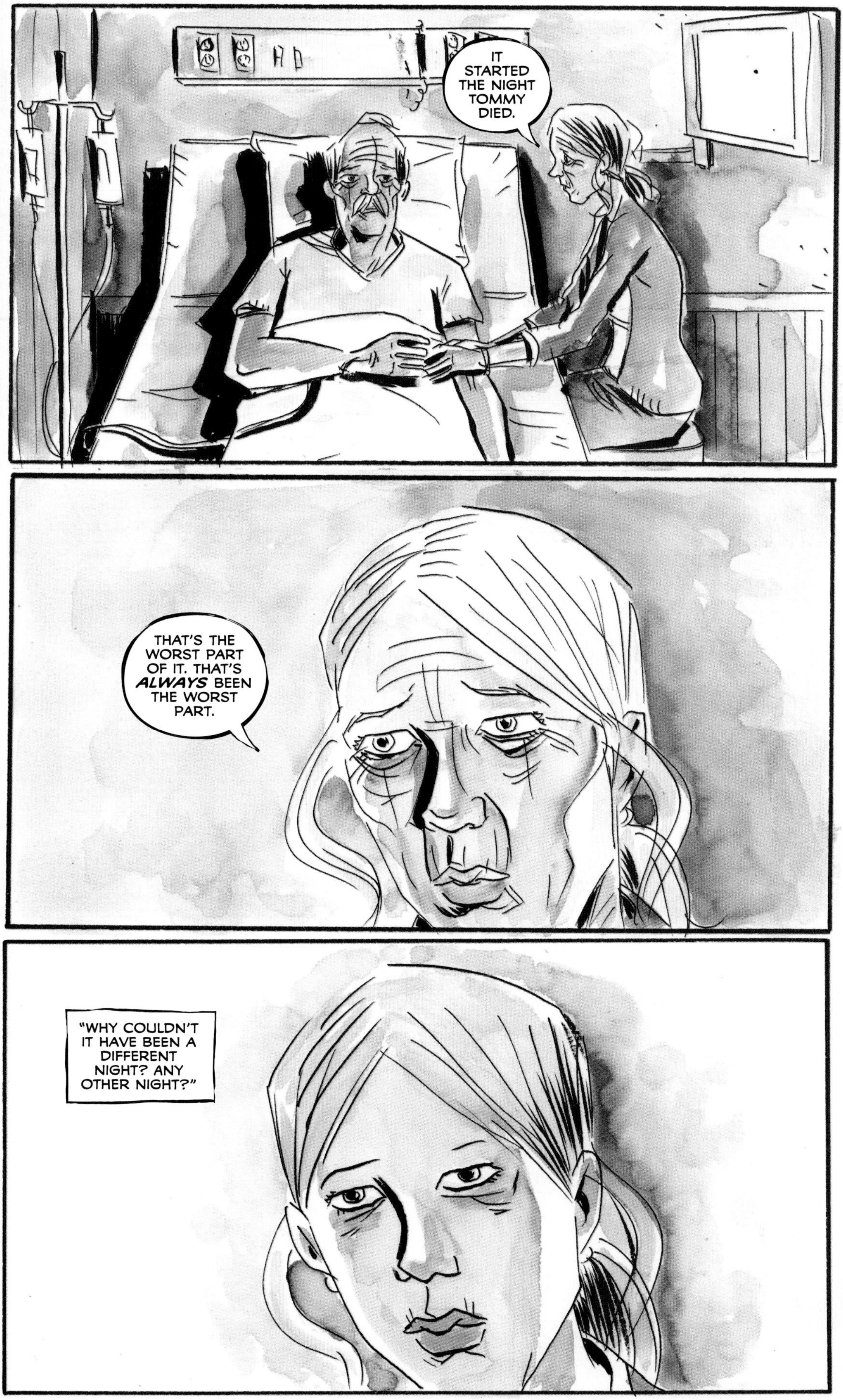
IT STARTED THE NIGHT TOMMY DIED.
THAT'S THE WORST PART OF IT. THAT'S *ALWAYS* BEEN THE WORST PART.
"WHY COULDN'T IT HAVE BEEN A DIFFERENT NIGHT? ANY OTHER NIGHT?"

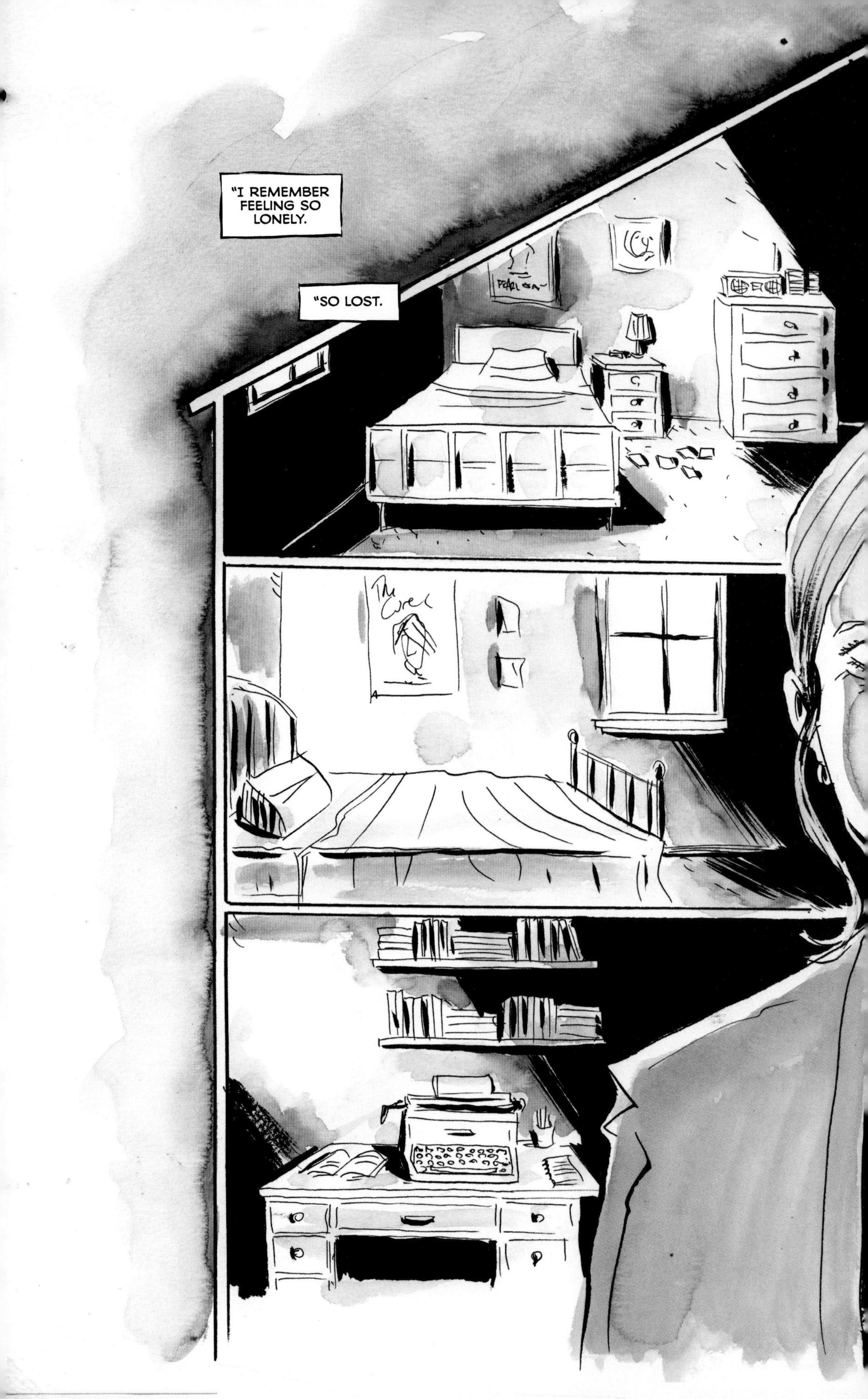
"I REMEMBER FEELING SO LONELY.
"SO LOST.

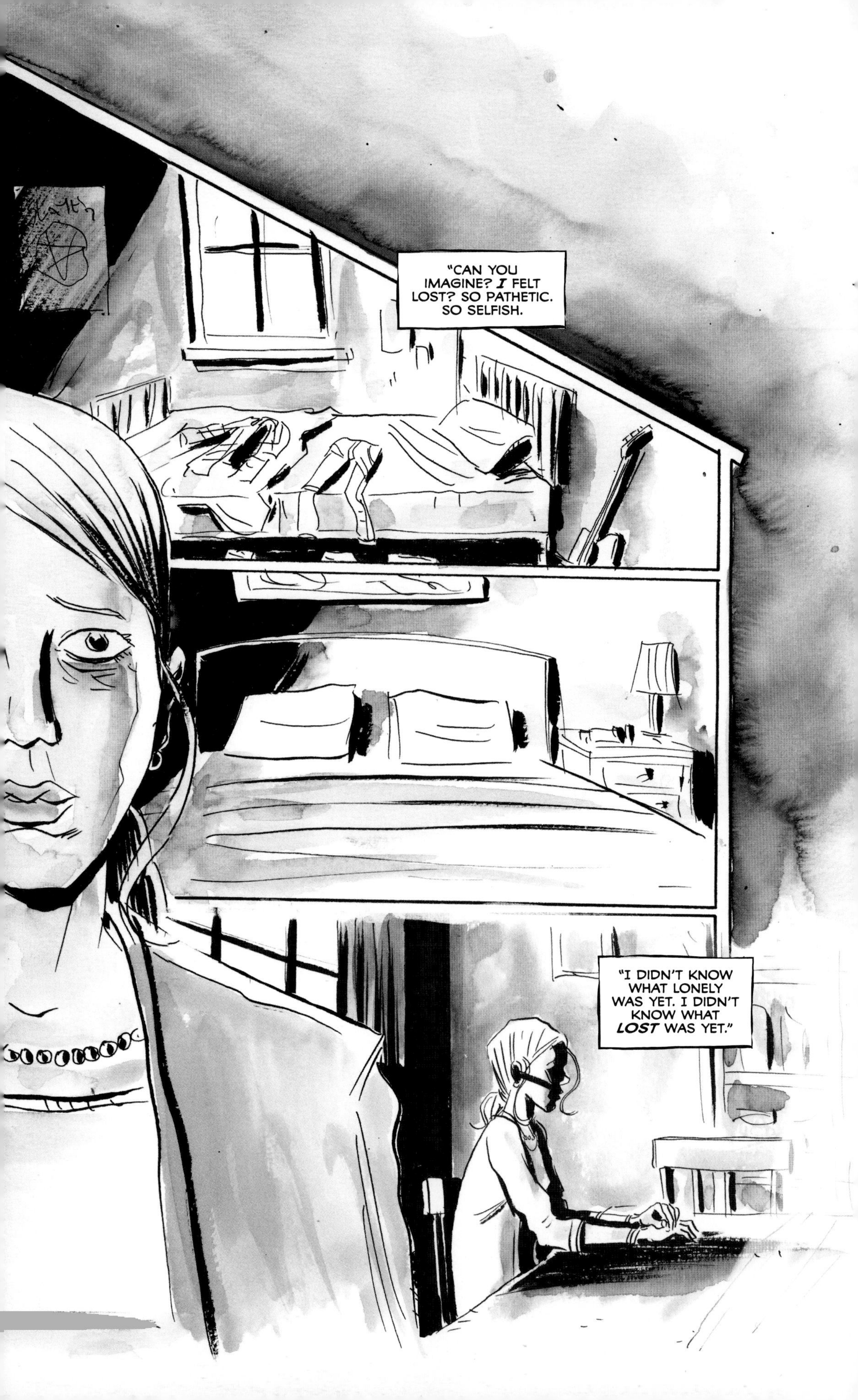
"CAN YOU IMAGINE? *I* FELT LOST? SO PATHETIC. SO SELFISH.
"I DIDN'T KNOW WHAT LONELY WAS YET. I DIDN'T KNOW WHAT *LOST* WAS YET."

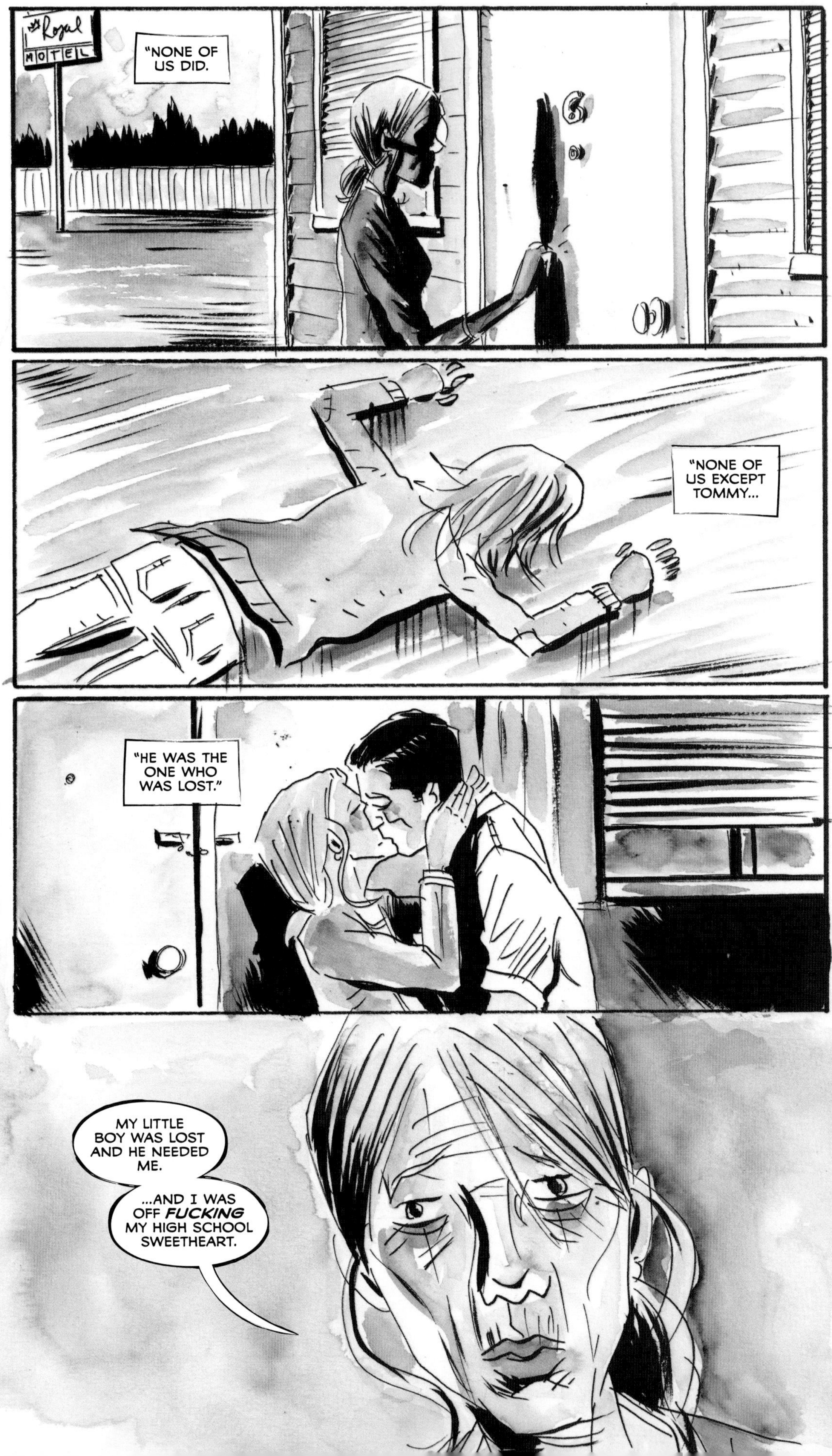
Royal
MOTEL
"NONE OF US DID.
"NONE OF US EXCEPT TOMMY...
"HE WAS THE ONE WHO WAS LOST."
MY LITTLE BOY WAS LOST AND HE NEEDED ME.
...AND I WAS OFF *FUCKING* MY HIGH SCHOOL SWEETHEART.

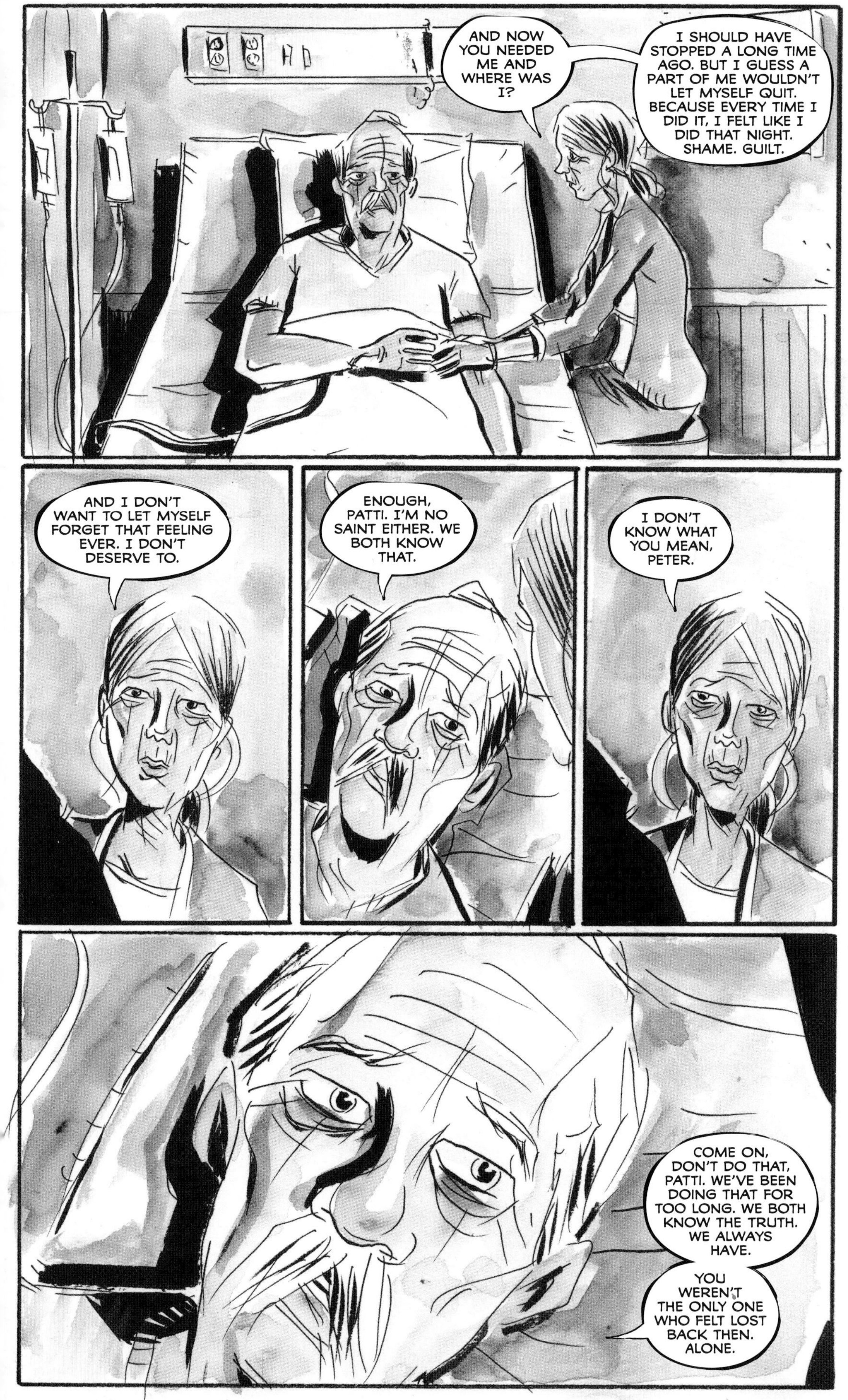
AND NOW YOU NEEDED ME AND WHERE WAS I?
I SHOULD HAVE STOPPED A LONG TIME AGO. BUT I GUESS A PART OF ME WOULDN'T LET MYSELF QUIT. BECAUSE EVERY TIME I DID IT, I FELT LIKE I DID THAT NIGHT. SHAME. GUILT.
AND I DON'T WANT TO LET MYSELF FORGET THAT FEELING EVER. I DON'T DESERVE TO.
ENOUGH, PATTI. I'M NO SAINT EITHER. WE BOTH KNOW THAT.
I DON'T KNOW WHAT YOU MEAN, PETER.
COME ON, DON'T DO THAT, PATTI. WE'VE BEEN DOING THAT FOR TOO LONG. WE BOTH KNOW THE TRUTH. WE ALWAYS HAVE.
YOU WEREN'T THE ONLY ONE WHO FELT LOST BACK THEN. ALONE.

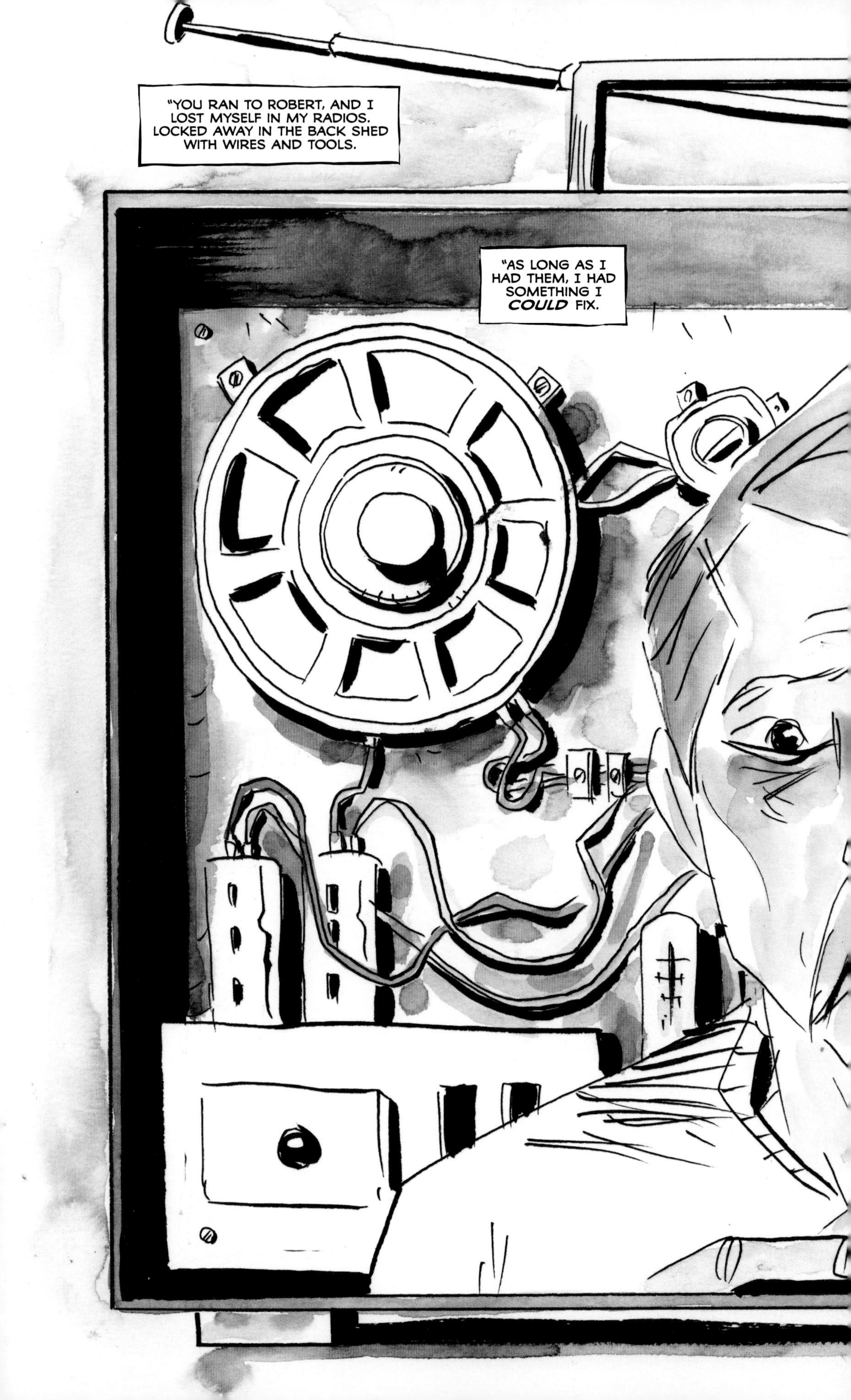
"YOU RAN TO ROBERT, AND I LOST MYSELF IN MY RADIOS. LOCKED AWAY IN THE BACK SHED WITH WIRES AND TOOLS.
"AS LONG AS I HAD THEM, I HAD SOMETHING I *COULD* FIX.

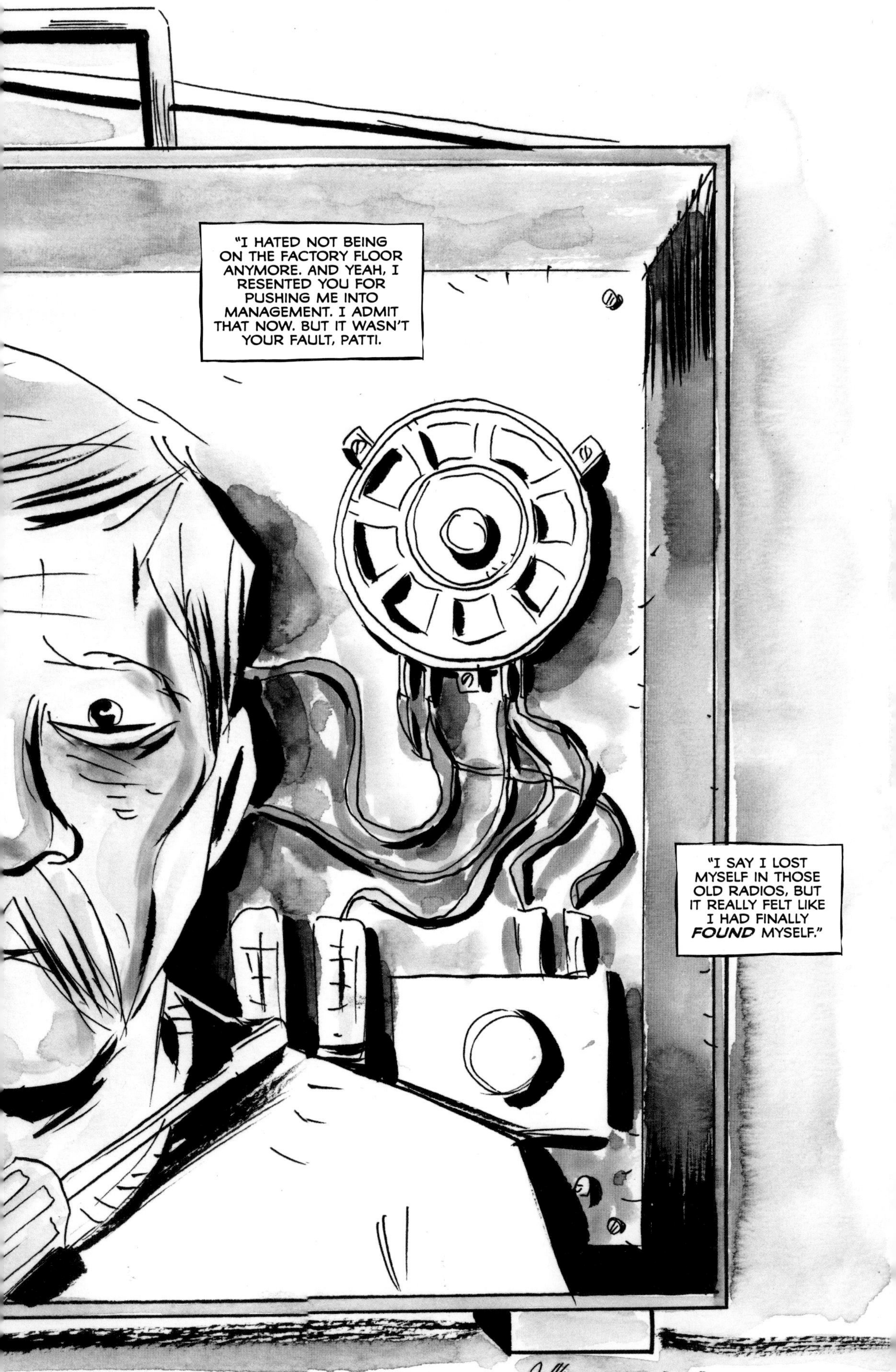
"I HATED NOT BEING ON THE FACTORY FLOOR ANYMORE. AND YEAH, I RESENTED YOU FOR PUSHING ME INTO MANAGEMENT. I ADMIT THAT NOW. BUT IT WASN'T YOUR FAULT, PATTI.
"I SAY I LOST MYSELF IN THOSE OLD RADIOS, BUT IT REALLY FELT LIKE I HAD FINALLY *FOUND* MYSELF."
2018

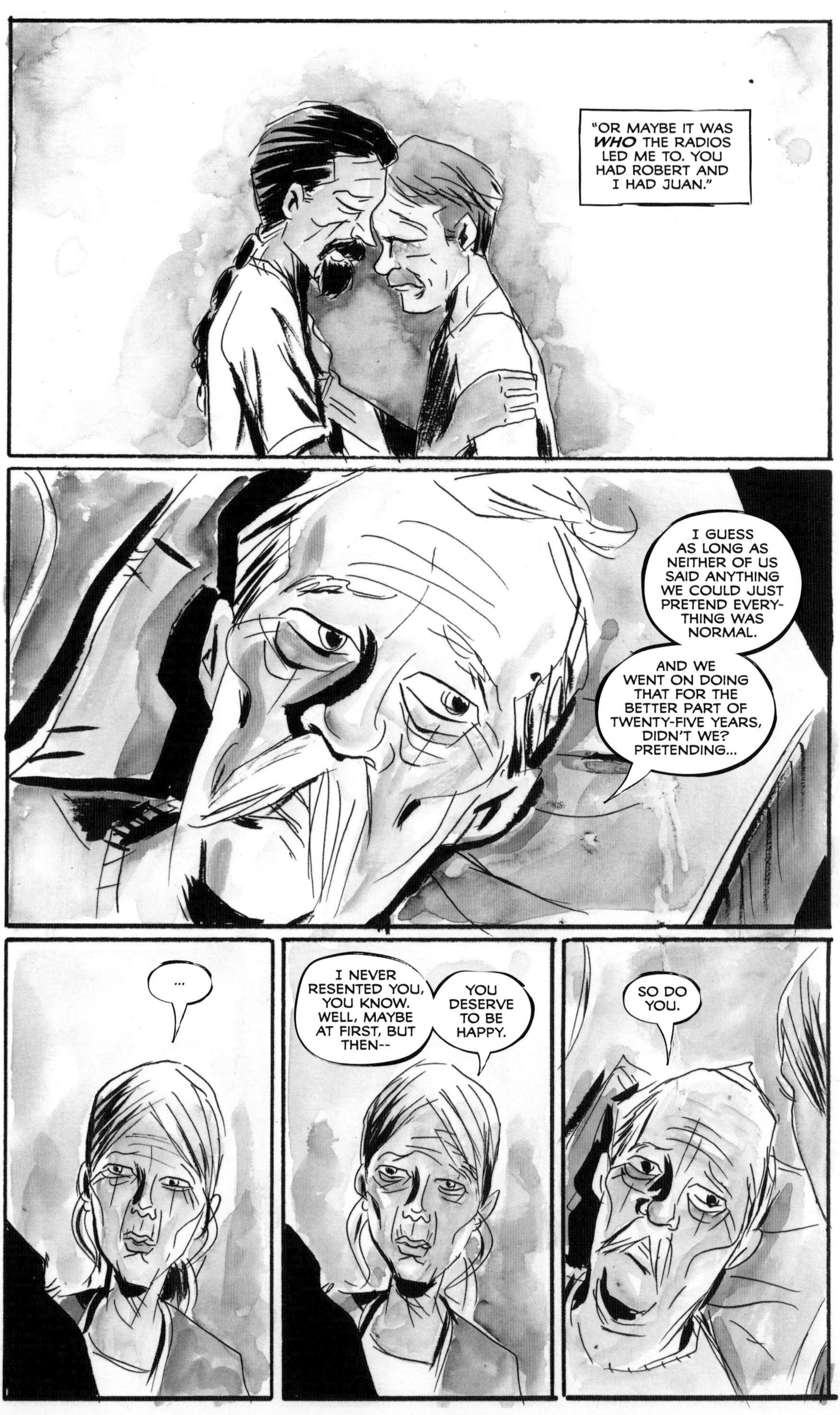
"OR MAYBE IT WAS *WHO* THE RADIOS LED ME TO. YOU HAD ROBERT AND I HAD JUAN."
I GUESS AS LONG AS NEITHER OF US SAID ANYTHING WE COULD JUST PRETEND EVERY-THING WAS NORMAL.
AND WE WENT ON DOING THAT FOR THE BETTER PART OF TWENTY-FIVE YEARS, DIDN'T WE? PRETENDING...
...
I NEVER RESENTED YOU, YOU KNOW. WELL, MAYBE AT FIRST, BUT THEN--
YOU DESERVE TO BE HAPPY.
SO DO YOU.

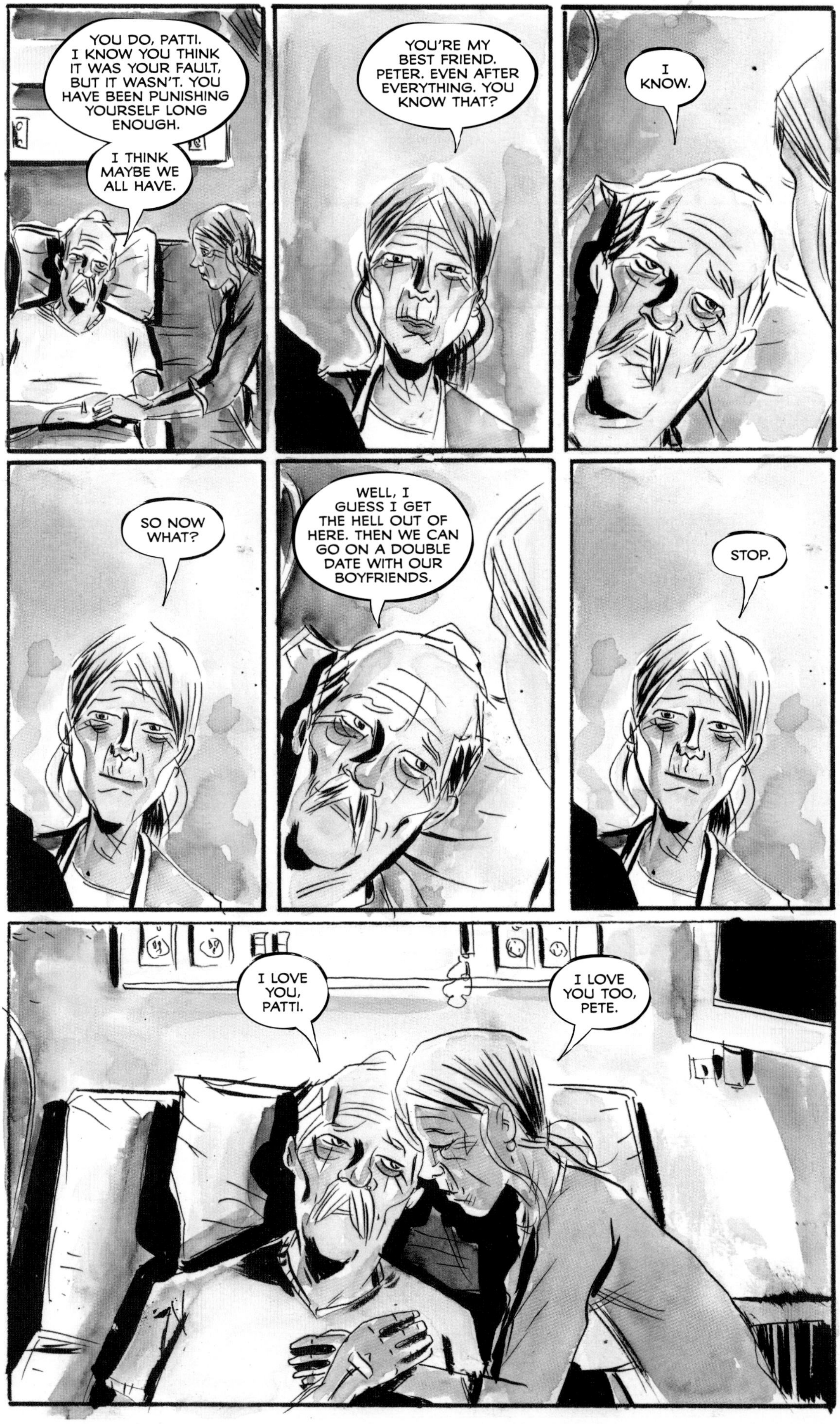
YOU DO, PATTI. I KNOW YOU THINK IT WAS YOUR FAULT, BUT IT WASN'T. YOU HAVE BEEN PUNISHING YOURSELF LONG ENOUGH.
I THINK MAYBE WE ALL HAVE.
YOU'RE MY BEST FRIEND. PETER. EVEN AFTER EVERYTHING. YOU KNOW THAT?
I KNOW.
SO NOW WHAT?
WELL, I GUESS I GET THE HELL OUT OF HERE. THEN WE CAN GO ON A DOUBLE DATE WITH OUR BOYFRIENDS.
STOP.
I LOVE YOU, PATTI.
I LOVE YOU TOO, PETE.

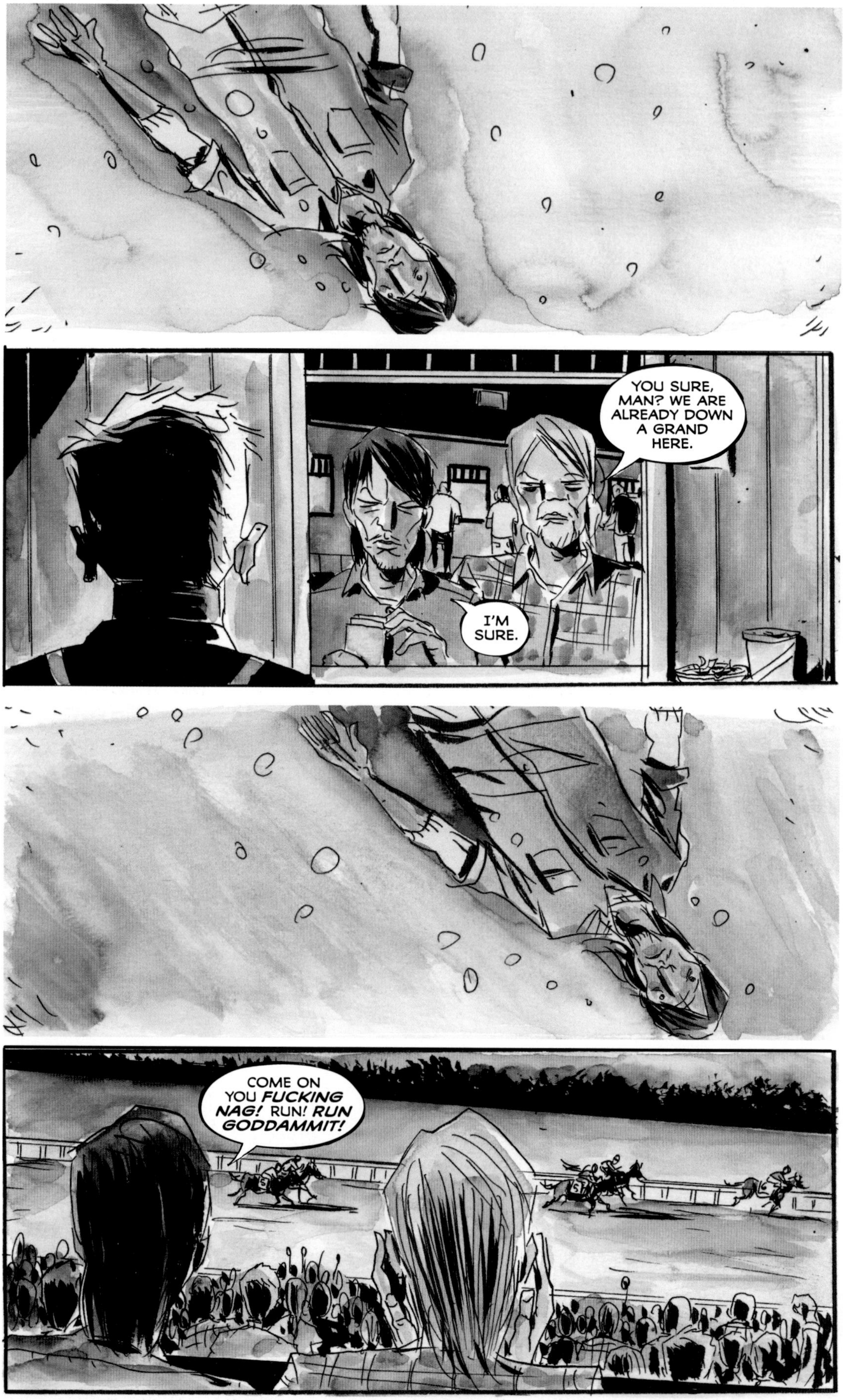
YOU SURE, MAN? WE ARE ALREADY DOWN A GRAND HERE.
I'M SURE.
COME ON YOU *FUCKING NAG!* RUN! *RUN GODDAMMIT!*

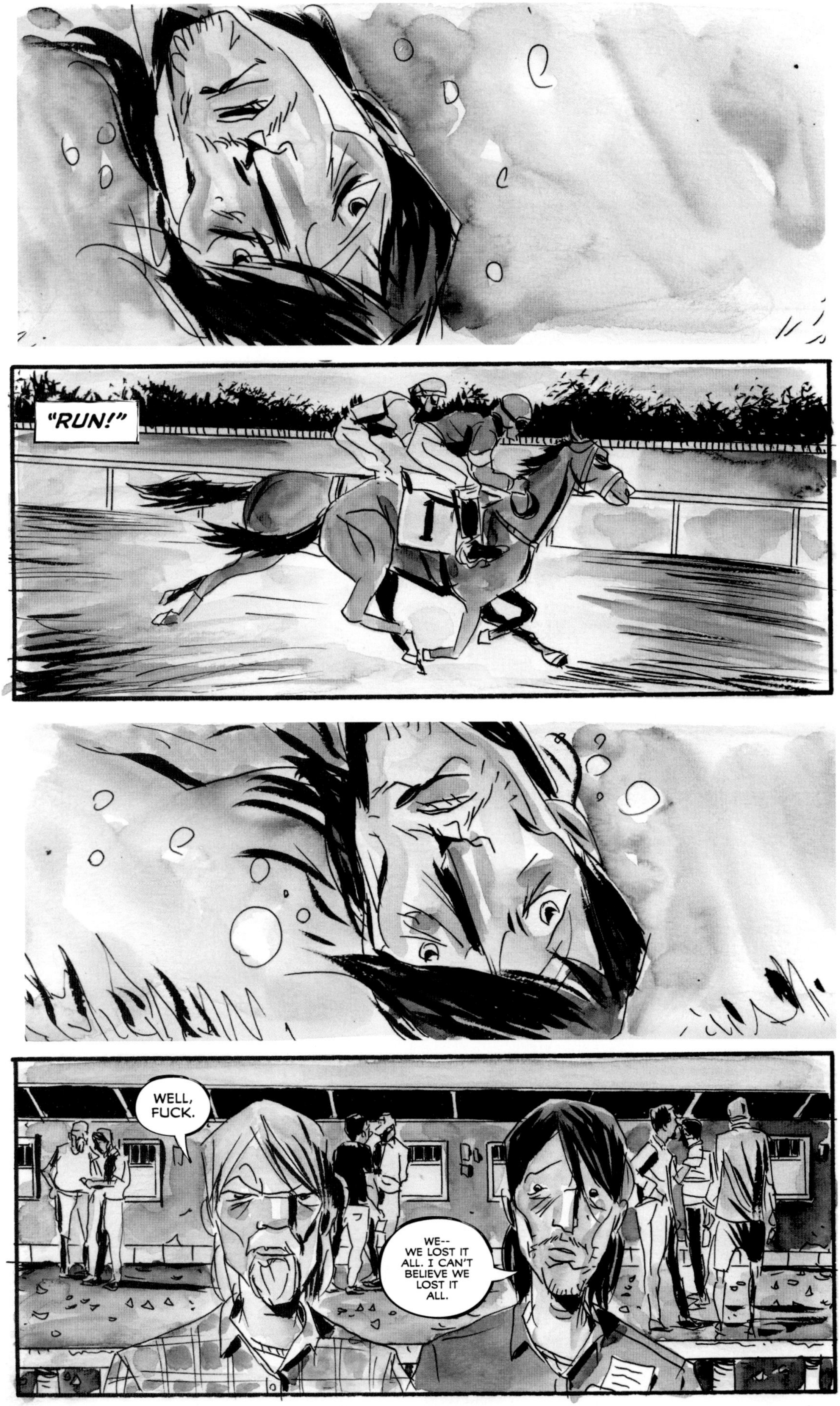
"RUN!"
WELL, FUCK.
WE-- WE LOST IT ALL. I CAN'T BELIEVE WE LOST IT ALL.

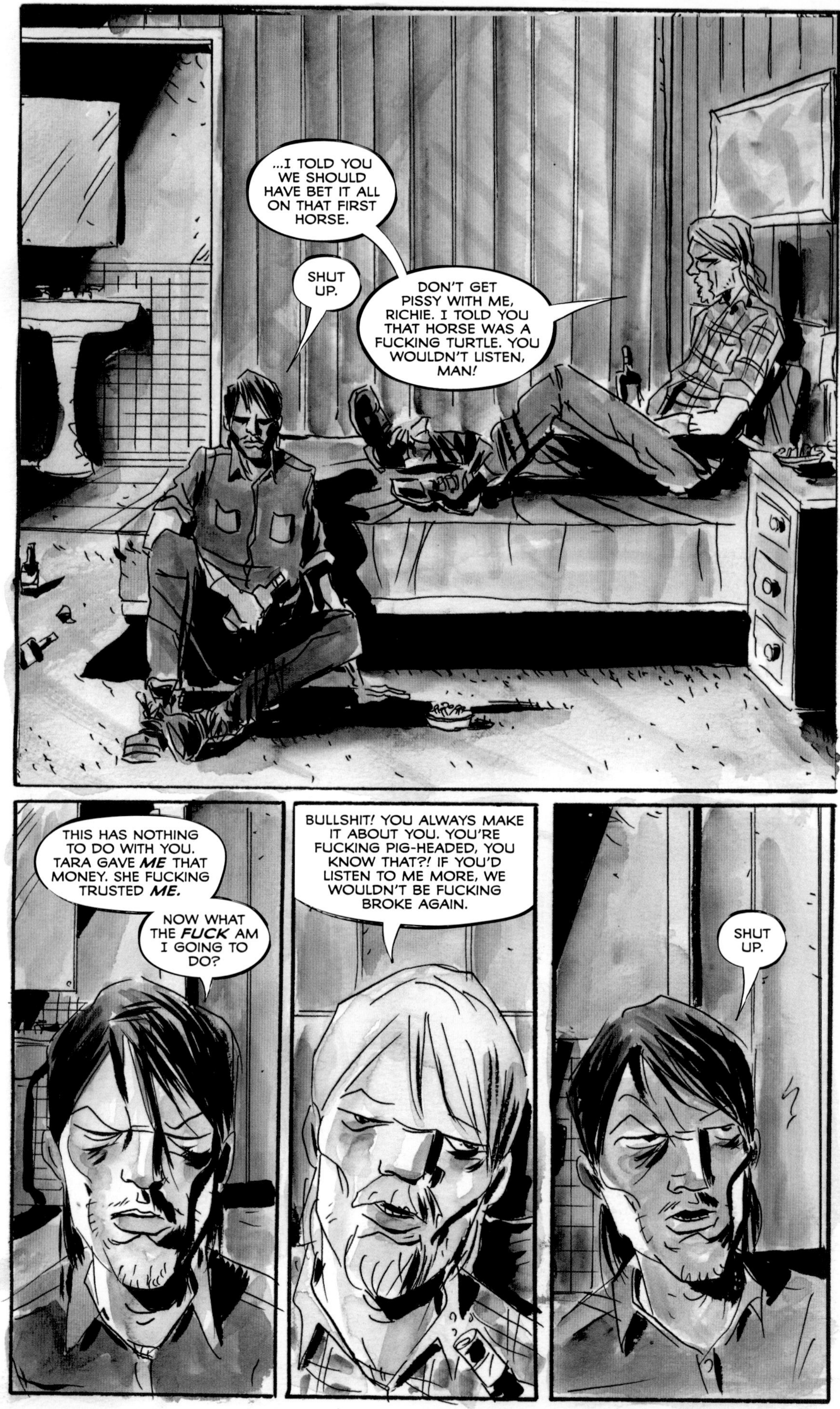
...I TOLD YOU WE SHOULD HAVE BET IT ALL ON THAT FIRST HORSE.
SHUT UP.
DON'T GET PISSY WITH ME, RICHIE. I TOLD YOU THAT HORSE WAS A FUCKING TURTLE. YOU WOULDN'T LISTEN, MAN!
THIS HAS NOTHING TO DO WITH YOU. TARA GAVE ME THAT MONEY. SHE FUCKING TRUSTED ME.
NOW WHAT THE FUCK AM I GOING TO DO?
BULLSHIT! YOU ALWAYS MAKE IT ABOUT YOU. YOU'RE FUCKING PIG-HEADED, YOU KNOW THAT?! IF YOU'D LISTEN TO ME MORE, WE WOULDN'T BE FUCKING BROKE AGAIN.
SHUT UP.

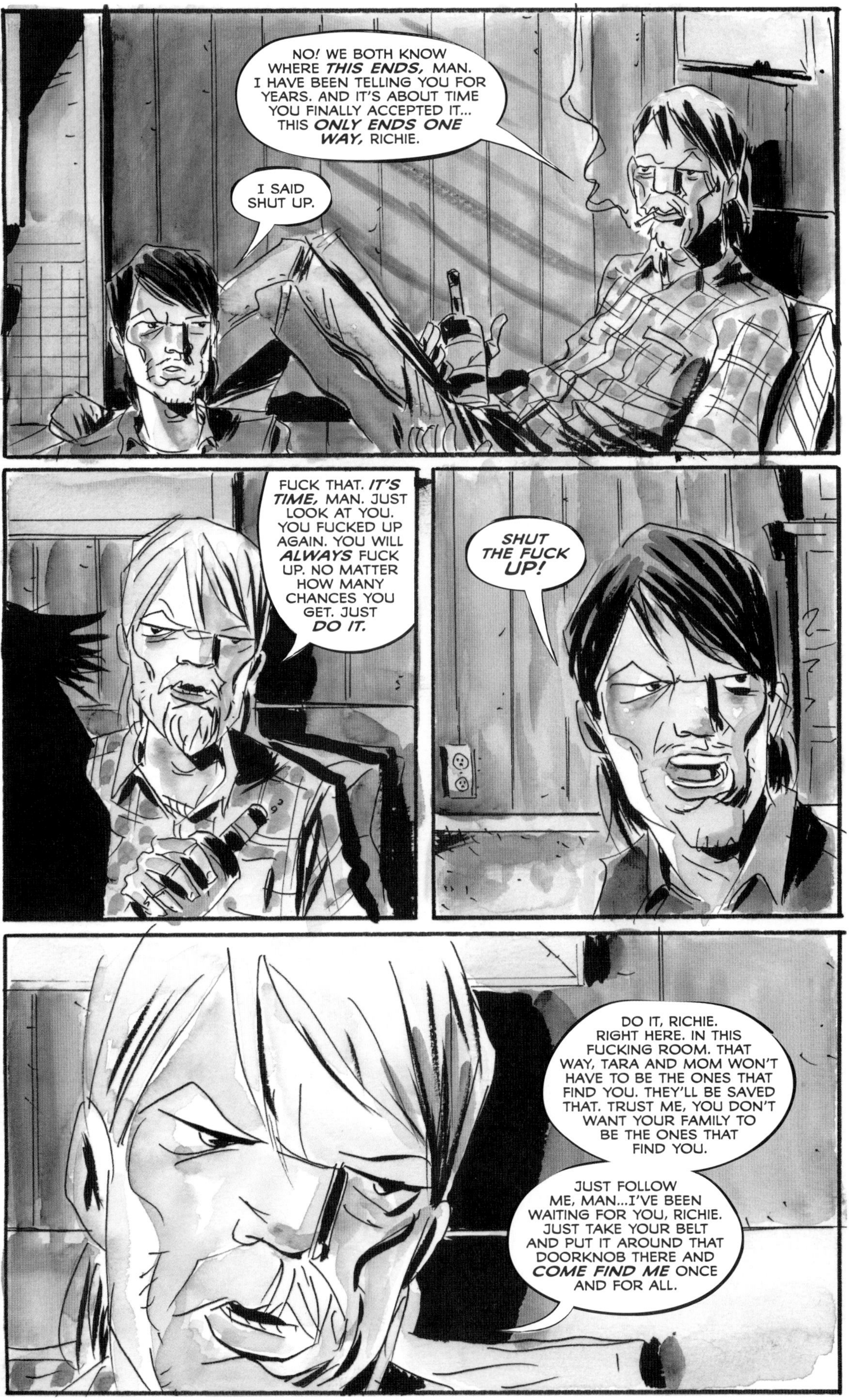
NO! WE BOTH KNOW WHERE THIS ENDS, MAN. I HAVE BEEN TELLING YOU FOR YEARS. AND IT'S ABOUT TIME YOU FINALLY ACCEPTED IT... THIS ONLY ENDS ONE WAY, RICHIE.
I SAID SHUT UP.
FUCK THAT. IT'S TIME, MAN. JUST LOOK AT YOU. YOU FUCKED UP AGAIN. YOU WILL ALWAYS FUCK UP. NO MATTER HOW MANY CHANCES YOU GET. JUST DO IT.
SHUT THE FUCK UP!
DO IT, RICHIE. RIGHT HERE. IN THIS FUCKING ROOM. THAT WAY, TARA AND MOM WON'T HAVE TO BE THE ONES THAT FIND YOU. THEY'LL BE SAVED THAT. TRUST ME, YOU DON'T WANT YOUR FAMILY TO BE THE ONES THAT FIND YOU.
JUST FOLLOW ME, MAN...I'VE BEEN WAITING FOR YOU, RICHIE. JUST TAKE YOUR BELT AND PUT IT AROUND THAT DOORKNOB THERE AND COME FIND ME ONCE AND FOR ALL.

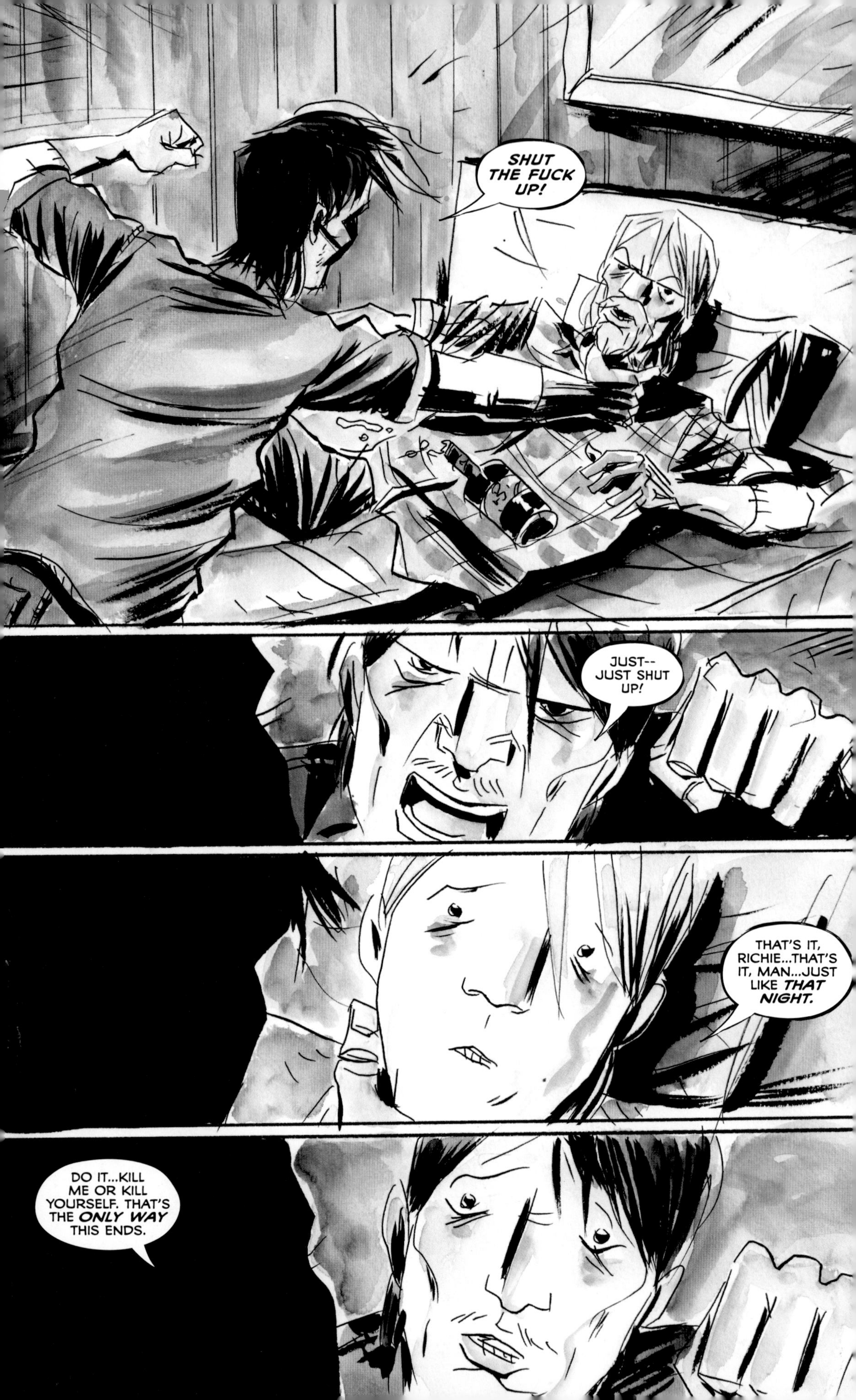
SHUT THE FUCK UP!
JUST-- JUST SHUT UP!
THAT'S IT, RICHIE...THAT'S IT, MAN...JUST LIKE THAT NIGHT.
DO IT...KILL ME OR KILL YOURSELF. THAT'S THE ONLY WAY THIS ENDS.

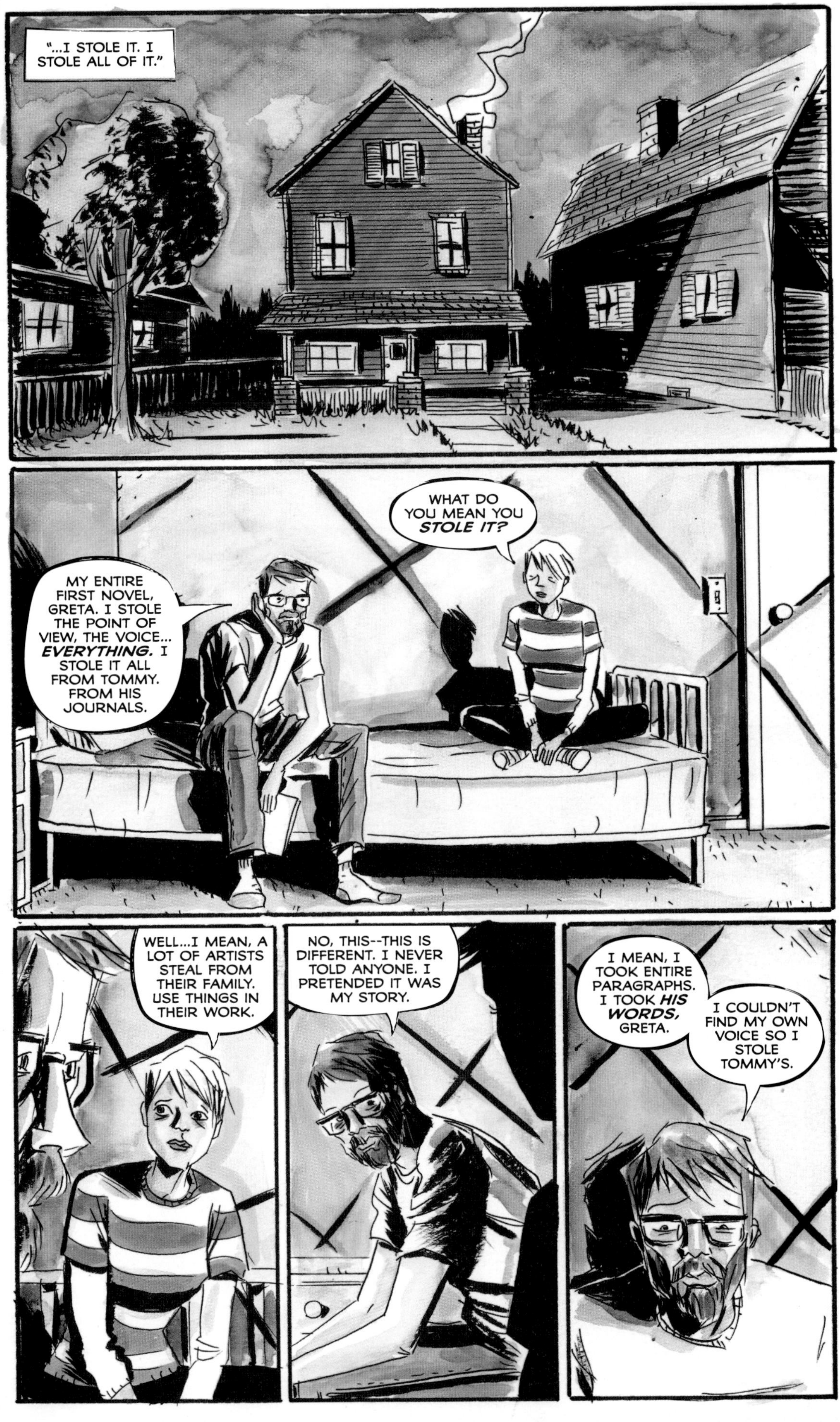
"...I STOLE IT. I STOLE ALL OF IT."
WHAT DO YOU MEAN YOU STOLE IT?
MY ENTIRE FIRST NOVEL, GRETA. I STOLE THE POINT OF VIEW, THE VOICE... EVERYTHING. I STOLE IT ALL FROM TOMMY. FROM HIS JOURNALS.
WELL...I MEAN, A LOT OF ARTISTS STEAL FROM THEIR FAMILY. USE THINGS IN THEIR WORK.
NO, THIS--THIS IS DIFFERENT. I NEVER TOLD ANYONE. I PRETENDED IT WAS MY STORY.
I MEAN, I TOOK ENTIRE PARAGRAPHS. I TOOK HIS WORDS, GRETA.
I COULDN'T FIND MY OWN VOICE SO I STOLE TOMMY'S.

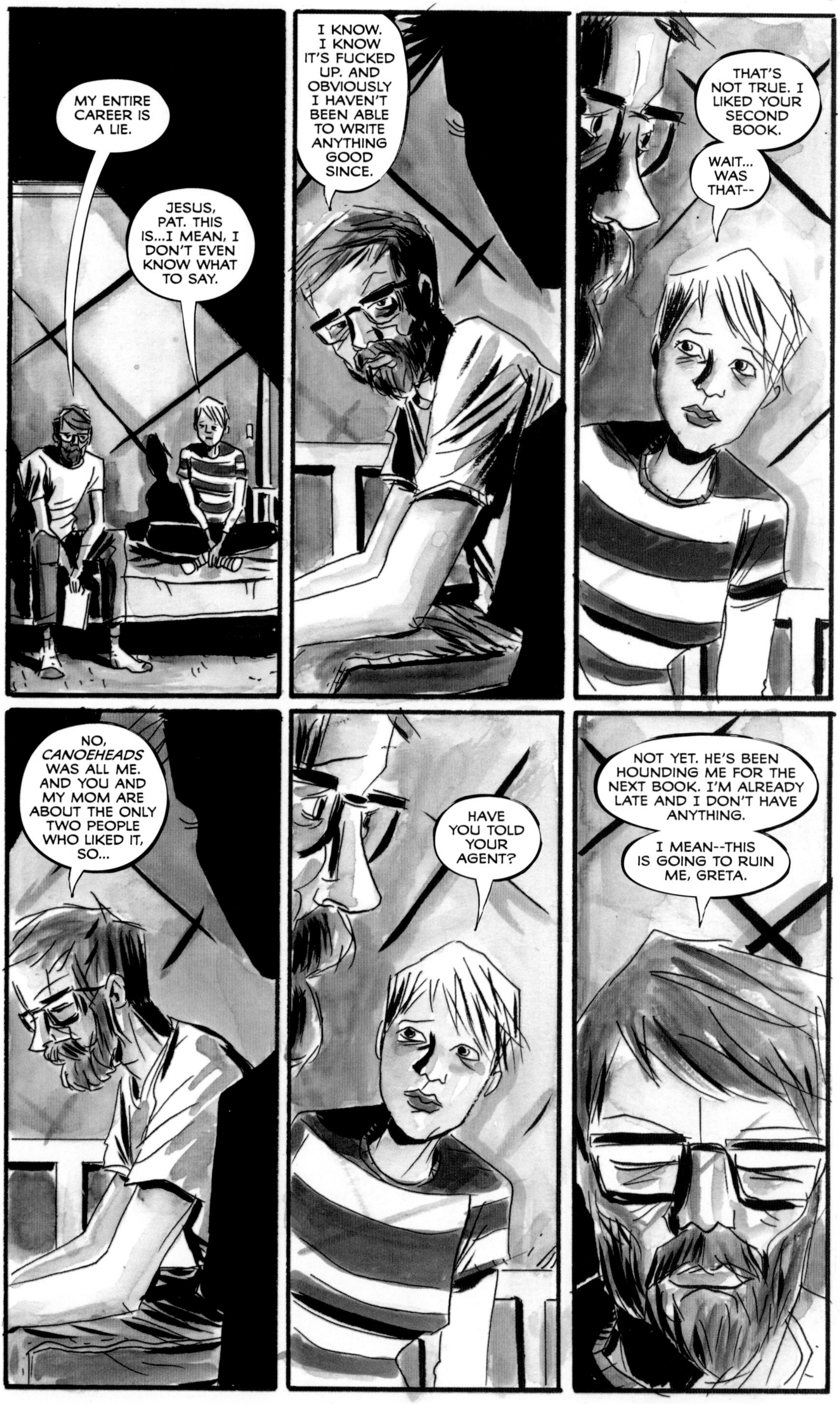
MY ENTIRE CAREER IS A LIE.
JESUS, PAT. THIS IS...I MEAN, I DON'T EVEN KNOW WHAT TO SAY.
I KNOW. I KNOW IT'S FUCKED UP. AND OBVIOUSLY I HAVEN'T BEEN ABLE TO WRITE ANYTHING GOOD SINCE.
THAT'S NOT TRUE. I LIKED YOUR SECOND BOOK.
WAIT... WAS THAT--
NO, *CANOEHEADS* WAS ALL ME. AND YOU AND MY MOM ARE ABOUT THE ONLY TWO PEOPLE WHO LIKED IT, SO...
HAVE YOU TOLD YOUR AGENT?
NOT YET. HE'S BEEN HOUNDING ME FOR THE NEXT BOOK. I'M ALREADY LATE AND I DON'T HAVE ANYTHING.
I MEAN--THIS IS GOING TO RUIN ME, GRETA.

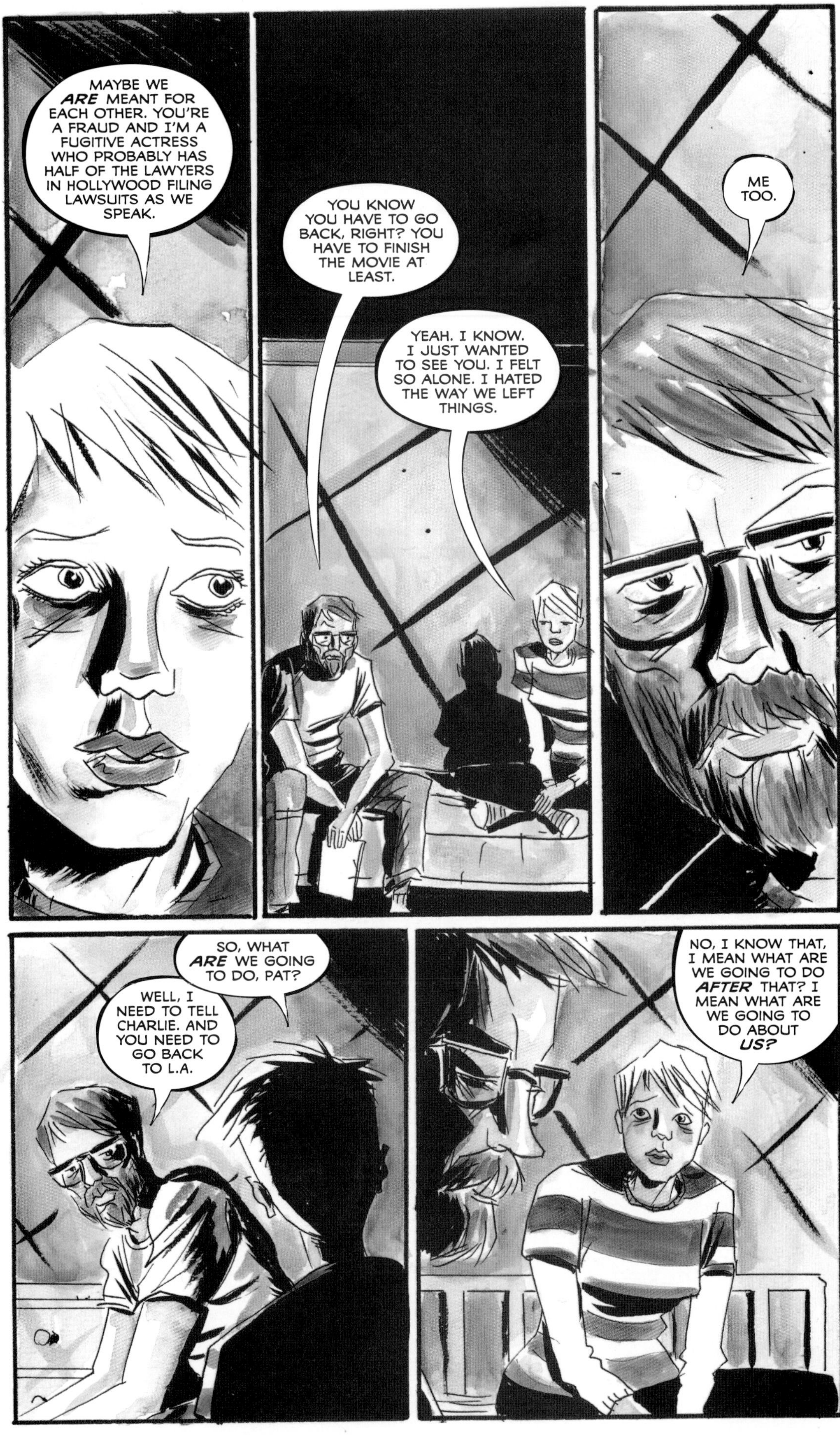
MAYBE WE *ARE* MEANT FOR EACH OTHER. YOU'RE A FRAUD AND I'M A FUGITIVE ACTRESS WHO PROBABLY HAS HALF OF THE LAWYERS IN HOLLYWOOD FILING LAWSUITS AS WE SPEAK.
YOU KNOW YOU HAVE TO GO BACK, RIGHT? YOU HAVE TO FINISH THE MOVIE AT LEAST.
YEAH. I KNOW. I JUST WANTED TO SEE YOU. I FELT SO ALONE. I HATED THE WAY WE LEFT THINGS.
ME TOO.
SO, WHAT *ARE* WE GOING TO DO, PAT?
WELL, I NEED TO TELL CHARLIE. AND YOU NEED TO GO BACK TO L.A.
NO, I KNOW THAT, I MEAN WHAT ARE WE GOING TO DO *AFTER* THAT? I MEAN WHAT ARE WE GOING TO DO ABOUT *US?*

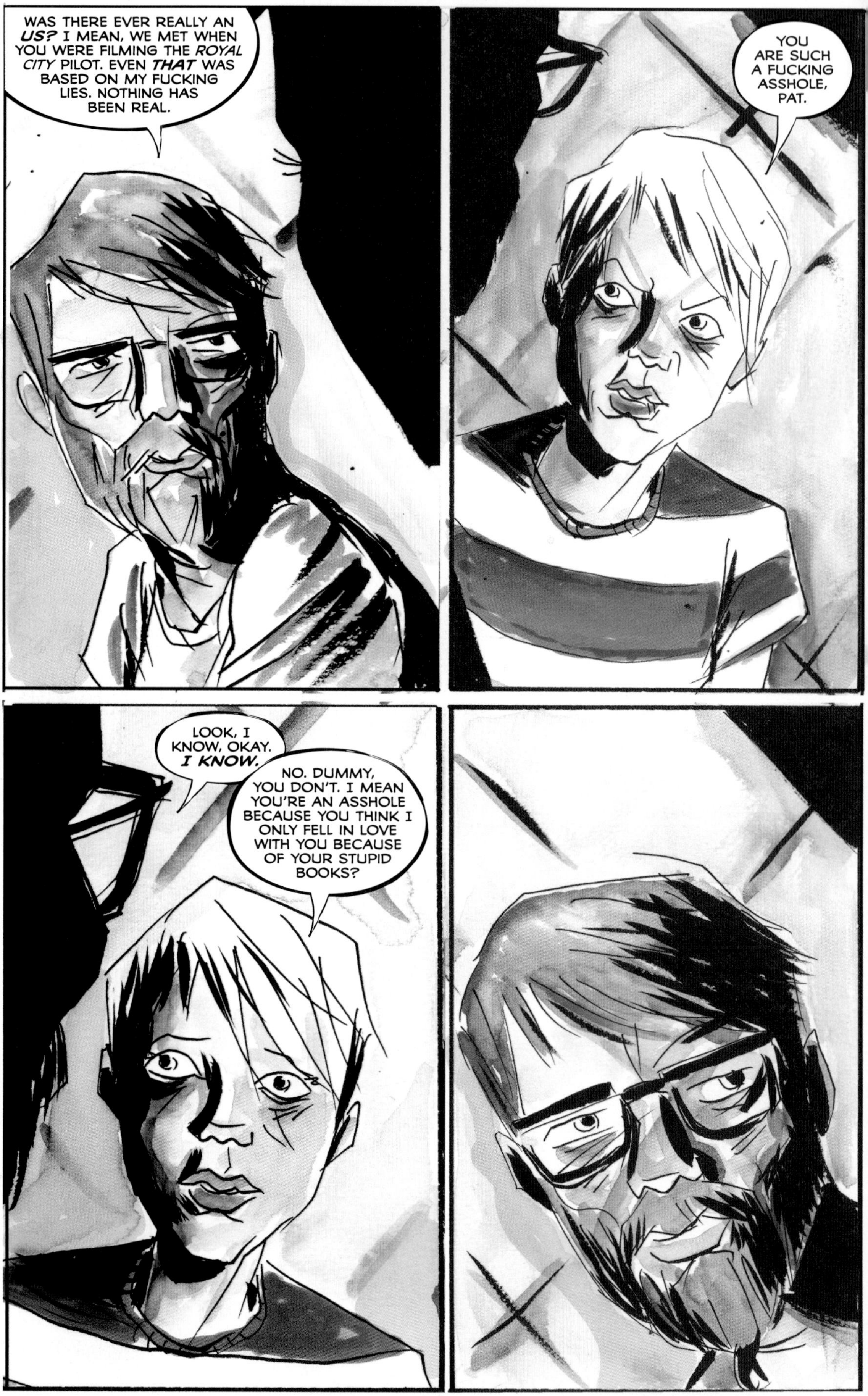
WAS THERE EVER REALLY AN *US?* I MEAN, WE MET WHEN YOU WERE FILMING THE *ROYAL CITY* PILOT. EVEN *THAT* WAS BASED ON MY FUCKING LIES. NOTHING HAS BEEN REAL.
YOU ARE SUCH A FUCKING ASSHOLE, PAT.
LOOK, I KNOW, OKAY. *I KNOW.*
NO. DUMMY, YOU DON'T. I MEAN YOU'RE AN ASSHOLE BECAUSE YOU THINK I ONLY FELL IN LOVE WITH YOU BECAUSE OF YOUR STUPID BOOKS?

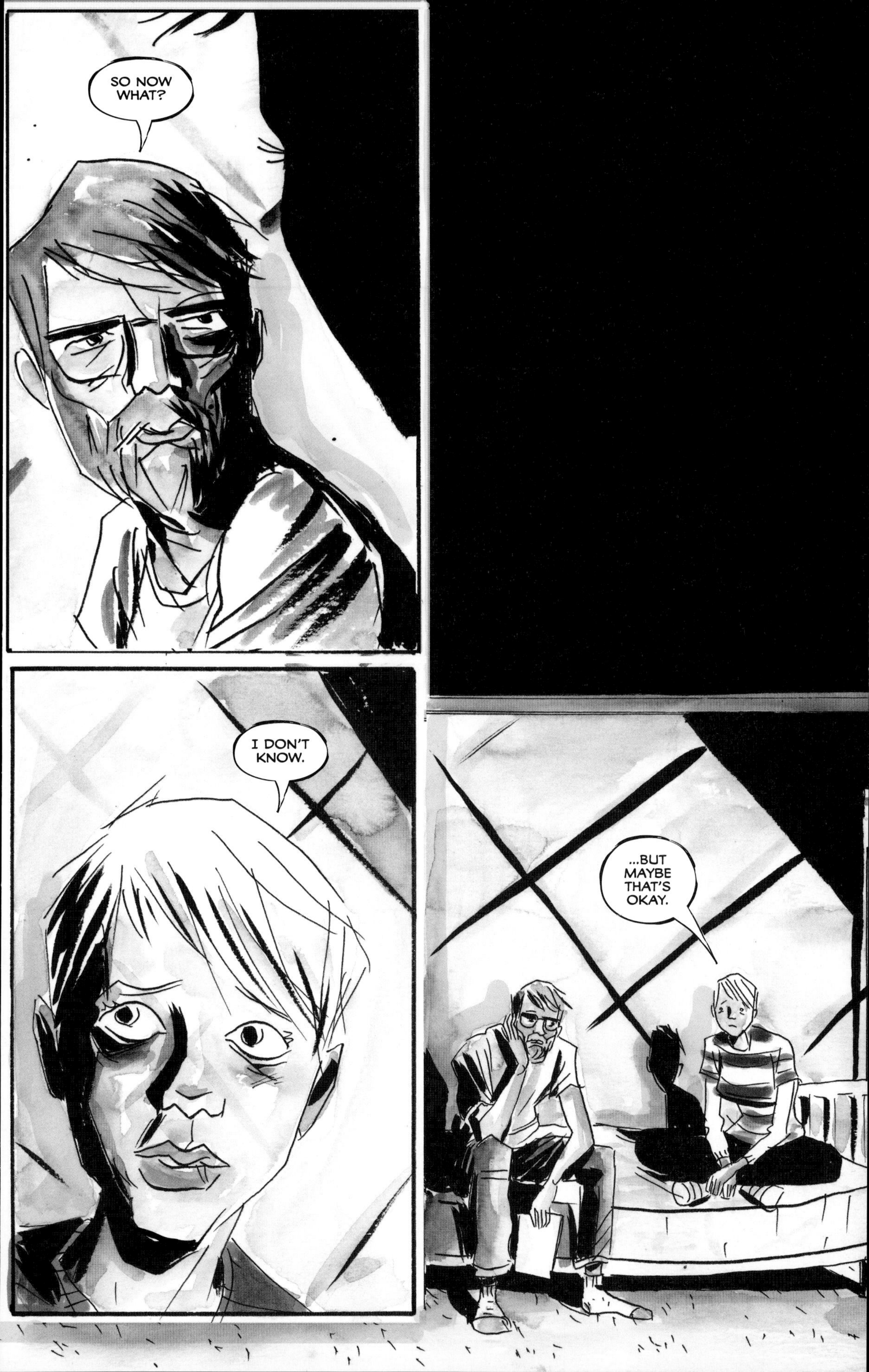
SO NOW WHAT?
I DON'T KNOW.
...BUT MAYBE THAT'S OKAY.

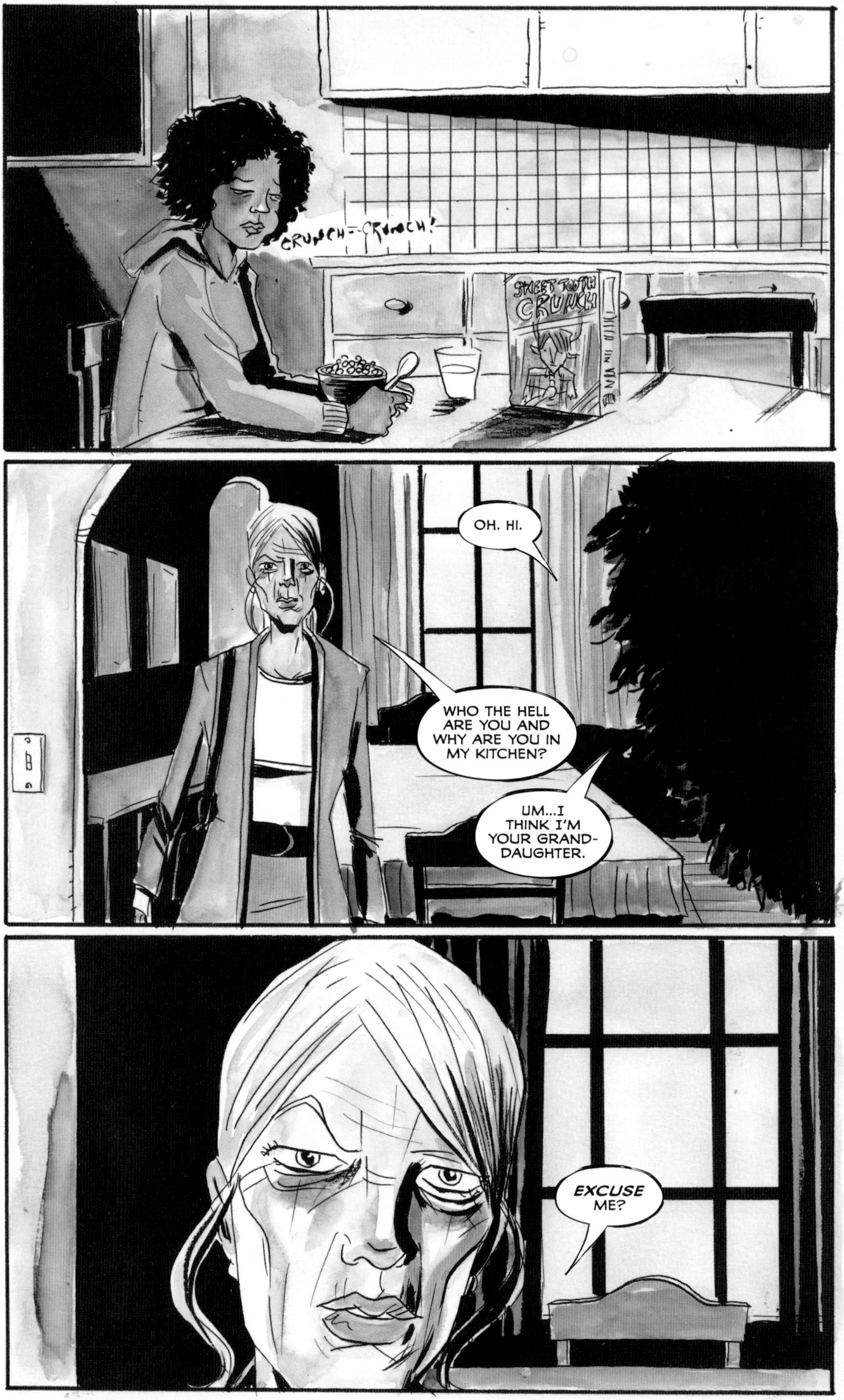
CRUNCH--CRUNCH!
SWEET TOOTH CRUNCH
OH. HI.
WHO THE HELL ARE YOU AND WHY ARE YOU IN MY KITCHEN?
UM...I THINK I'M YOUR GRAND-DAUGHTER.
EXCUSE ME?

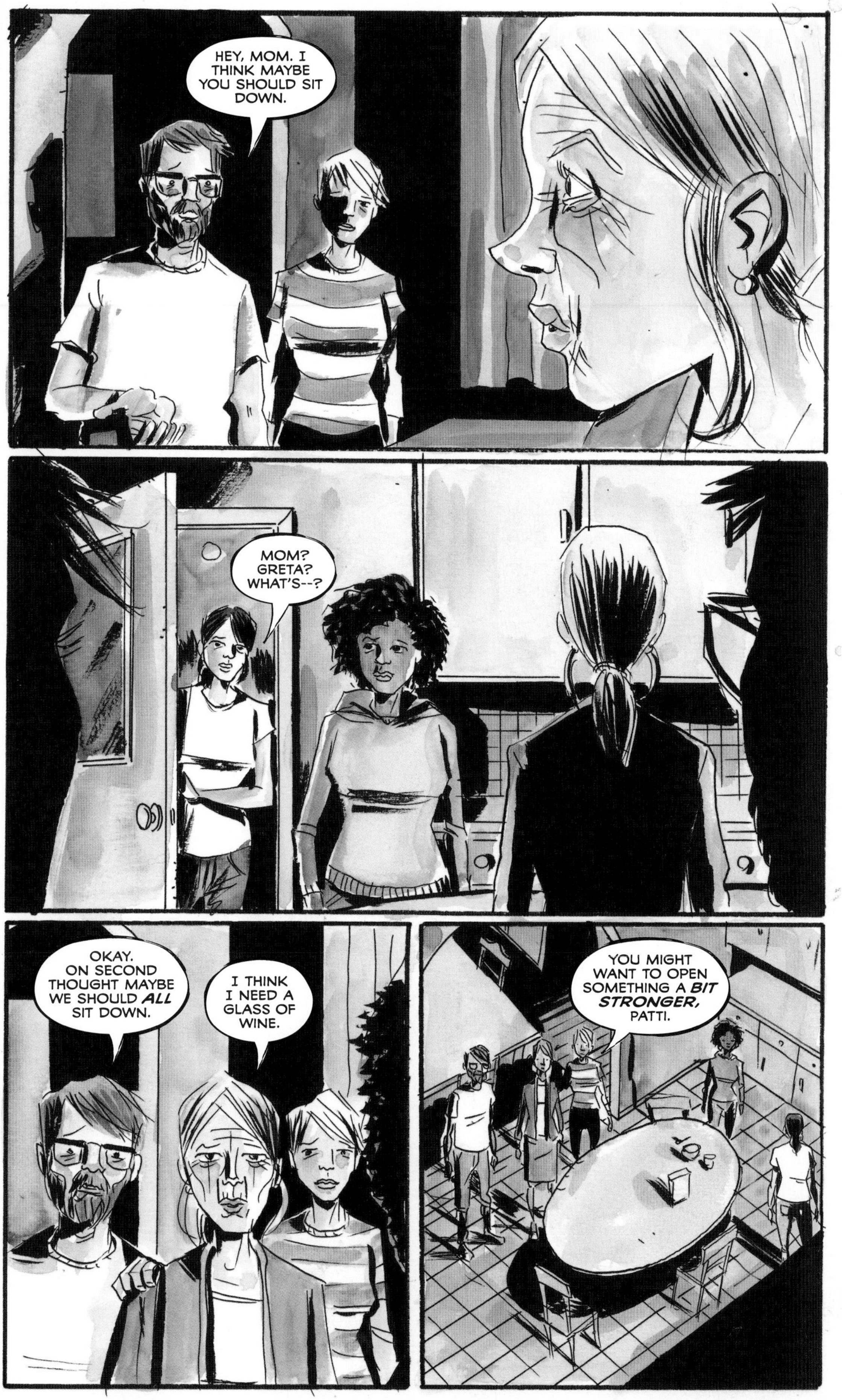
HEY, MOM. I THINK MAYBE YOU SHOULD SIT DOWN.
MOM? GRETA? WHAT'S--?
OKAY. ON SECOND THOUGHT MAYBE WE SHOULD *ALL* SIT DOWN.
I THINK I NEED A GLASS OF WINE.
YOU MIGHT WANT TO OPEN SOMETHING A ***BIT STRONGER,*** PATTI.

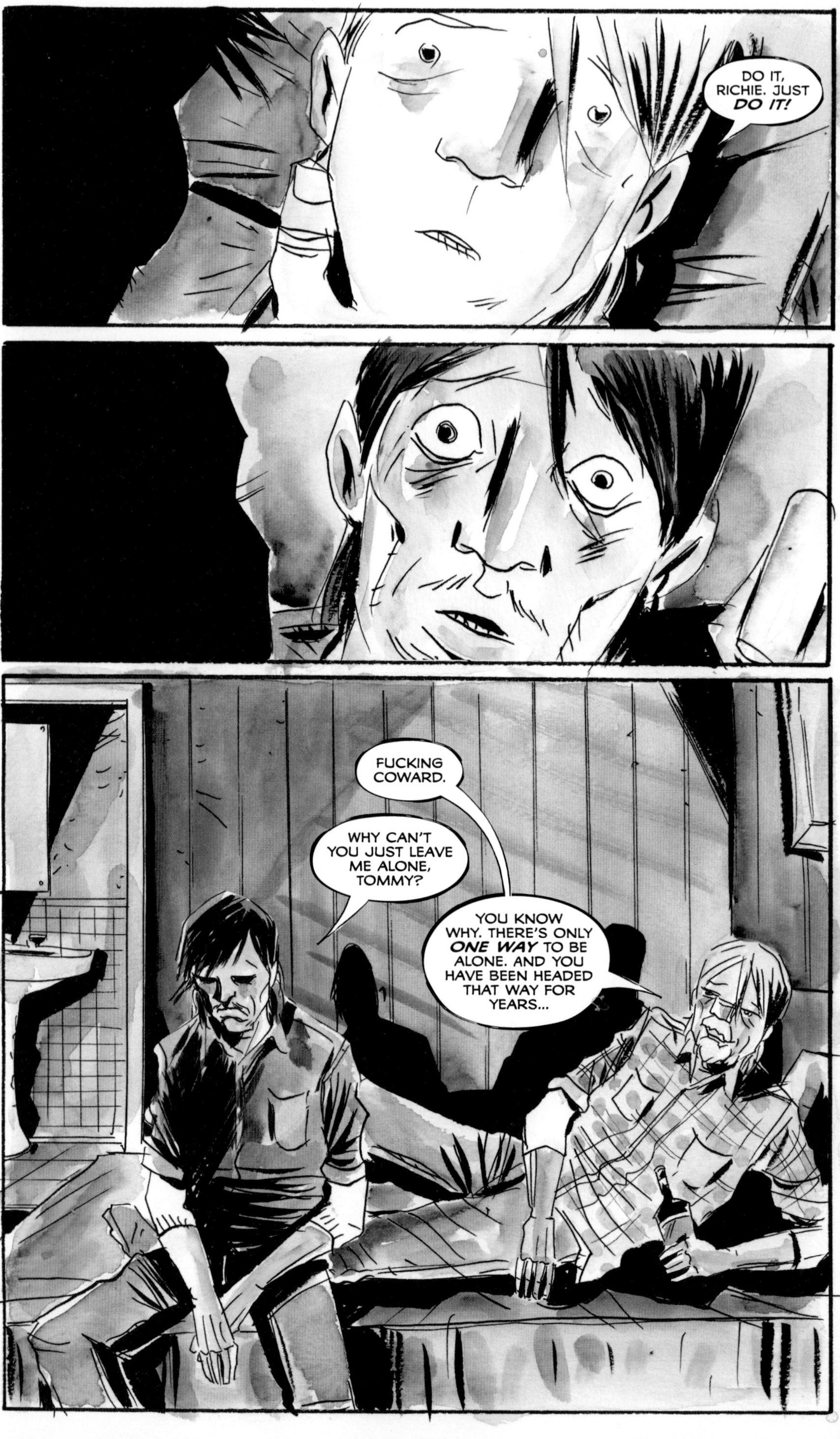
DO IT, RICHIE. JUST *DO IT!*
FUCKING COWARD.
WHY CAN'T YOU JUST LEAVE ME ALONE, TOMMY?
YOU KNOW WHY. THERE'S ONLY *ONE WAY* TO BE ALONE. AND YOU HAVE BEEN HEADED THAT WAY FOR YEARS...

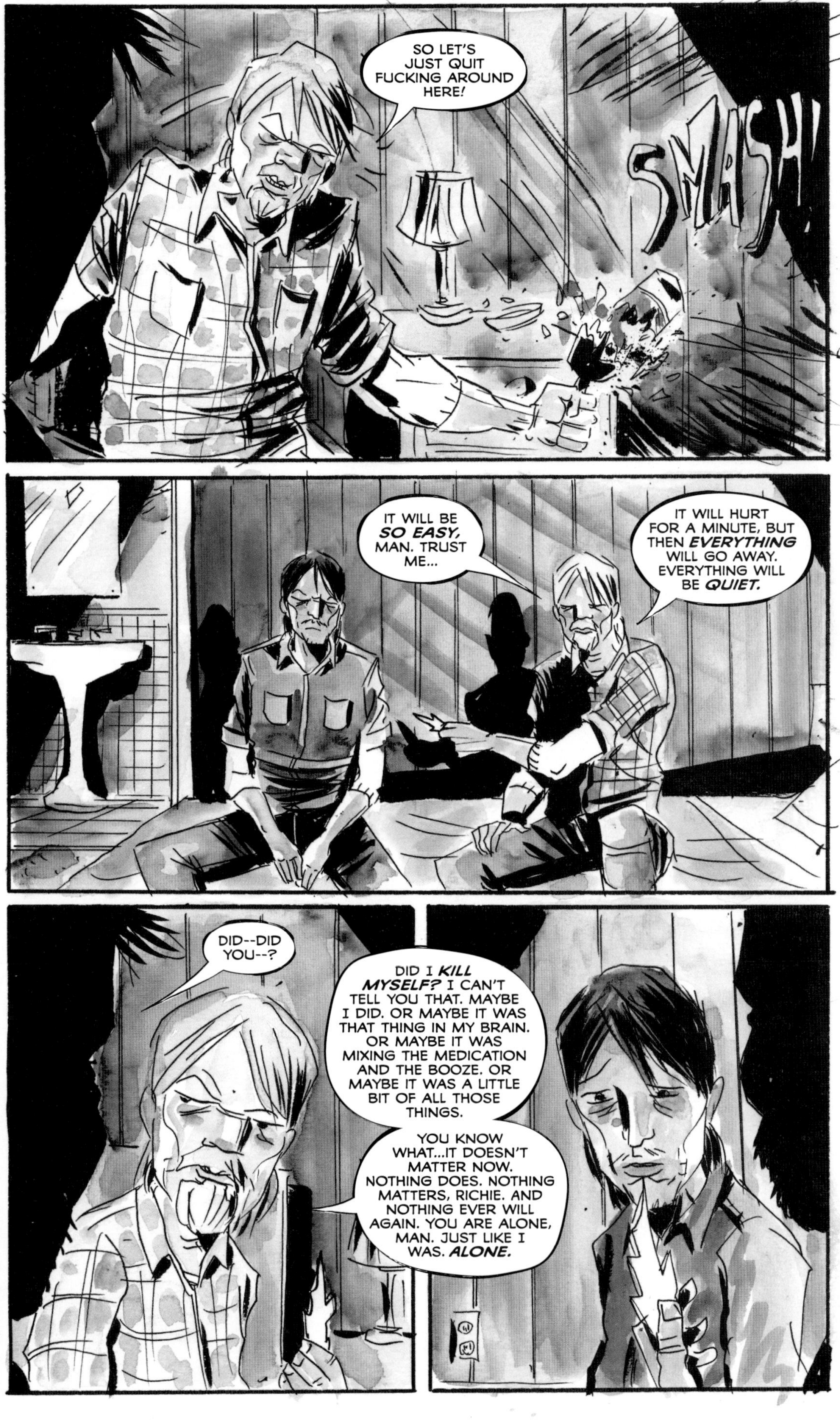
SO LET'S JUST QUIT FUCKING AROUND HERE!
SMASH!
IT WILL BE SO EASY, MAN. TRUST ME...
IT WILL HURT FOR A MINUTE, BUT THEN EVERYTHING WILL GO AWAY. EVERYTHING WILL BE QUIET.
DID--DID YOU--?
DID I KILL MYSELF? I CAN'T TELL YOU THAT. MAYBE I DID. OR MAYBE IT WAS THAT THING IN MY BRAIN. OR MAYBE IT WAS MIXING THE MEDICATION AND THE BOOZE. OR MAYBE IT WAS A LITTLE BIT OF ALL THOSE THINGS.
YOU KNOW WHAT...IT DOESN'T MATTER NOW. NOTHING DOES. NOTHING MATTERS, RICHIE. AND NOTHING EVER WILL AGAIN. YOU ARE ALONE, MAN. JUST LIKE I WAS. ALONE.

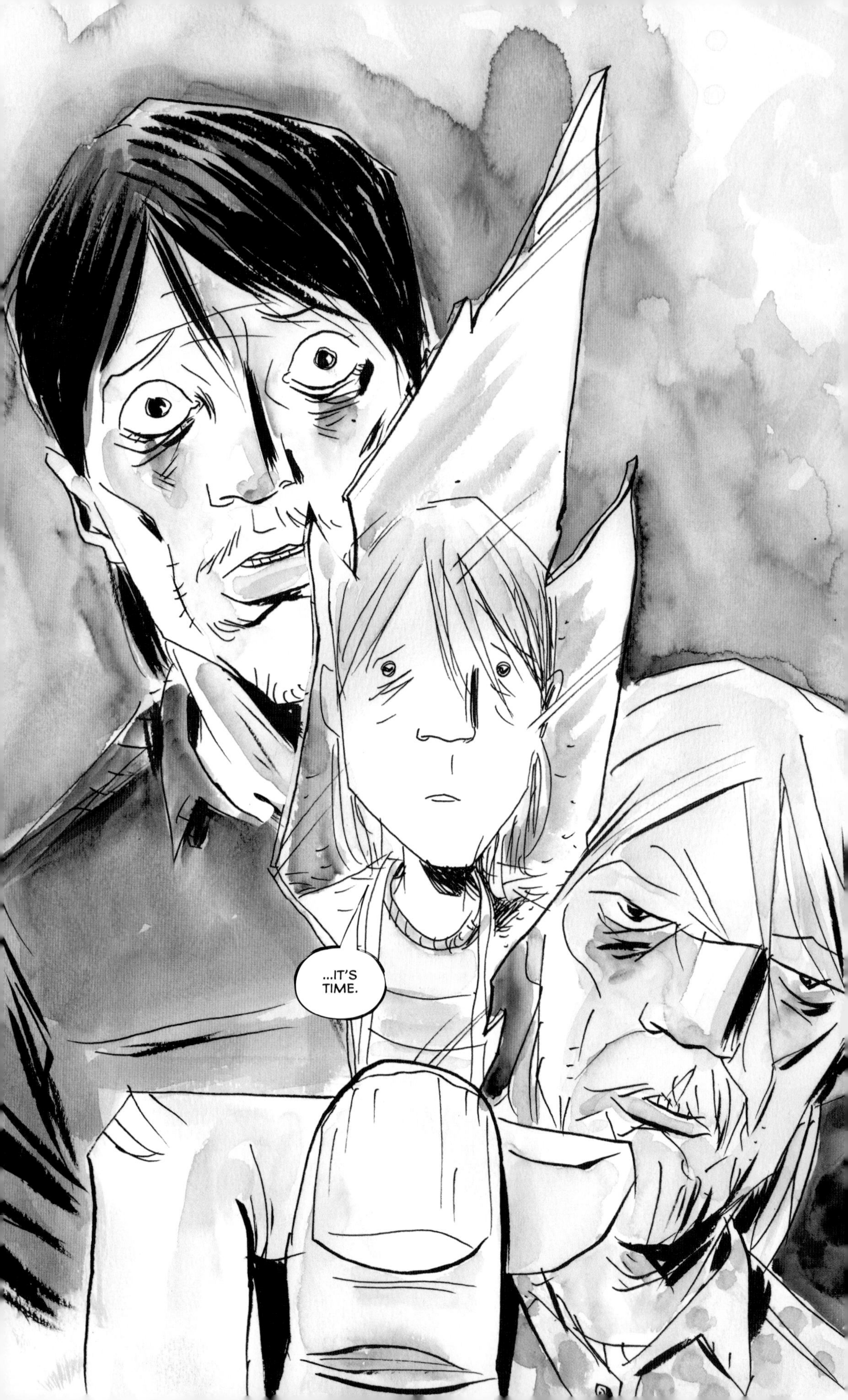
...IT'S TIME.

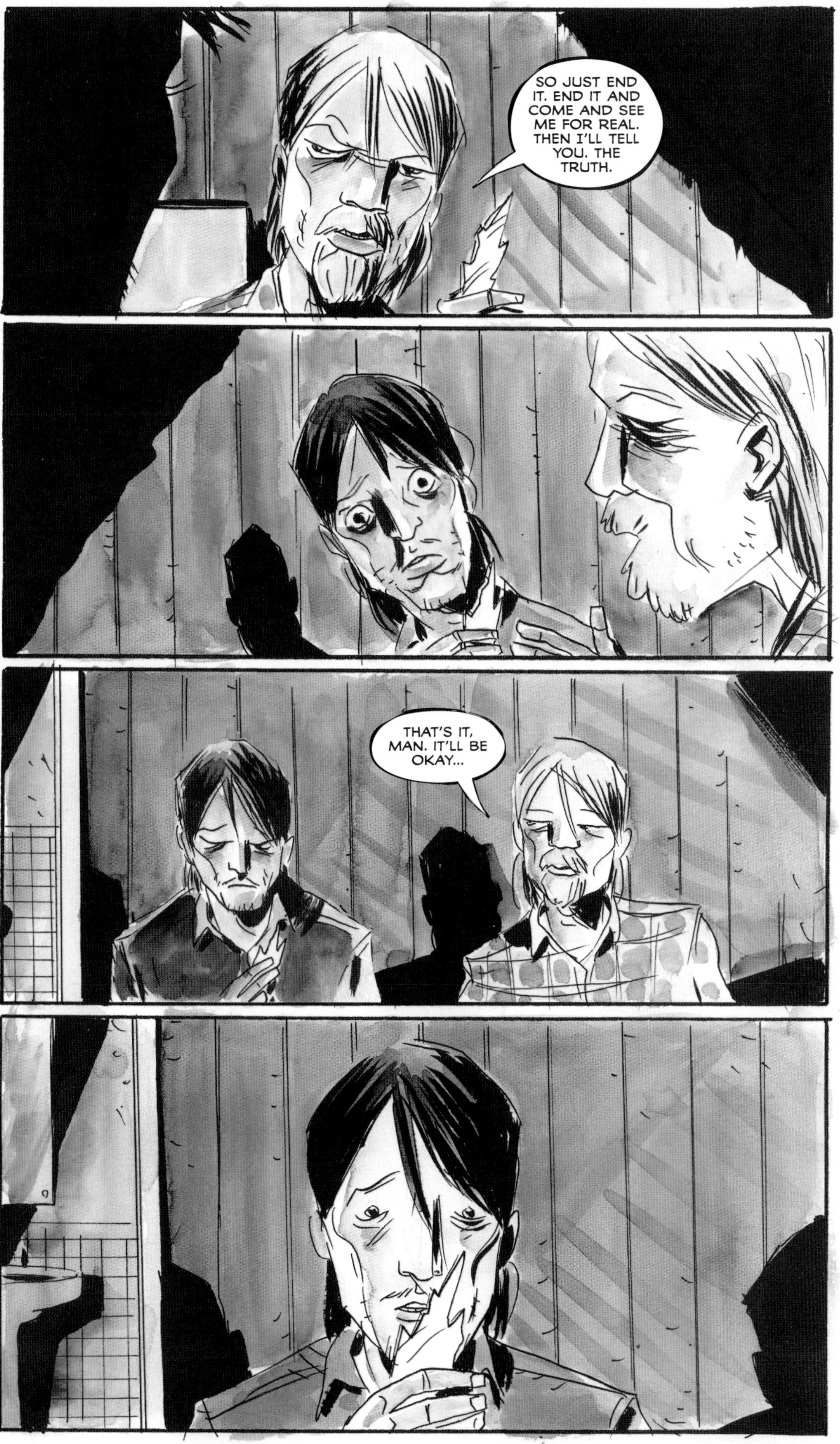
SO JUST END IT. END IT AND COME AND SEE ME FOR REAL. THEN I'LL TELL YOU. THE TRUTH.
THAT'S IT, MAN. IT'LL BE OKAY...

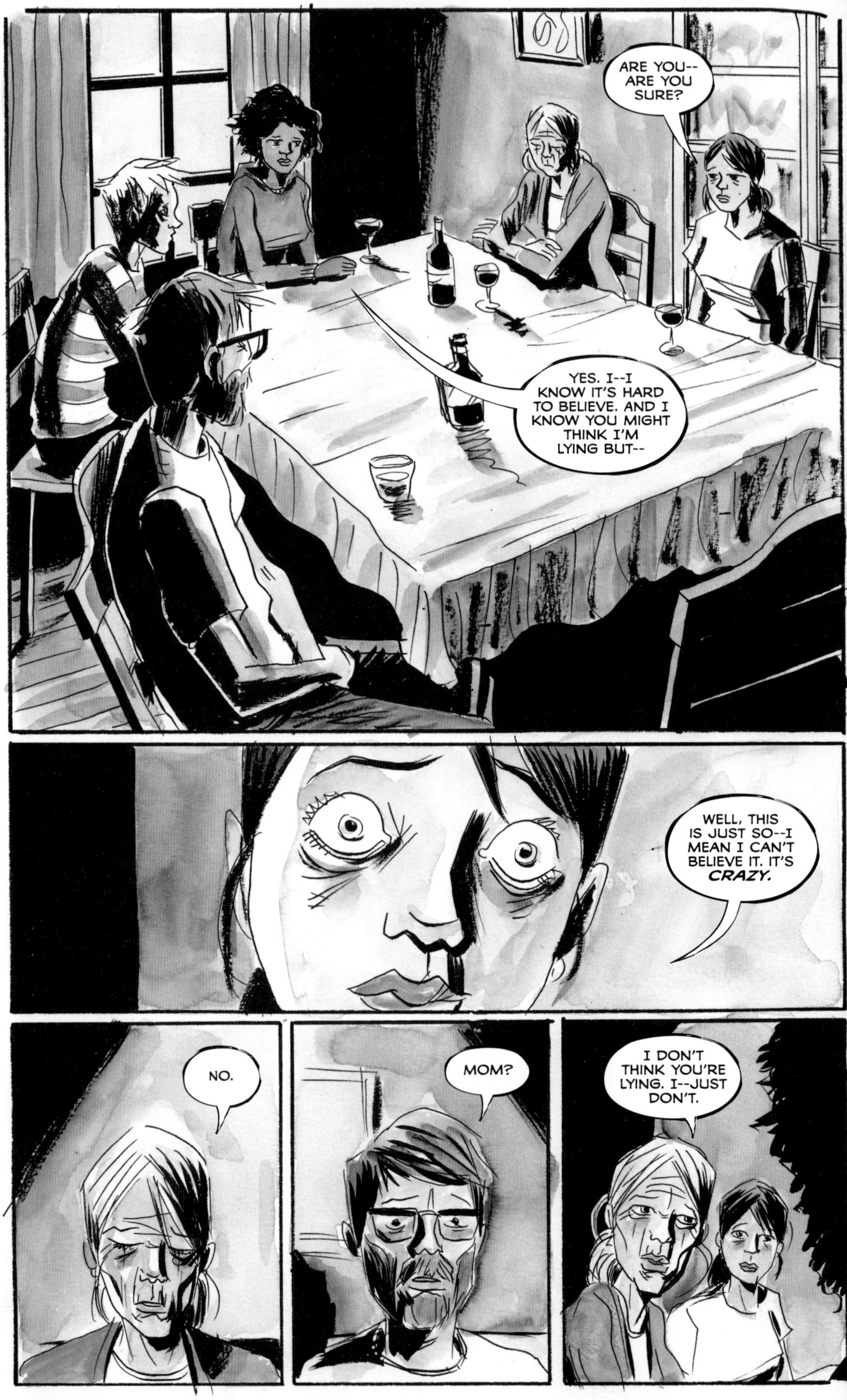
ARE YOU--
ARE YOU
SURE?
YES. I--I KNOW IT'S HARD TO BELIEVE. AND I KNOW YOU MIGHT THINK I'M LYING BUT--
WELL, THIS IS JUST SO--I MEAN I CAN'T BELIEVE IT. IT'S *CRAZY.*
NO.
MOM?
I DON'T THINK YOU'RE LYING. I--JUST DON'T.

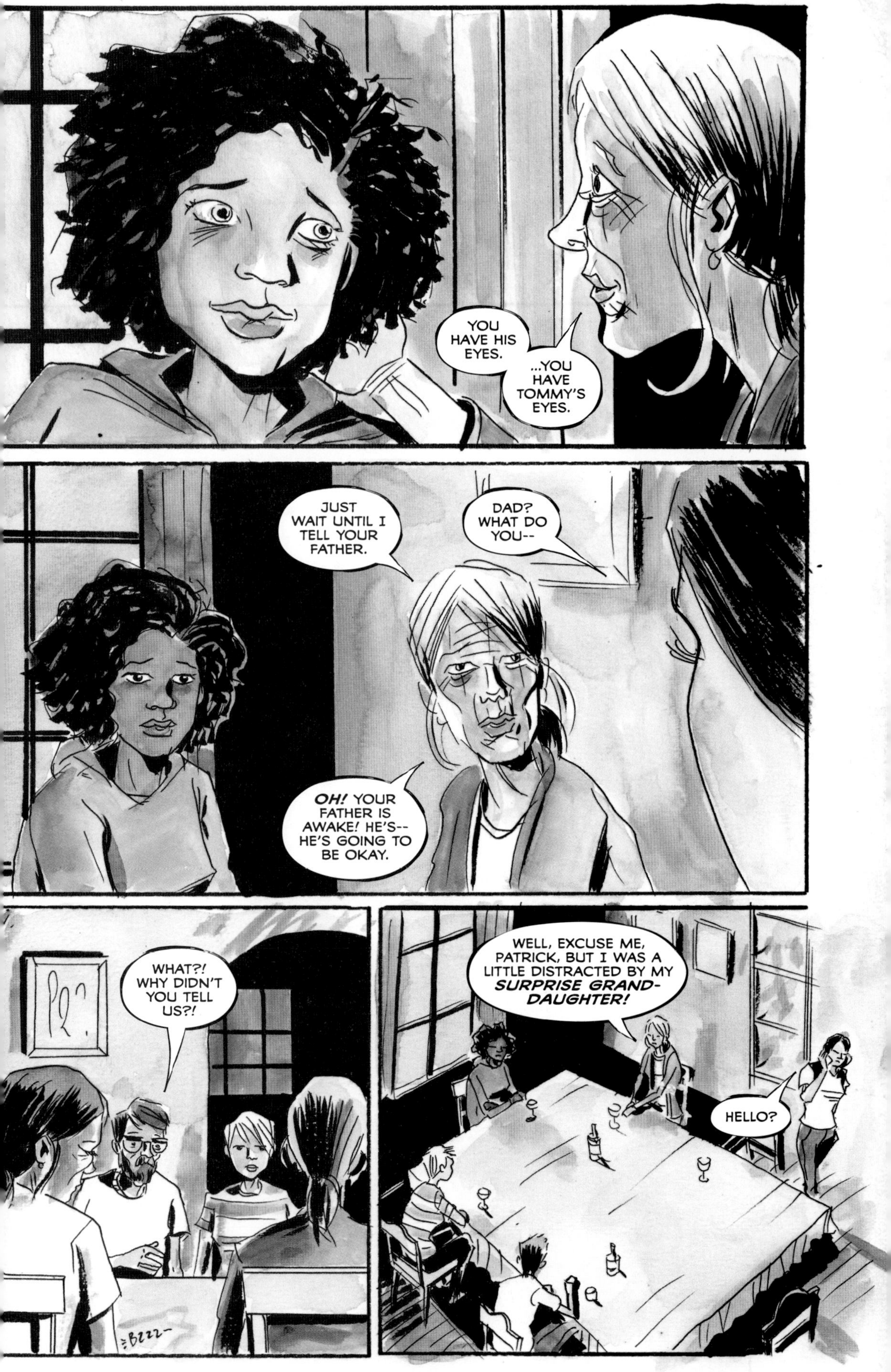
YOU HAVE HIS EYES.
...YOU HAVE TOMMY'S EYES.
JUST WAIT UNTIL I TELL YOUR FATHER.
DAD? WHAT DO YOU--
OH! YOUR FATHER IS AWAKE! HE'S-- HE'S GOING TO BE OKAY.
WHAT?! WHY DIDN'T YOU TELL US?!
BZZZ-
WELL, EXCUSE ME, PATRICK, BUT I WAS A LITTLE DISTRACTED BY MY SURPRISE GRAND-DAUGHTER!
HELLO?

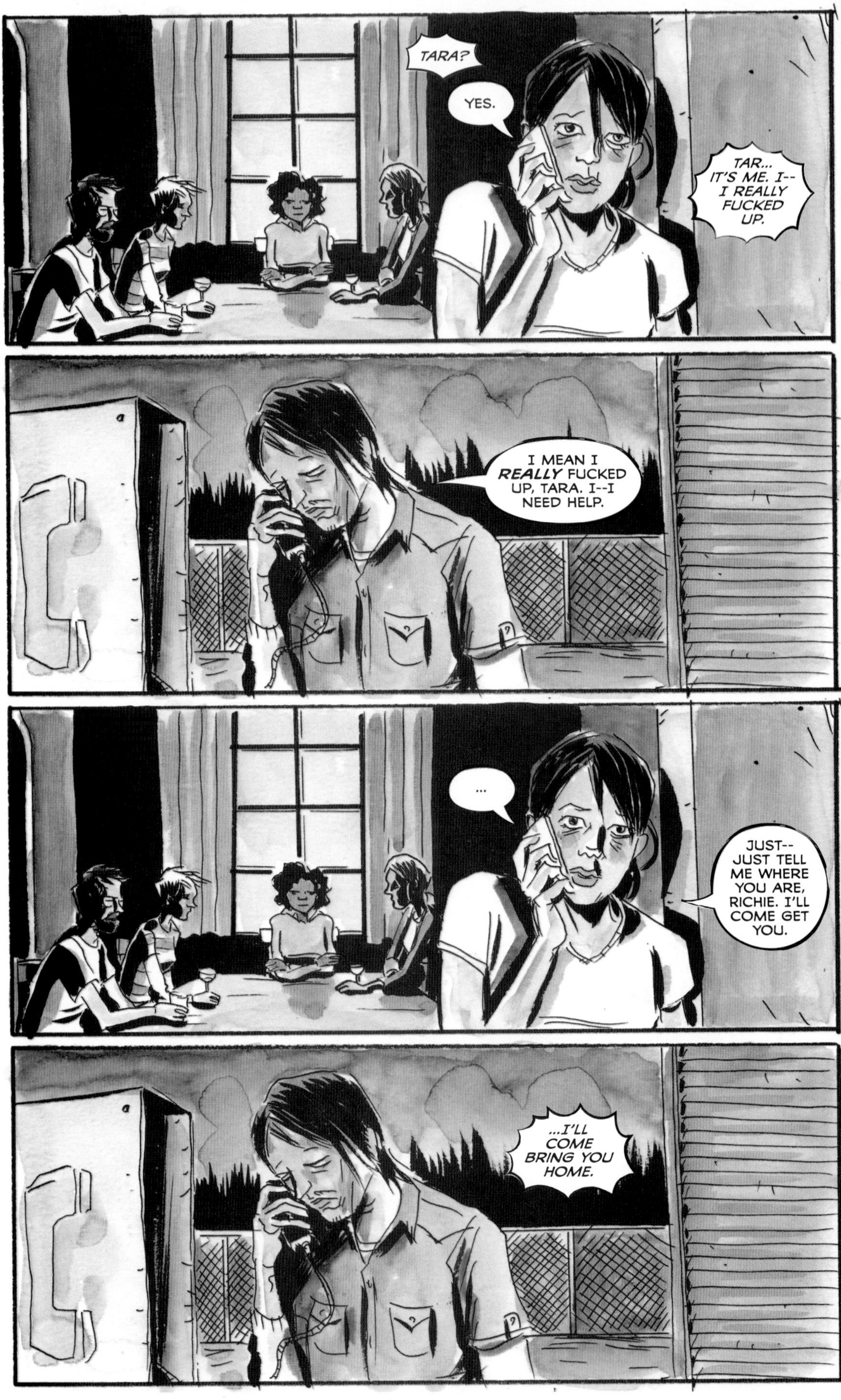
TARA?
YES.
TAR... IT'S ME. I-- I REALLY FUCKED UP.
I MEAN I *REALLY* FUCKED UP, TARA. I--I NEED HELP.
...
JUST-- JUST TELL ME WHERE YOU ARE, RICHIE. I'LL COME GET YOU.
...I'LL COME BRING YOU HOME.

JEFF LEMIRE

ROYAL CITY™

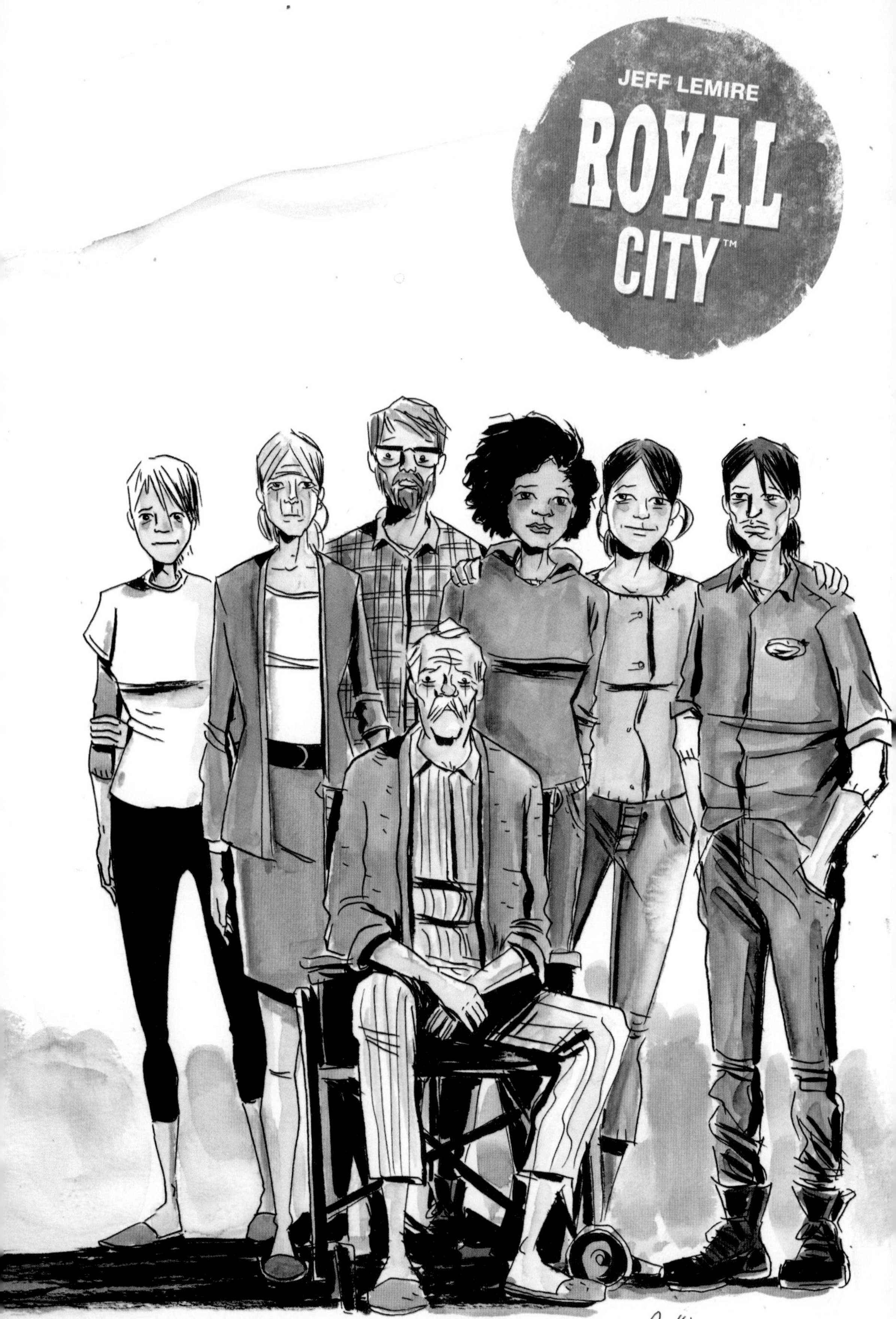

CHAPTER FOURTEEN

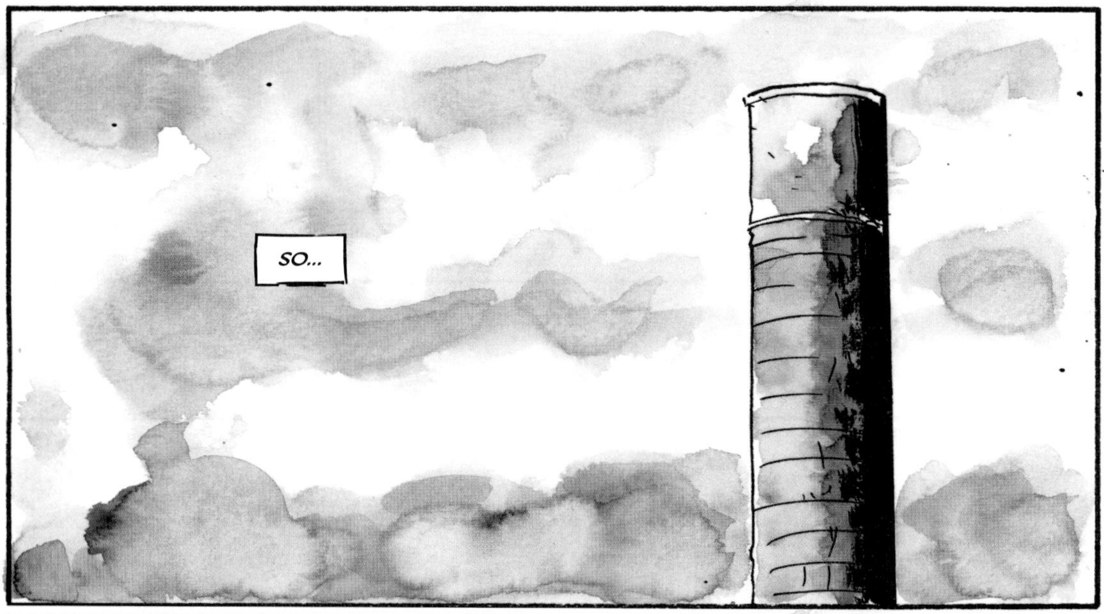
SO...

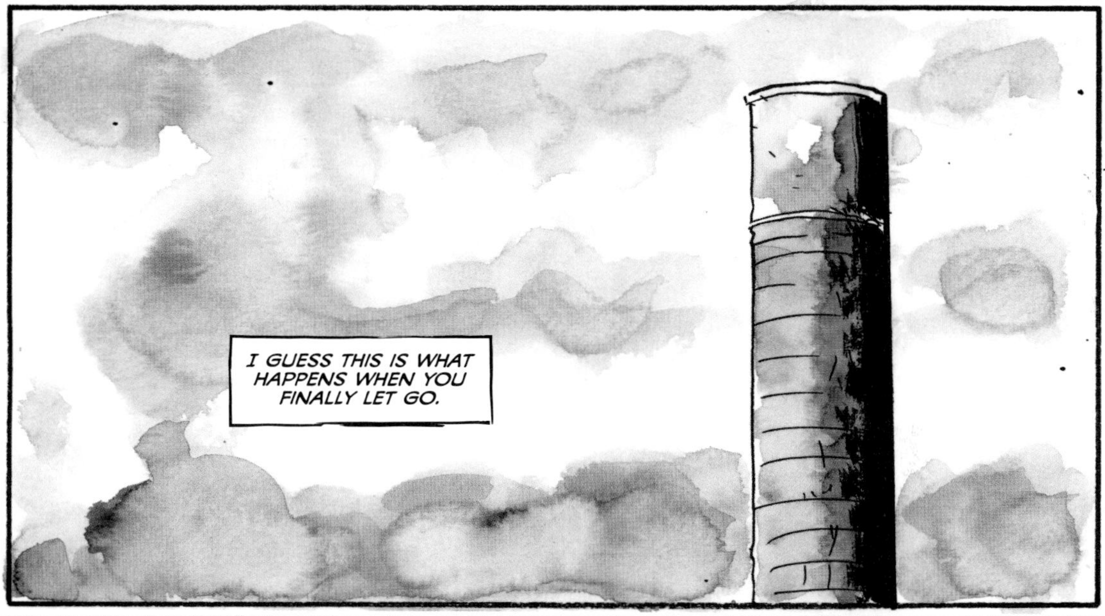
I GUESS THIS IS WHAT HAPPENS WHEN YOU FINALLY LET GO.

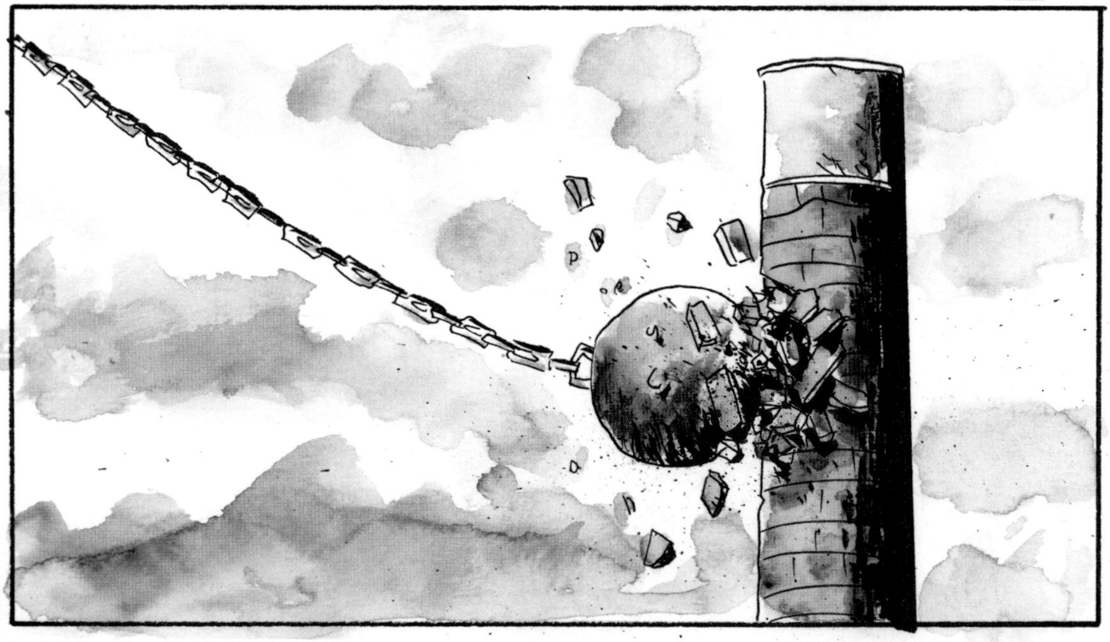

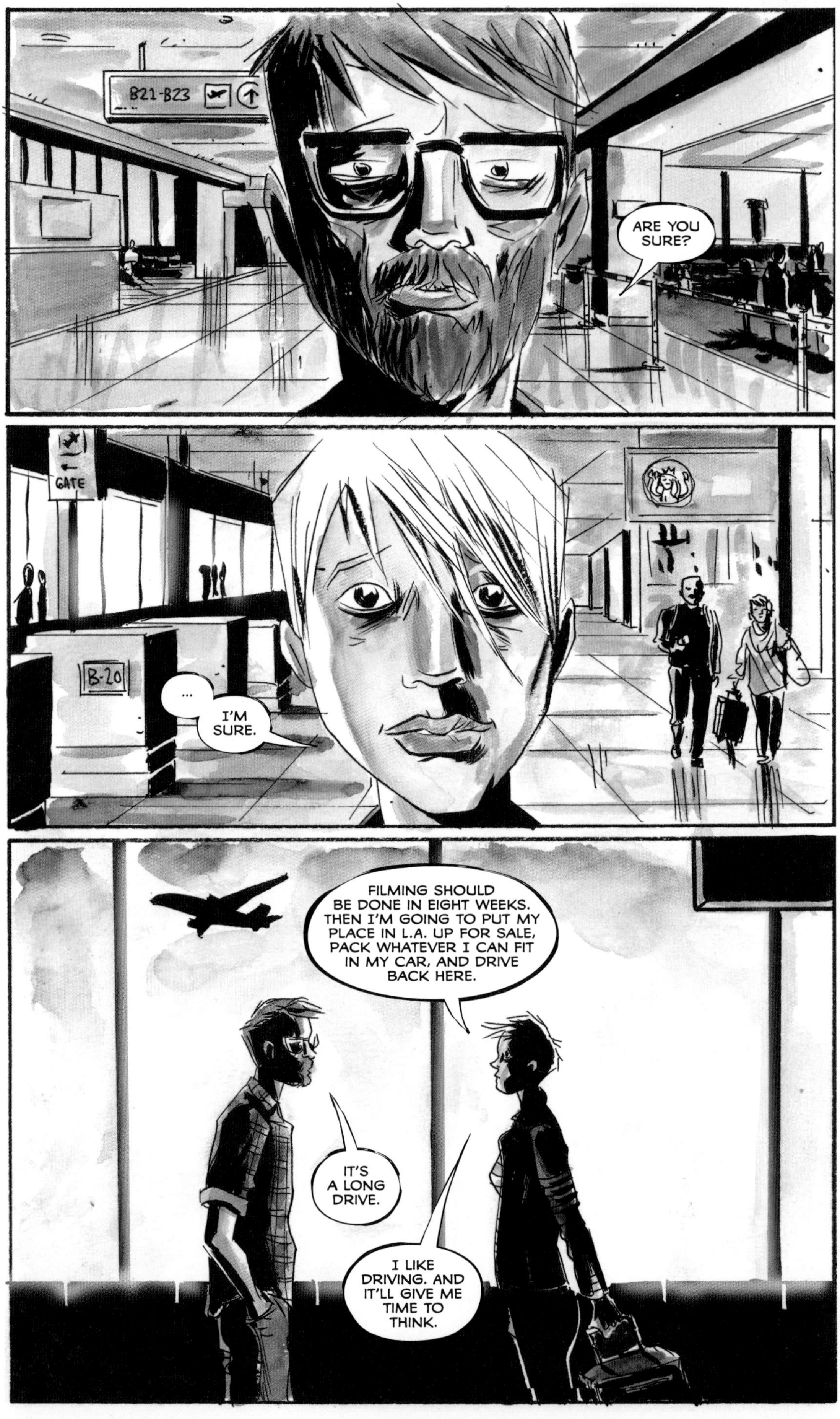
B21-B23
ARE YOU SURE?
GATE
B-20
...
I'M SURE.
FILMING SHOULD BE DONE IN EIGHT WEEKS. THEN I'M GOING TO PUT MY PLACE IN L.A. UP FOR SALE, PACK WHATEVER I CAN FIT IN MY CAR, AND DRIVE BACK HERE.
IT'S A LONG DRIVE.
I LIKE DRIVING. AND IT'LL GIVE ME TIME TO THINK.

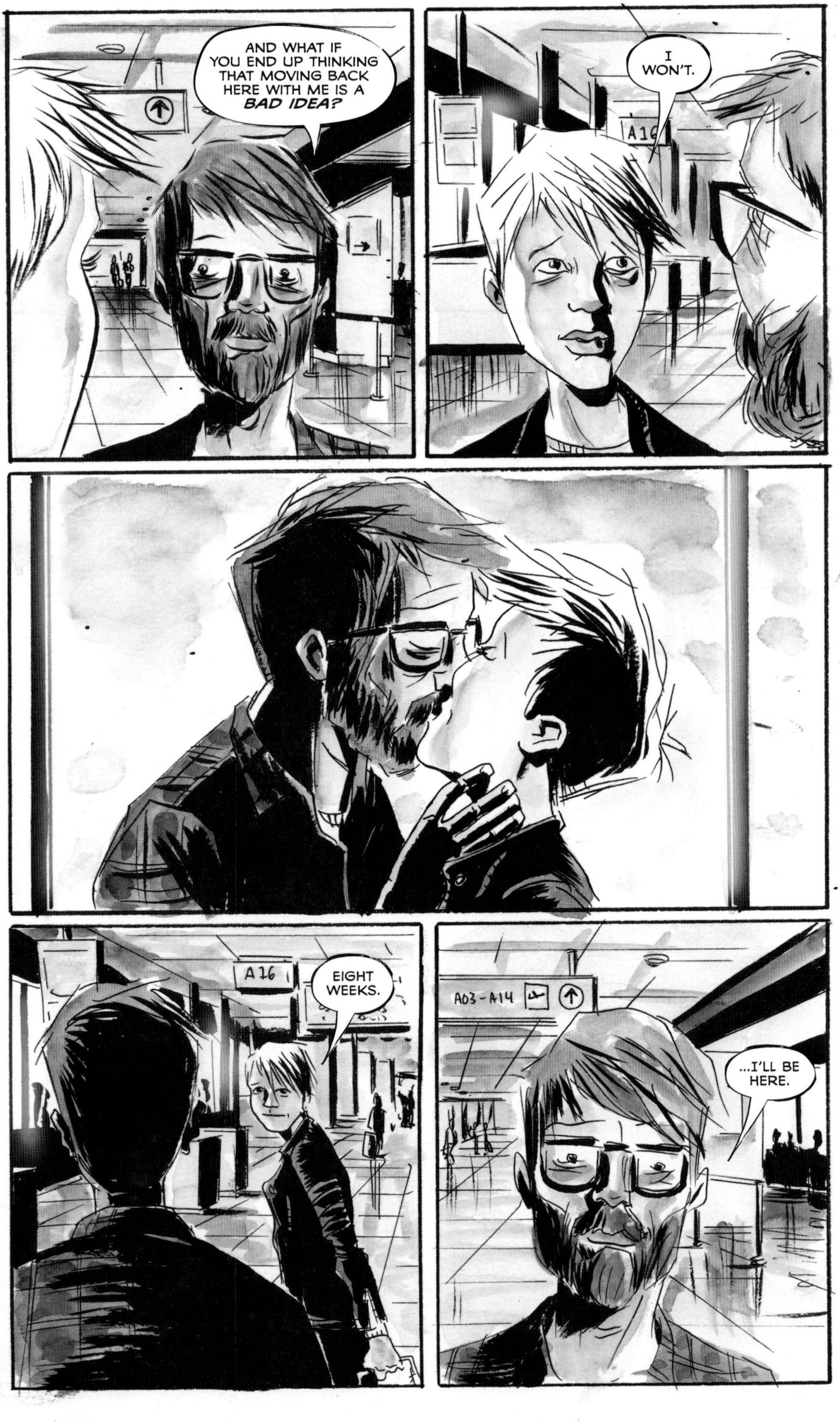
AND WHAT IF YOU END UP THINKING THAT MOVING BACK HERE WITH ME IS A BAD IDEA?
I WON'T.
A16
A16
EIGHT WEEKS.
A03-A14
...I'LL BE HERE.

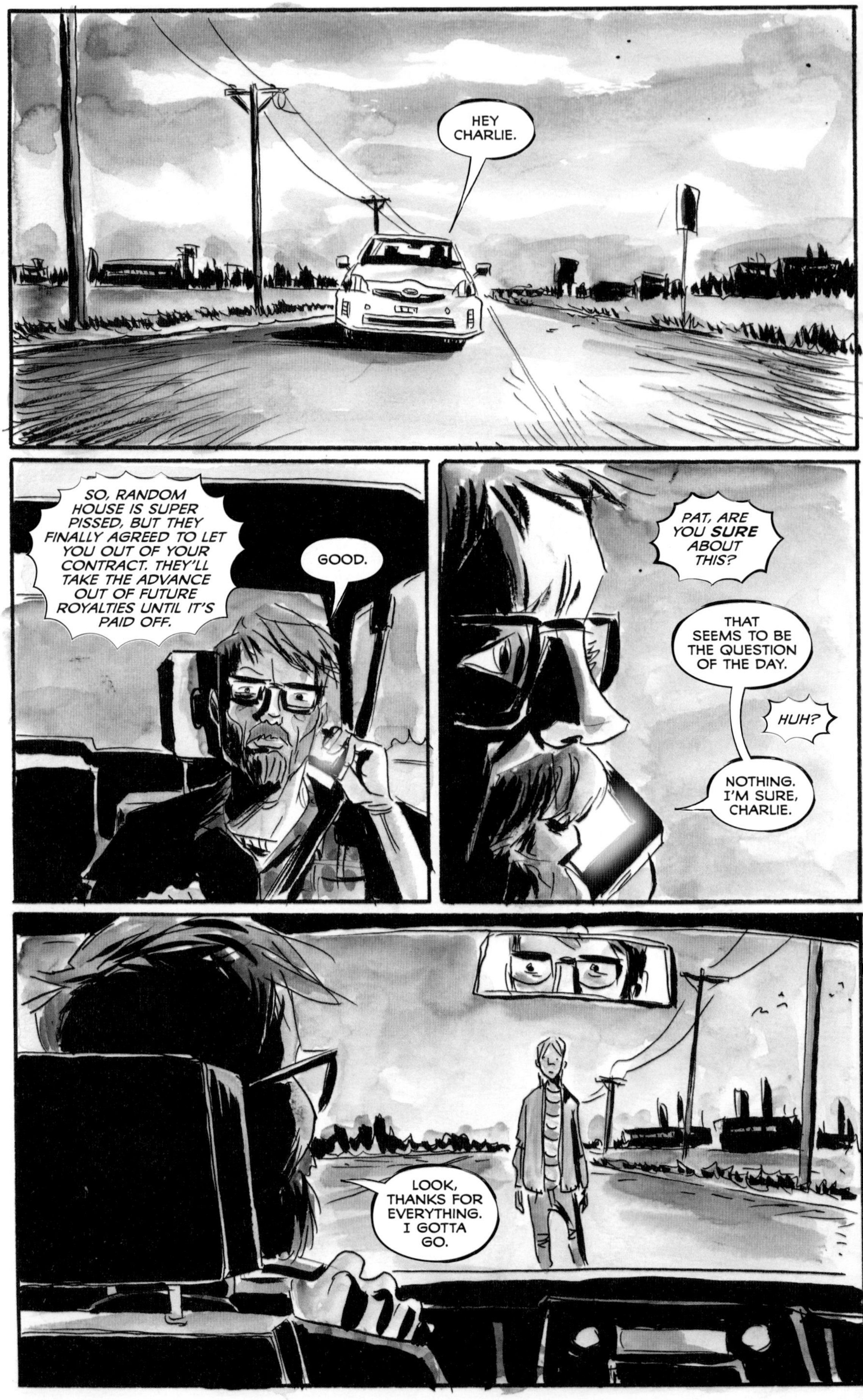
HEY CHARLIE.
SO, RANDOM HOUSE IS SUPER PISSED, BUT THEY FINALLY AGREED TO LET YOU OUT OF YOUR CONTRACT. THEY'LL TAKE THE ADVANCE OUT OF FUTURE ROYALTIES UNTIL IT'S PAID OFF.
GOOD.
PAT, ARE YOU SURE ABOUT THIS?
THAT SEEMS TO BE THE QUESTION OF THE DAY.
HUH?
NOTHING. I'M SURE, CHARLIE.
LOOK, THANKS FOR EVERYTHING. I GOTTA GO.

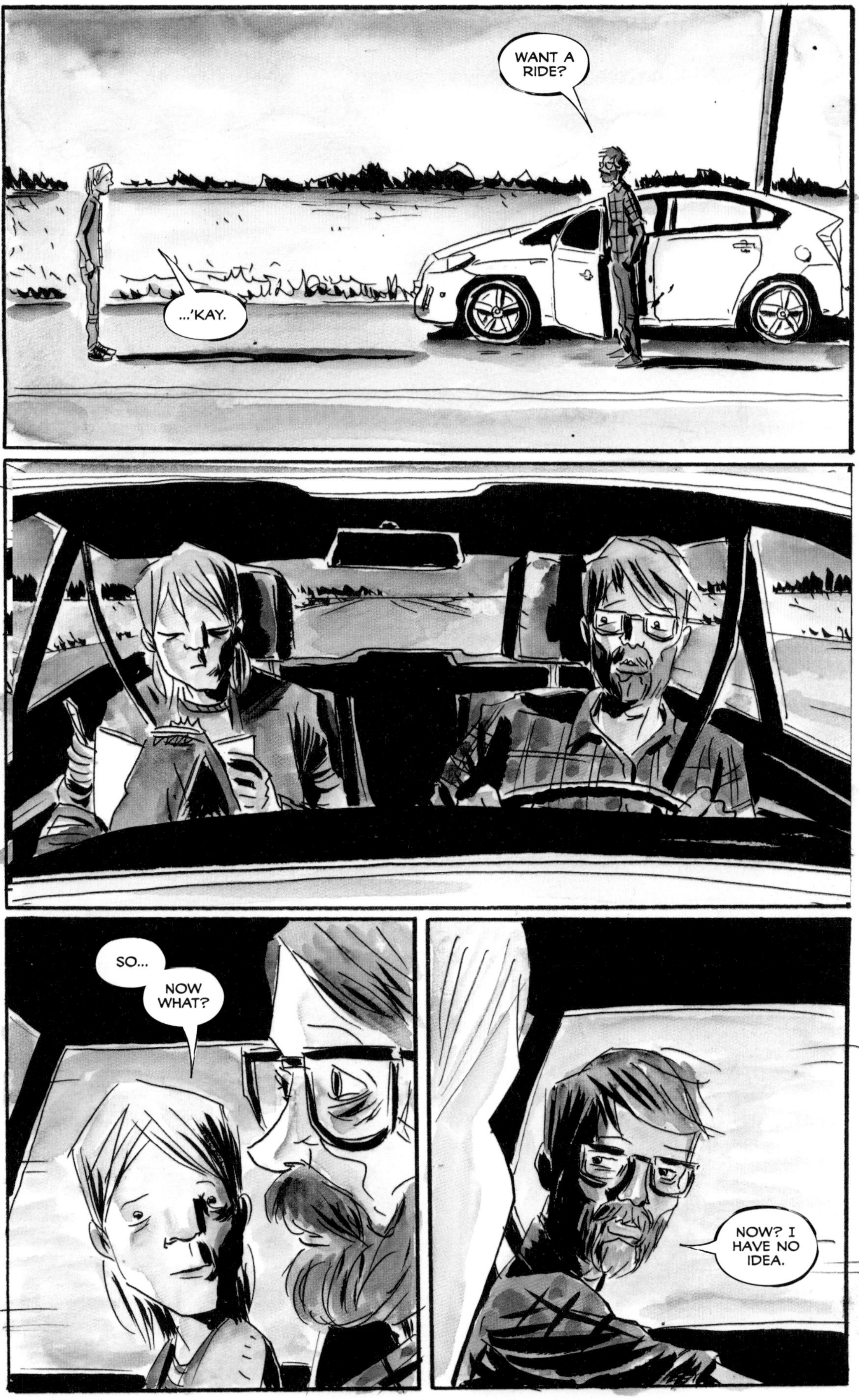
WANT A RIDE?
...'KAY.
SO...
NOW WHAT?
NOW? I HAVE NO IDEA.

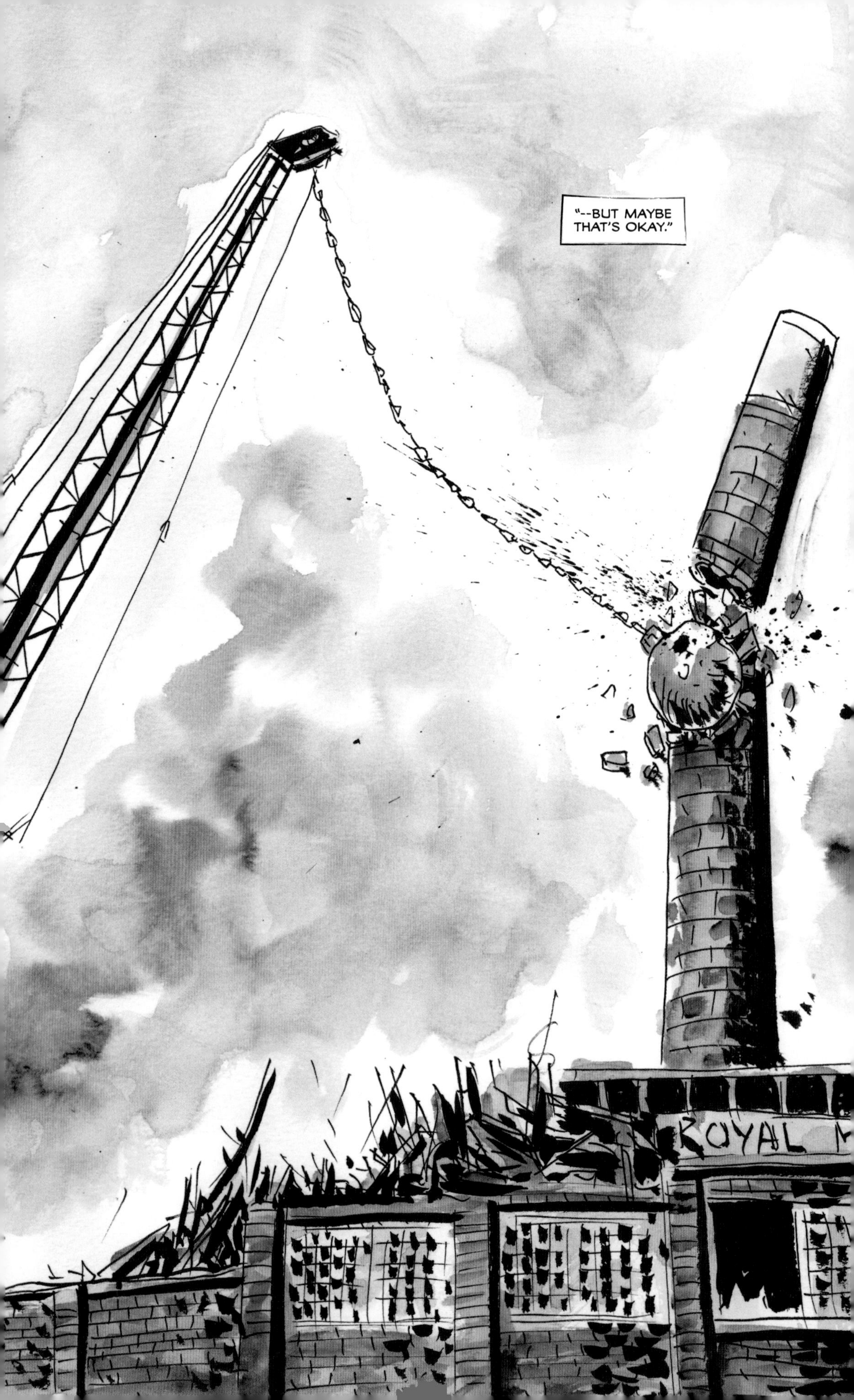
"--BUT MAYBE THAT'S OKAY."
ROYAL

THIS ONE OVER HERE, DAD?

YEAH WITH THE OTHER PHILCO. BE CAREFUL.

I AM.

I DON'T KNOW WHY YOU WANT TO KEEP ALL THESE OLD THINGS, PETER.

MOM.

≥SIGH≤ FINE. BUT THEY STAY IN THIS ROOM. I DON'T WANT RADIO PARTS ALL OVER MY HOUSE.

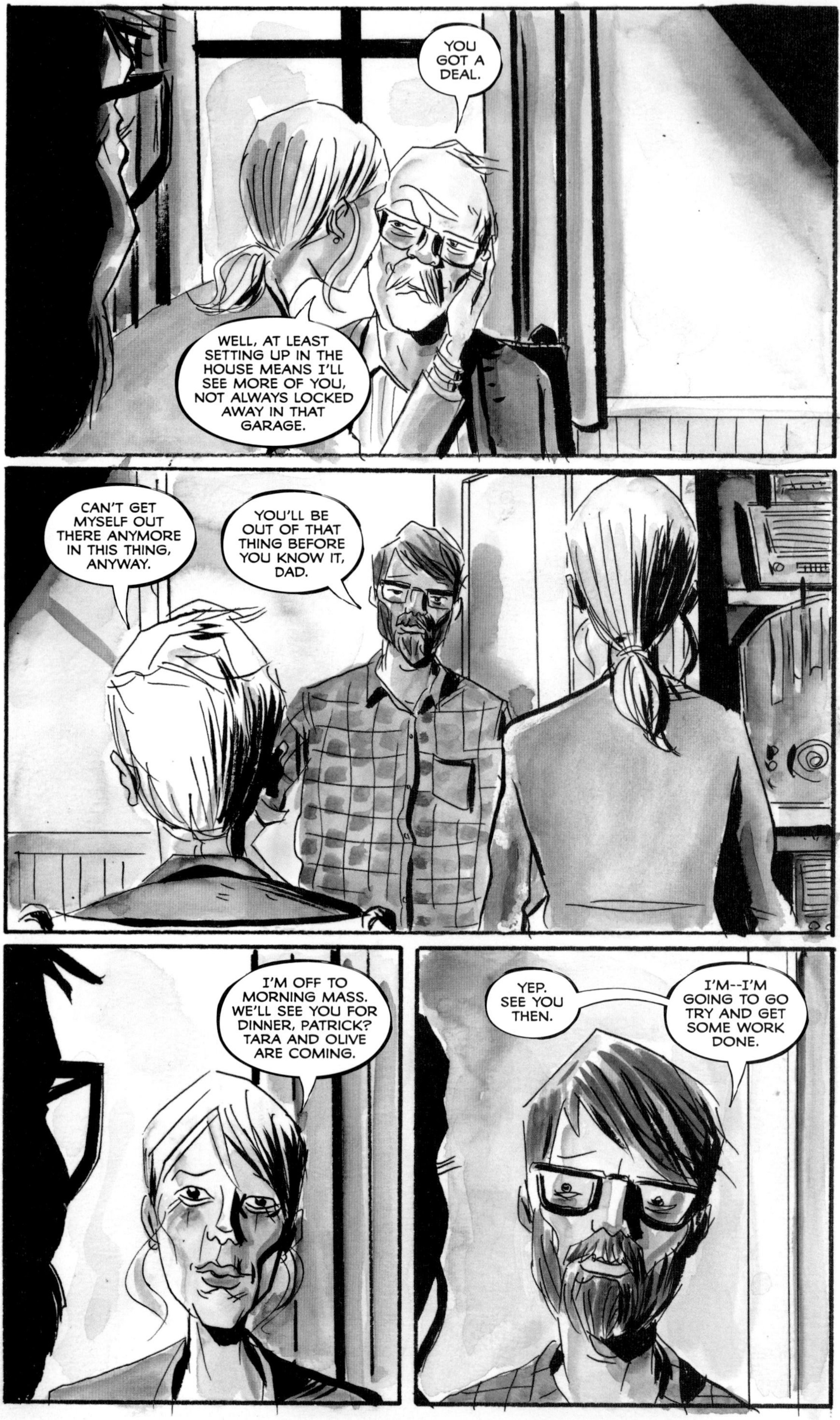
YOU GOT A DEAL.
WELL, AT LEAST SETTING UP IN THE HOUSE MEANS I'LL SEE MORE OF YOU, NOT ALWAYS LOCKED AWAY IN THAT GARAGE.
CAN'T GET MYSELF OUT THERE ANYMORE IN THIS THING, ANYWAY.
YOU'LL BE OUT OF THAT THING BEFORE YOU KNOW IT, DAD.
I'M OFF TO MORNING MASS. WE'LL SEE YOU FOR DINNER, PATRICK? TARA AND OLIVE ARE COMING.
YEP. SEE YOU THEN.
I'M--I'M GOING TO GO TRY AND GET SOME WORK DONE.

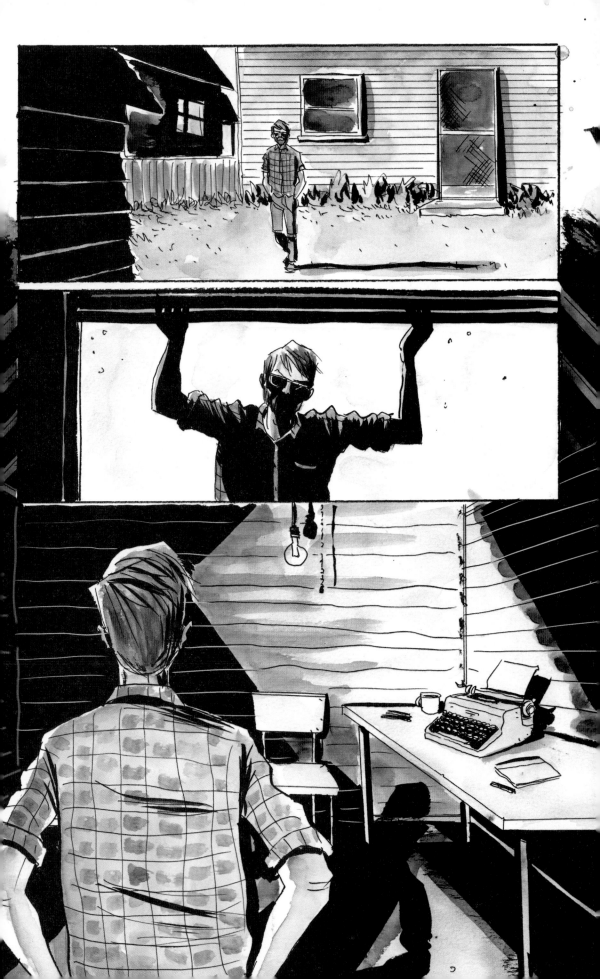

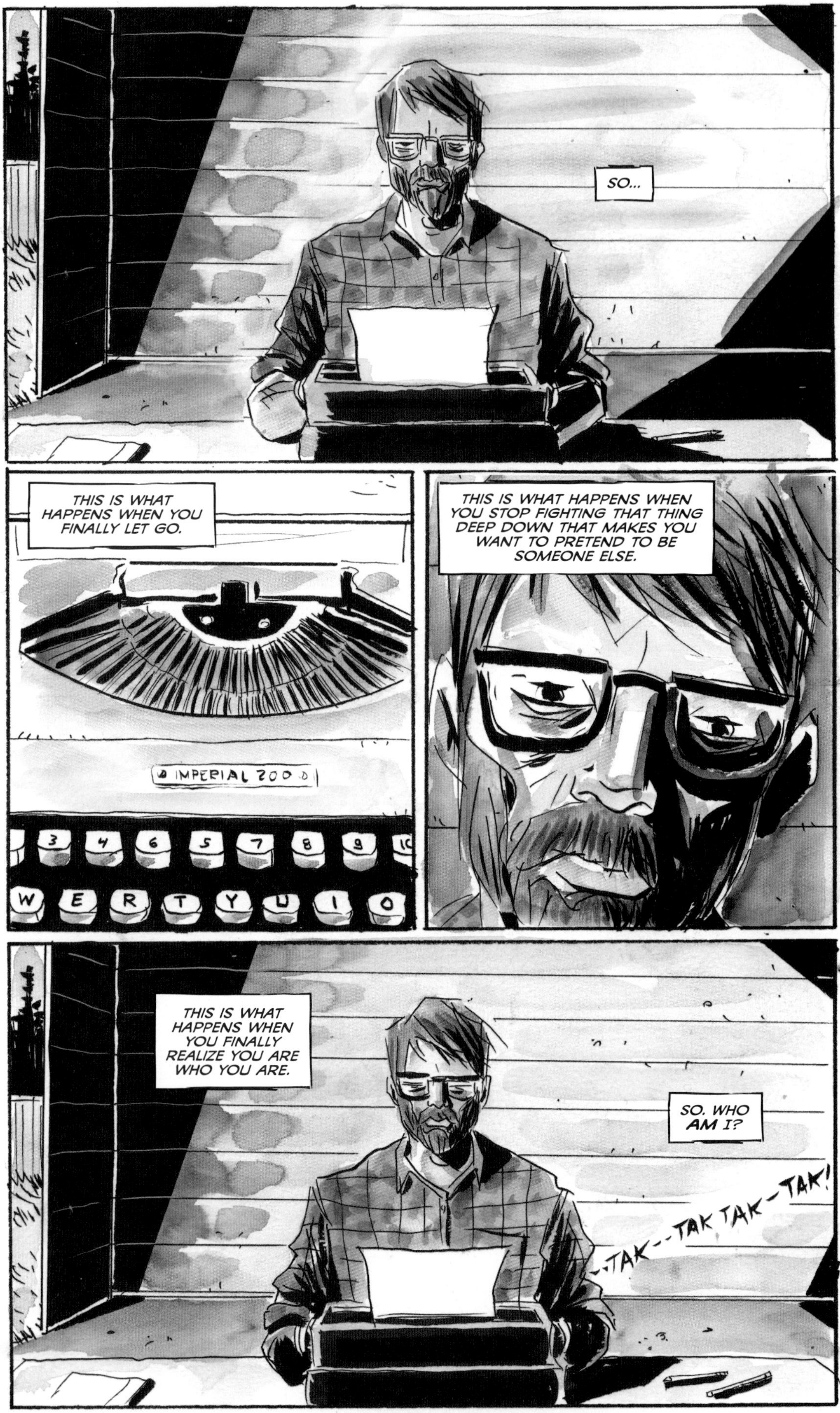
SO...
THIS IS WHAT HAPPENS WHEN YOU FINALLY LET GO.
IMPERIAL 200
THIS IS WHAT HAPPENS WHEN YOU STOP FIGHTING THAT THING DEEP DOWN THAT MAKES YOU WANT TO PRETEND TO BE SOMEONE ELSE.
THIS IS WHAT HAPPENS WHEN YOU FINALLY REALIZE YOU ARE WHO YOU ARE.
SO. WHO AM I?
--TAK--TAK TAK-TAK!

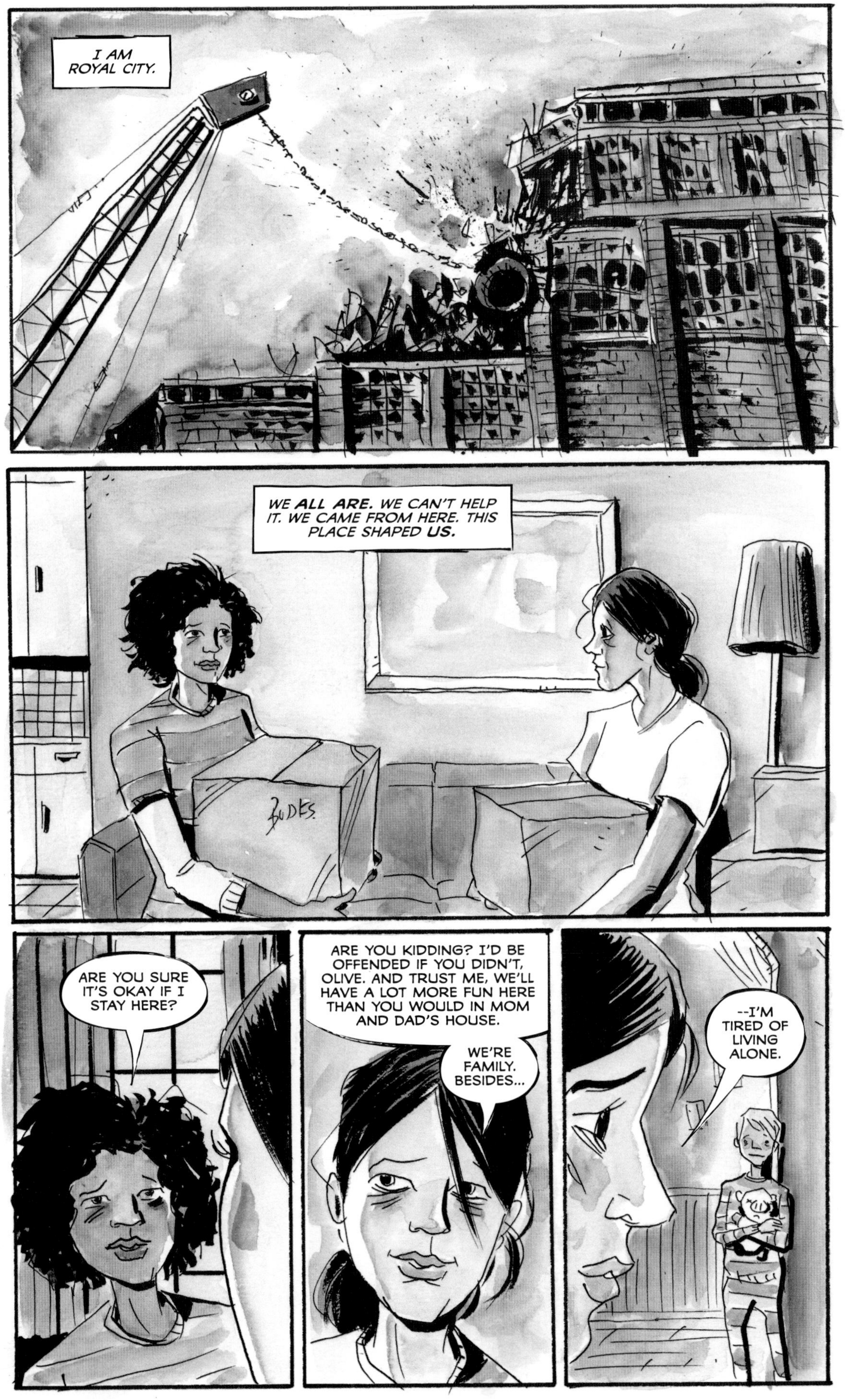
I AM ROYAL CITY.
WE ALL ARE. WE CAN'T HELP IT. WE CAME FROM HERE. THIS PLACE SHAPED US.
ARE YOU SURE IT'S OKAY IF I STAY HERE?
ARE YOU KIDDING? I'D BE OFFENDED IF YOU DIDN'T, OLIVE. AND TRUST ME, WE'LL HAVE A LOT MORE FUN HERE THAN YOU WOULD IN MOM AND DAD'S HOUSE.
WE'RE FAMILY. BESIDES...
--I'M TIRED OF LIVING ALONE.

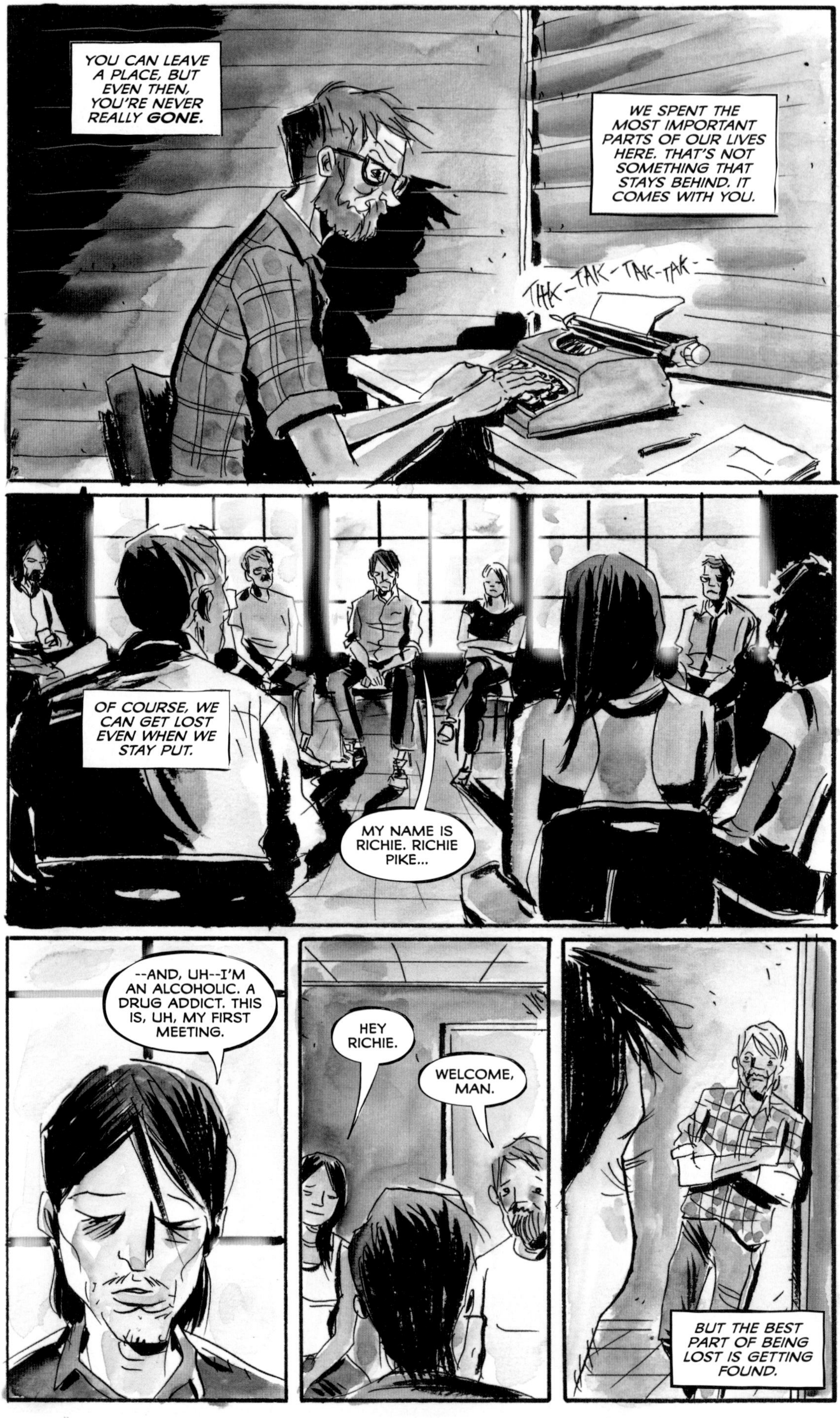
YOU CAN LEAVE A PLACE, BUT EVEN THEN, YOU'RE NEVER REALLY **GONE.**
WE SPENT THE MOST IMPORTANT PARTS OF OUR LIVES HERE. THAT'S NOT SOMETHING THAT STAYS BEHIND. IT COMES WITH YOU.
THK--TAK--TAK--TAK--
OF COURSE, WE CAN GET LOST EVEN WHEN WE STAY PUT.
MY NAME IS RICHIE. RICHIE PIKE...
--AND, UH--I'M AN ALCOHOLIC. A DRUG ADDICT. THIS IS, UH, MY FIRST MEETING.
HEY RICHIE.
WELCOME, MAN.
BUT THE BEST PART OF BEING LOST IS GETTING FOUND.

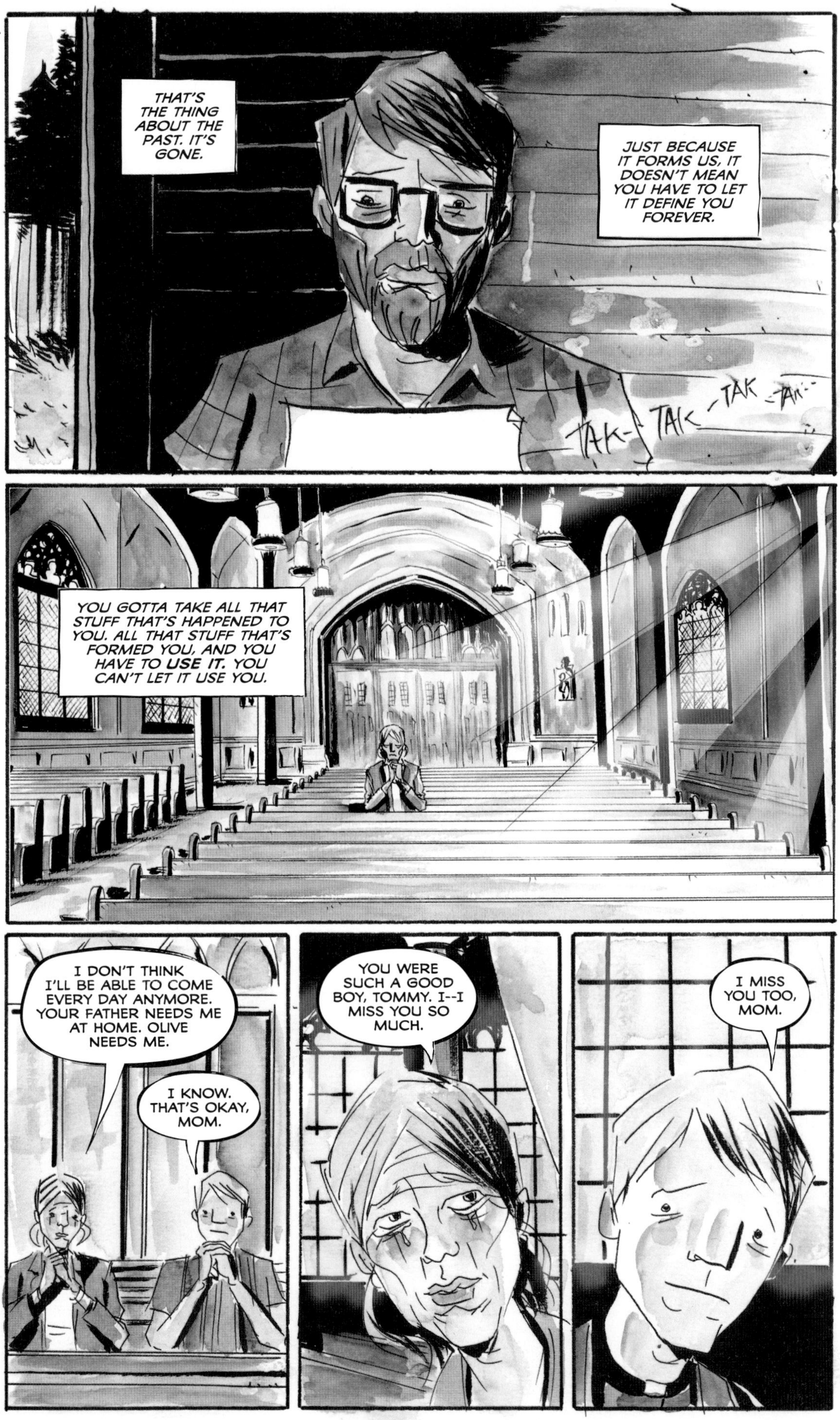
THAT'S THE THING ABOUT THE PAST. IT'S GONE.
JUST BECAUSE IT FORMS US, IT DOESN'T MEAN YOU HAVE TO LET IT DEFINE YOU FOREVER.
TAK- TAK -TAK -TAK-
YOU GOTTA TAKE ALL THAT STUFF THAT'S HAPPENED TO YOU. ALL THAT STUFF THAT'S FORMED YOU, AND YOU HAVE TO USE IT. YOU CAN'T LET IT USE YOU.
I DON'T THINK I'LL BE ABLE TO COME EVERY DAY ANYMORE. YOUR FATHER NEEDS ME AT HOME. OLIVE NEEDS ME.
I KNOW. THAT'S OKAY, MOM.
YOU WERE SUCH A GOOD BOY, TOMMY. I--I MISS YOU SO MUCH.
I MISS YOU TOO, MOM.

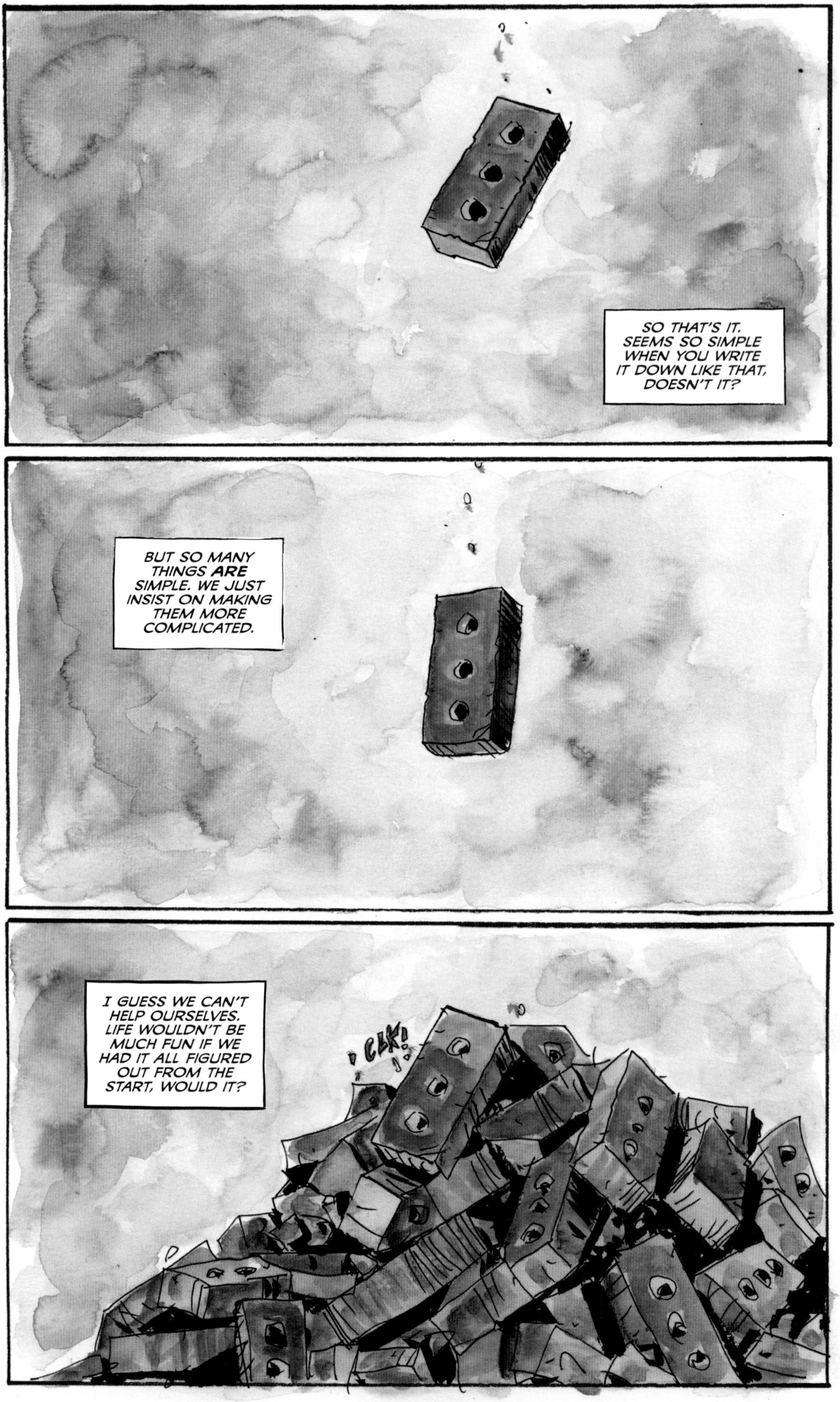
SO THAT'S IT. SEEMS SO SIMPLE WHEN YOU WRITE IT DOWN LIKE THAT, DOESN'T IT?
BUT SO MANY THINGS **ARE** SIMPLE. WE JUST INSIST ON MAKING THEM MORE COMPLICATED.
I GUESS WE CAN'T HELP OURSELVES. LIFE WOULDN'T BE MUCH FUN IF WE HAD IT ALL FIGURED OUT FROM THE START, WOULD IT?
CLK!

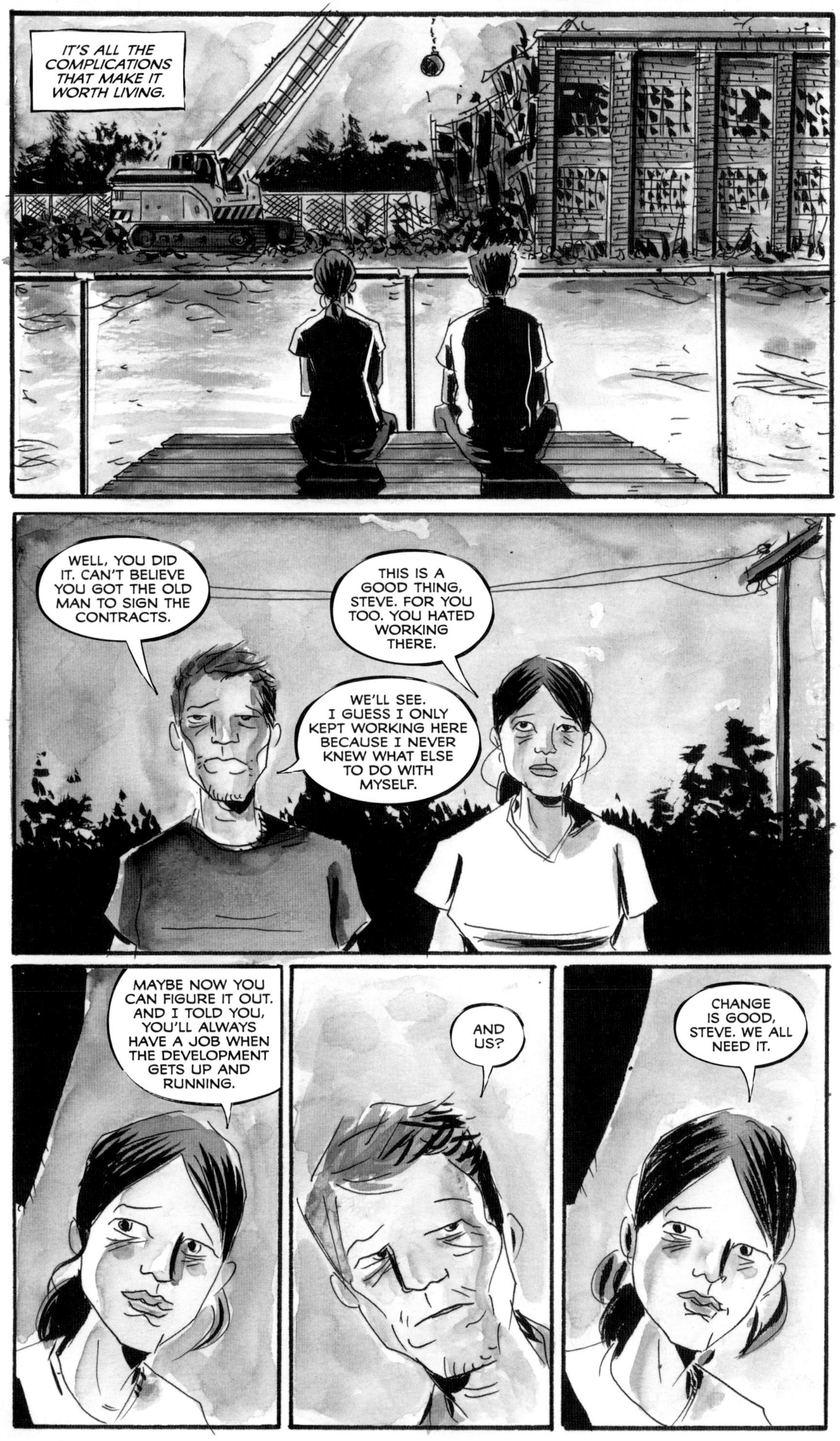
IT'S ALL THE COMPLICATIONS THAT MAKE IT WORTH LIVING.
WELL, YOU DID IT. CAN'T BELIEVE YOU GOT THE OLD MAN TO SIGN THE CONTRACTS.
THIS IS A GOOD THING, STEVE. FOR YOU TOO. YOU HATED WORKING THERE.
WE'LL SEE. I GUESS I ONLY KEPT WORKING HERE BECAUSE I NEVER KNEW WHAT ELSE TO DO WITH MYSELF.
MAYBE NOW YOU CAN FIGURE IT OUT. AND I TOLD YOU, YOU'LL ALWAYS HAVE A JOB WHEN THE DEVELOPMENT GETS UP AND RUNNING.
AND US?
CHANGE IS GOOD, STEVE. WE ALL NEED IT.

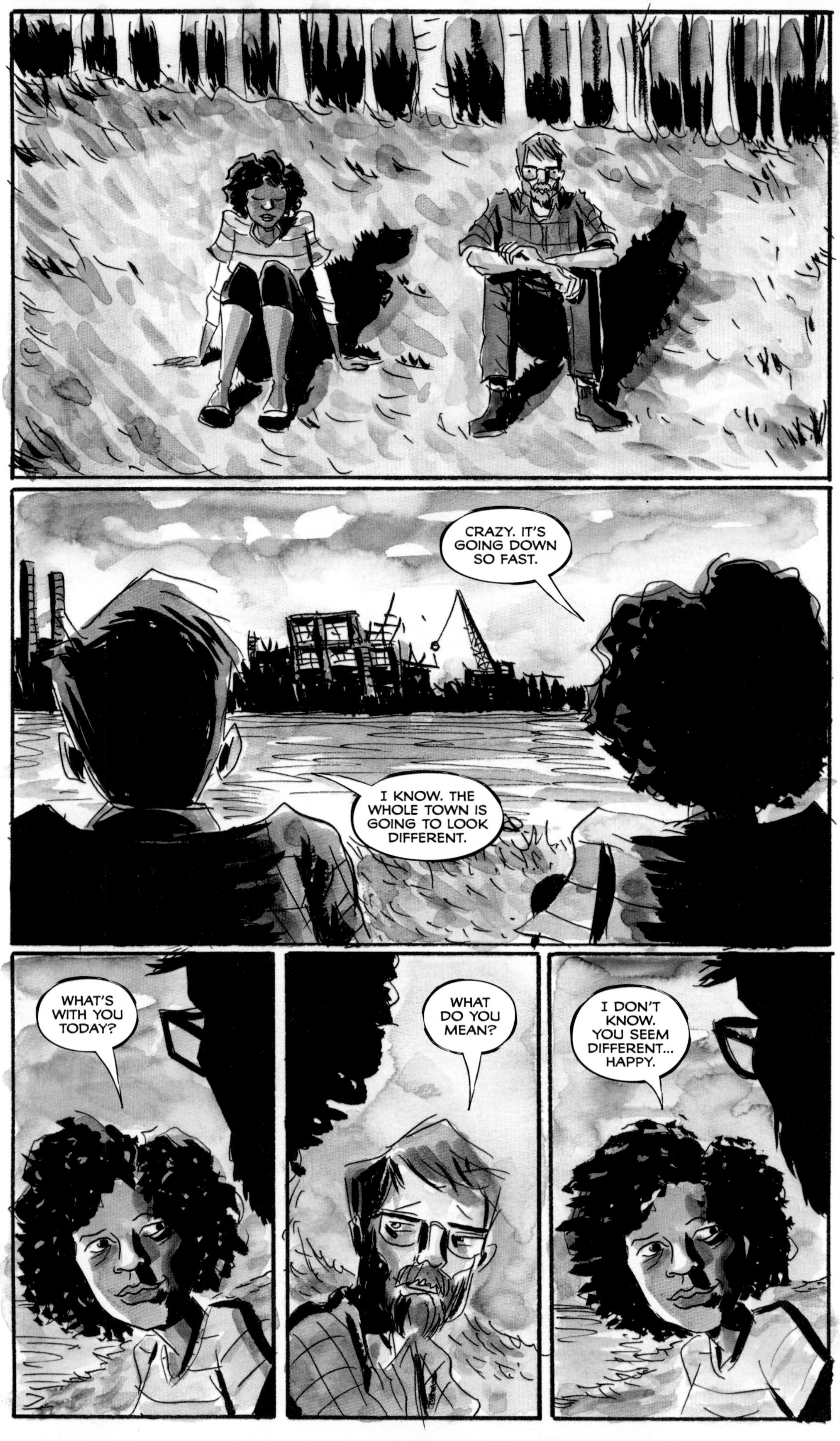
CRAZY. IT'S GOING DOWN SO FAST.
I KNOW. THE WHOLE TOWN IS GOING TO LOOK DIFFERENT.
WHAT'S WITH YOU TODAY?
WHAT DO YOU MEAN?
I DON'T KNOW. YOU SEEM DIFFERENT... HAPPY.

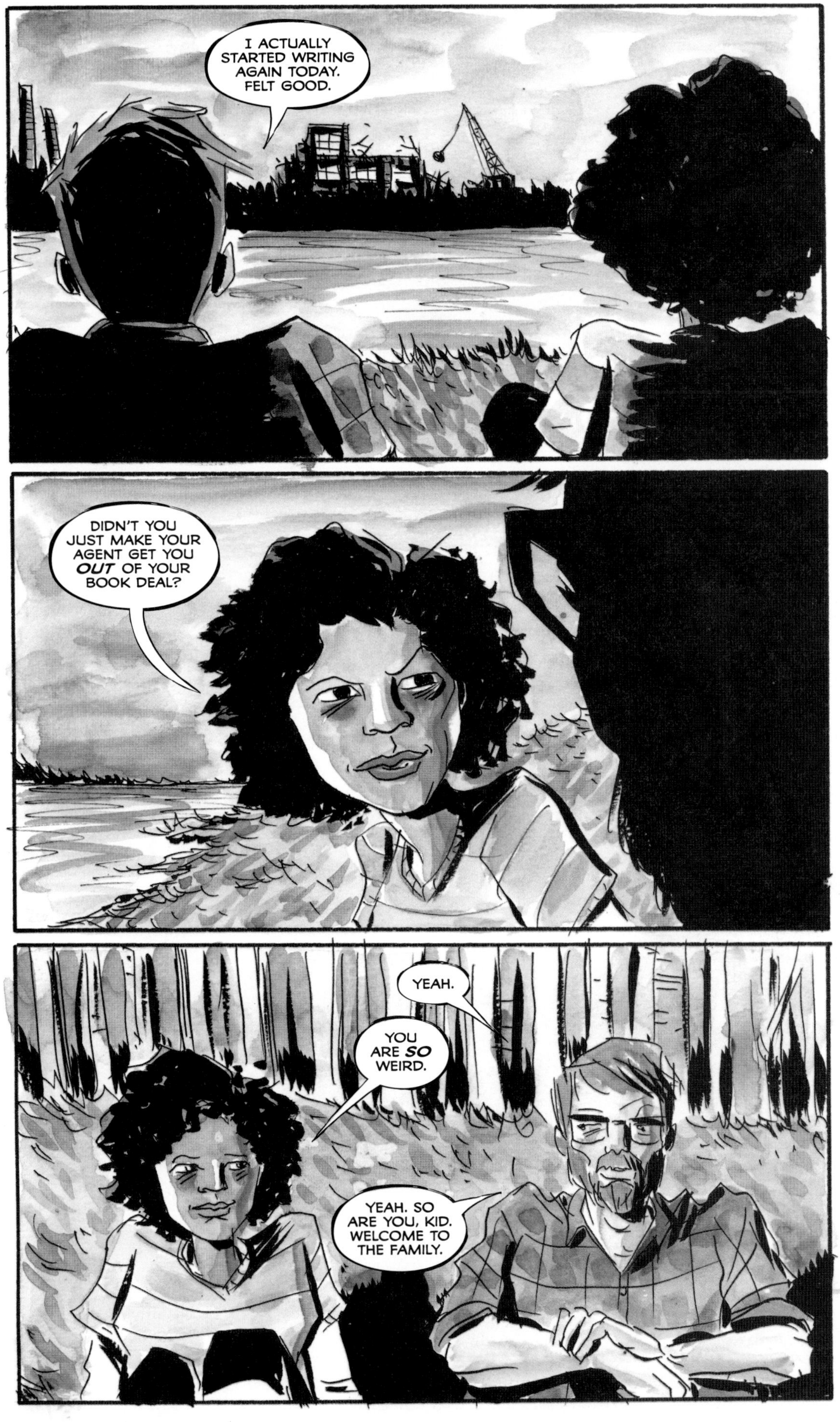
I ACTUALLY STARTED WRITING AGAIN TODAY. FELT GOOD.
DIDN'T YOU JUST MAKE YOUR AGENT GET YOU *OUT* OF YOUR BOOK DEAL?
YEAH.
YOU ARE *SO* WEIRD.
YEAH. SO ARE YOU, KID. WELCOME TO THE FAMILY.

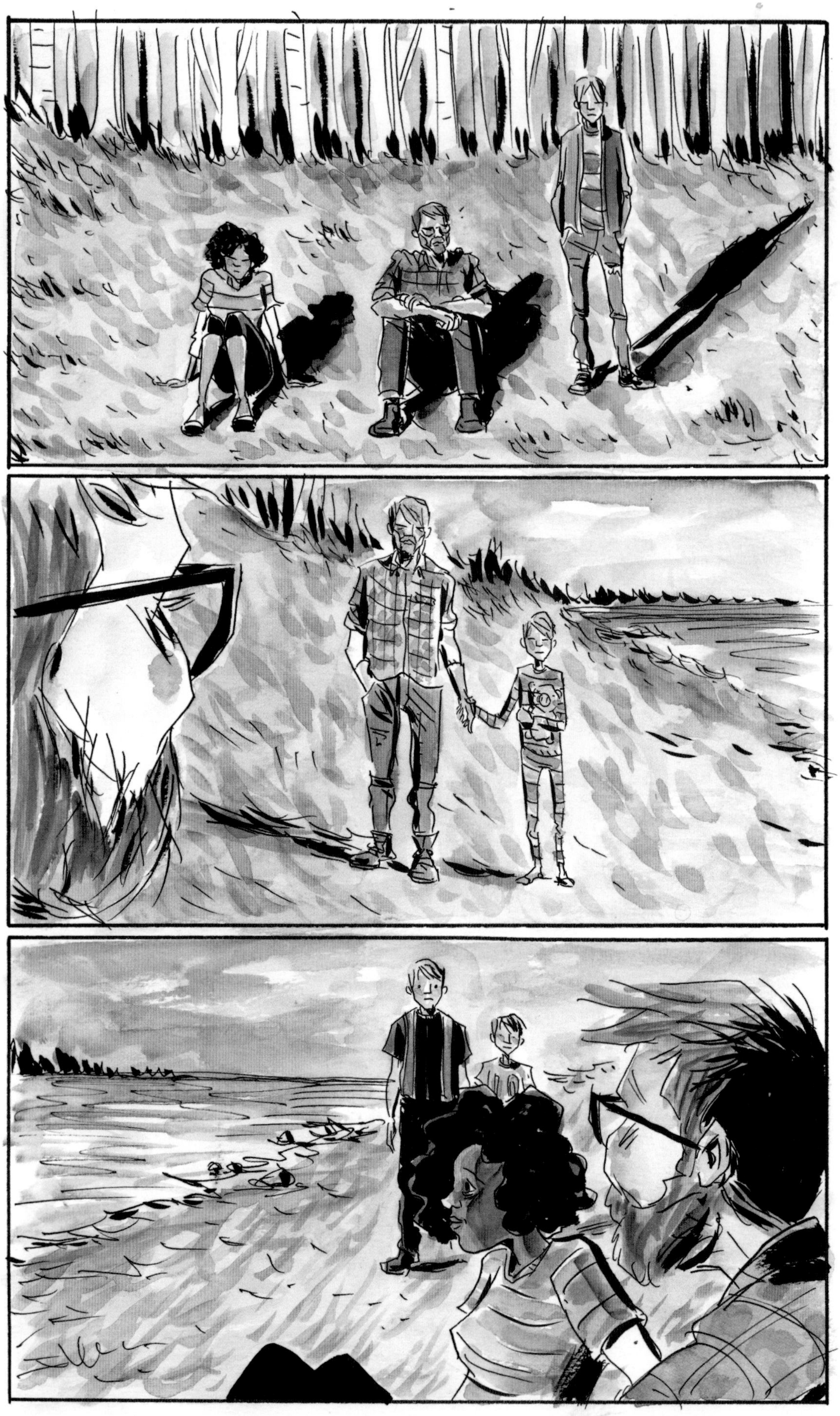

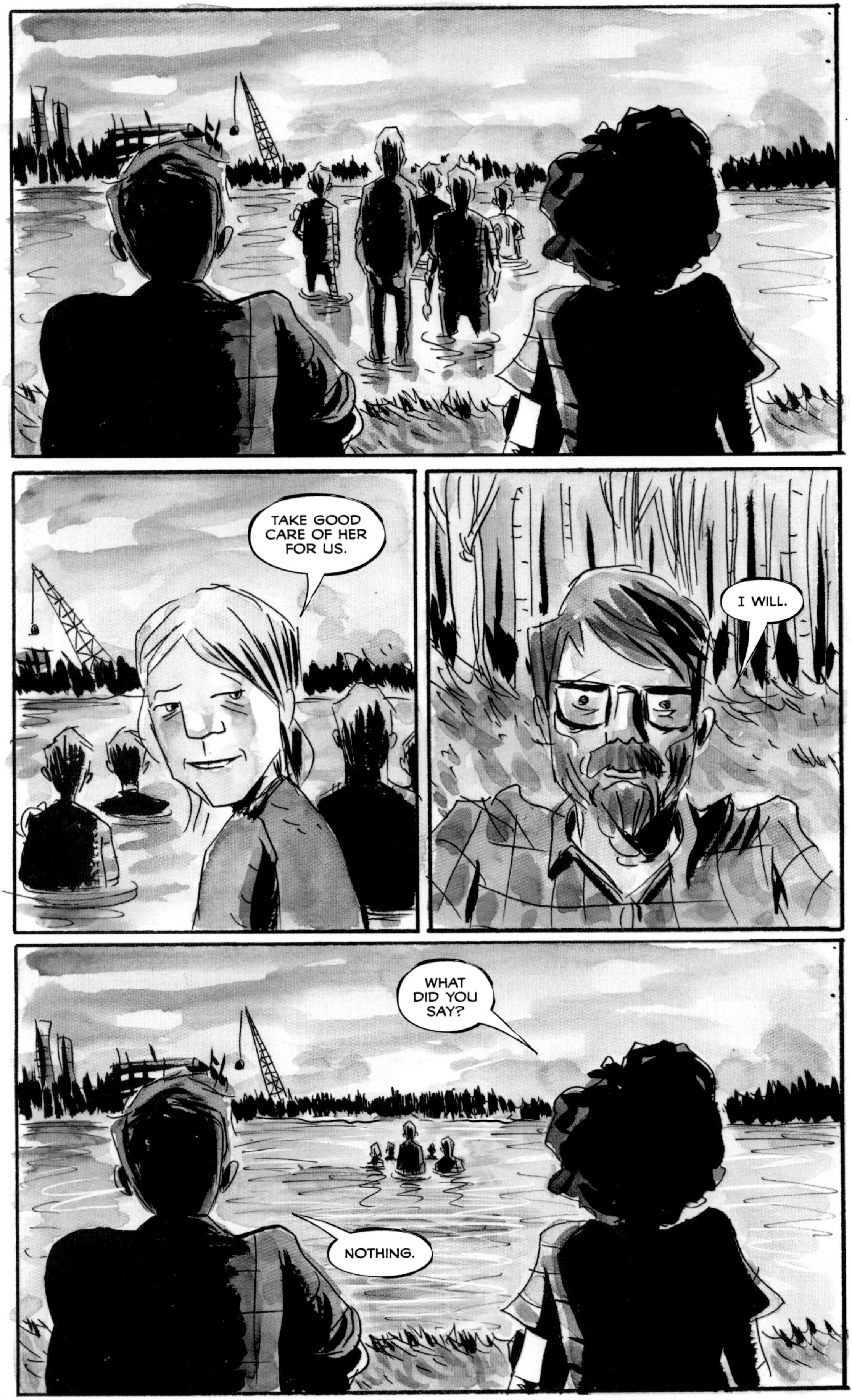
TAKE GOOD CARE OF HER FOR US.
I WILL.
WHAT DID YOU SAY?
NOTHING.

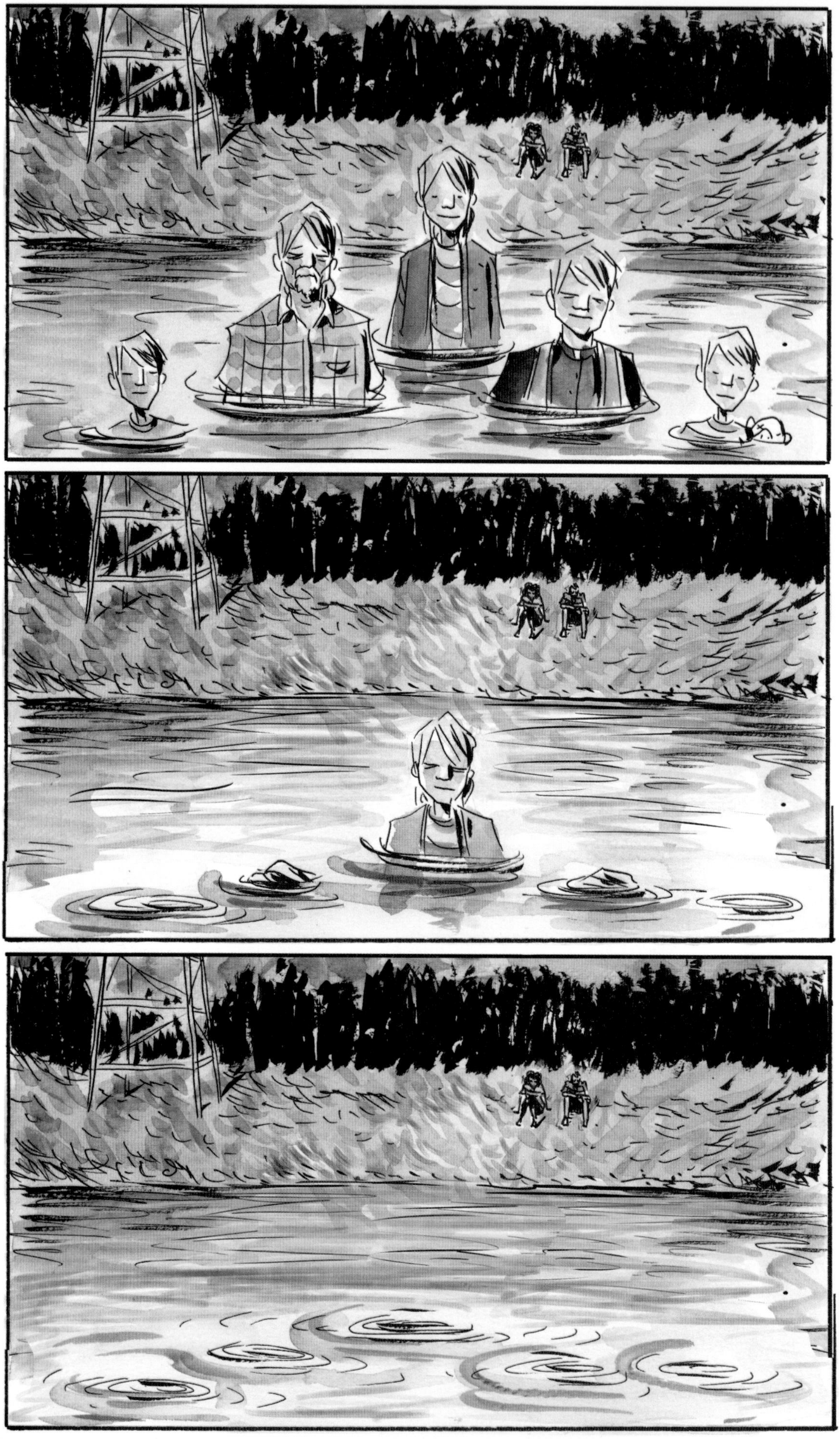

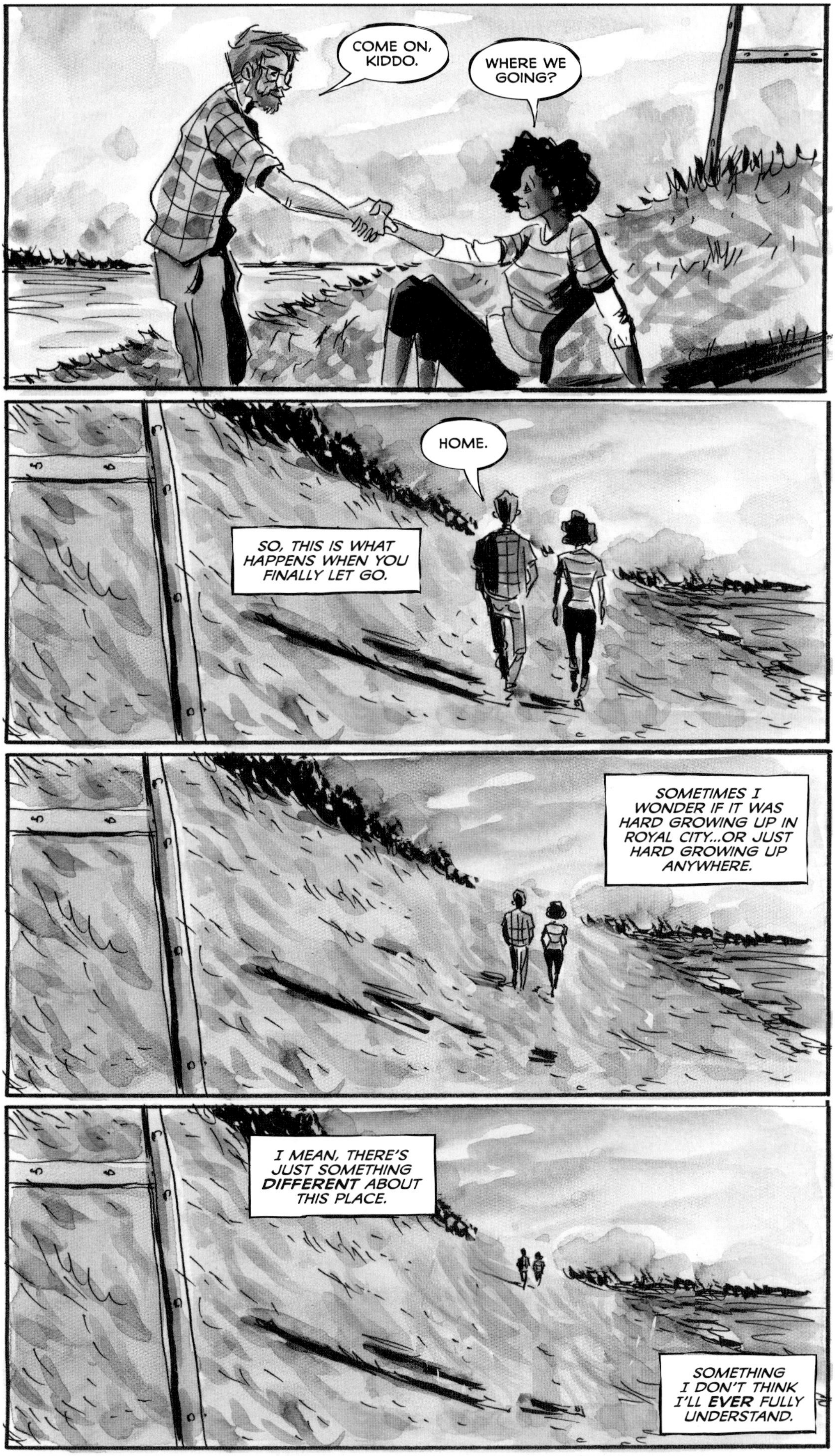
COME ON, KIDDO.
WHERE WE GOING?
HOME.
SO, THIS IS WHAT HAPPENS WHEN YOU FINALLY LET GO.
SOMETIMES I WONDER IF IT WAS HARD GROWING UP IN ROYAL CITY...OR JUST HARD GROWING UP ANYWHERE.
I MEAN, THERE'S JUST SOMETHING **DIFFERENT** ABOUT THIS PLACE.
SOMETHING I DON'T THINK I'LL **EVER** FULLY UNDERSTAND.

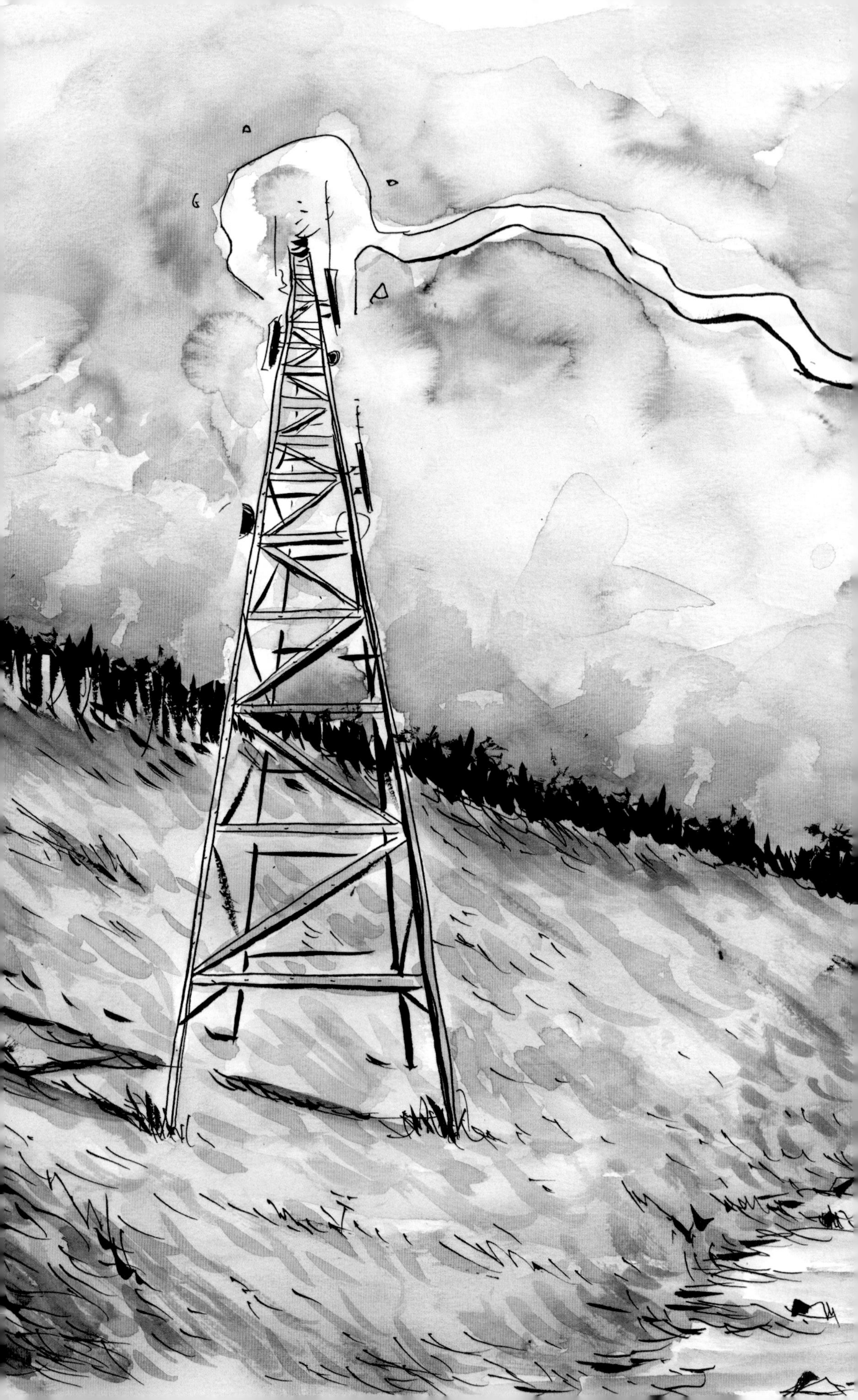

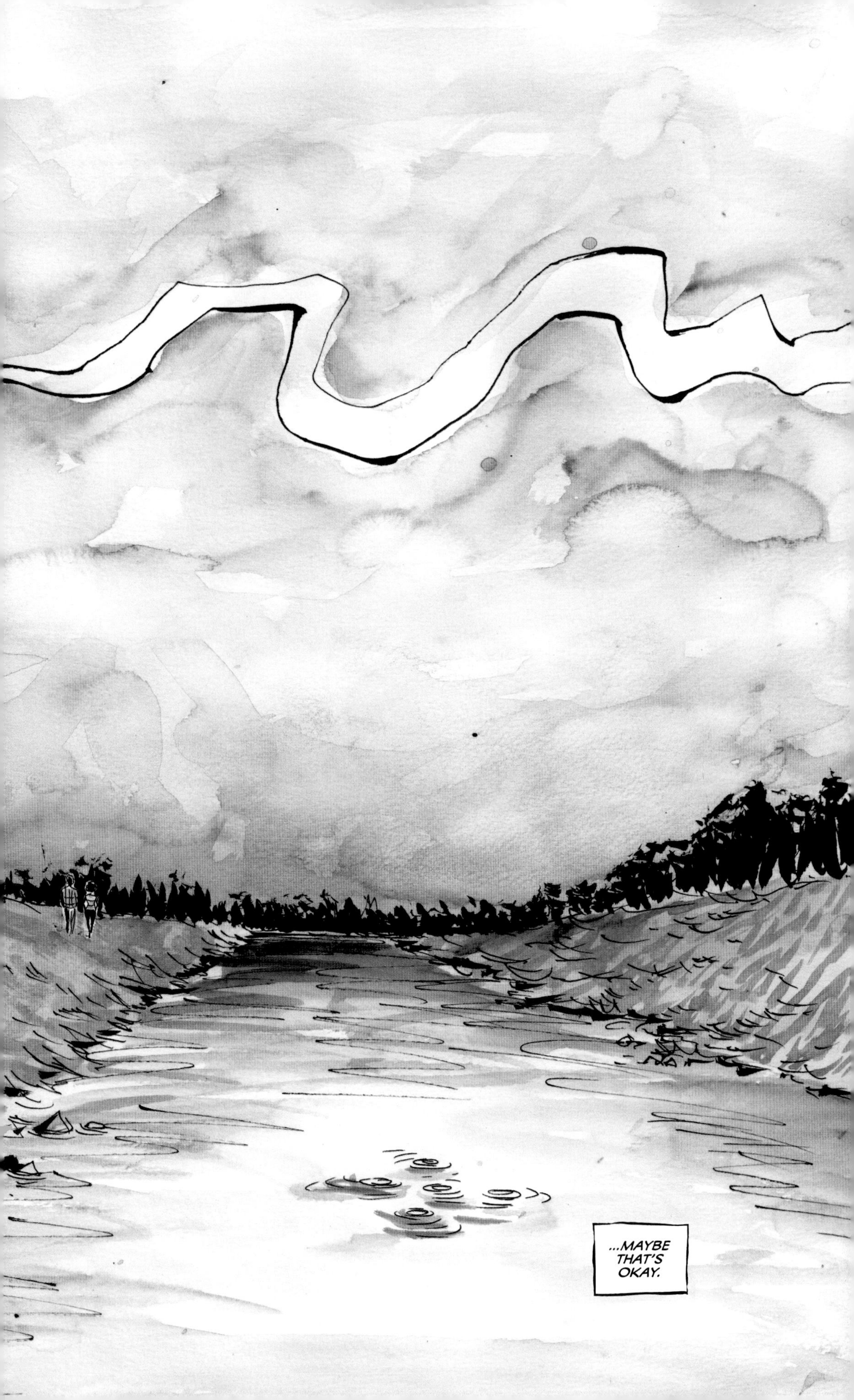
...MAYBE THAT'S OKAY.

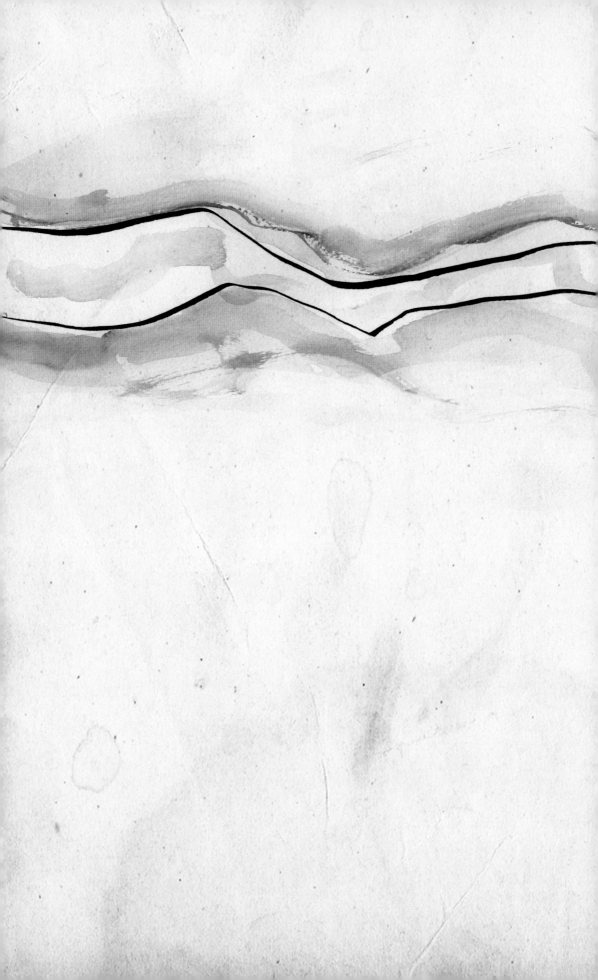

JEFF LEMIRE

ROYAL CITY

Jeff Lemire 2016-2018

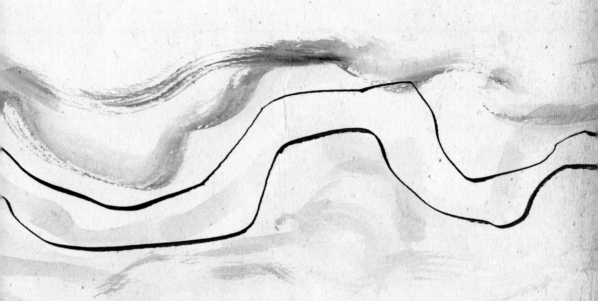

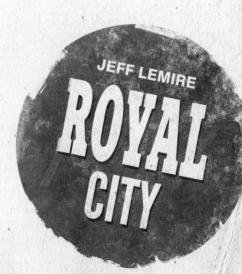

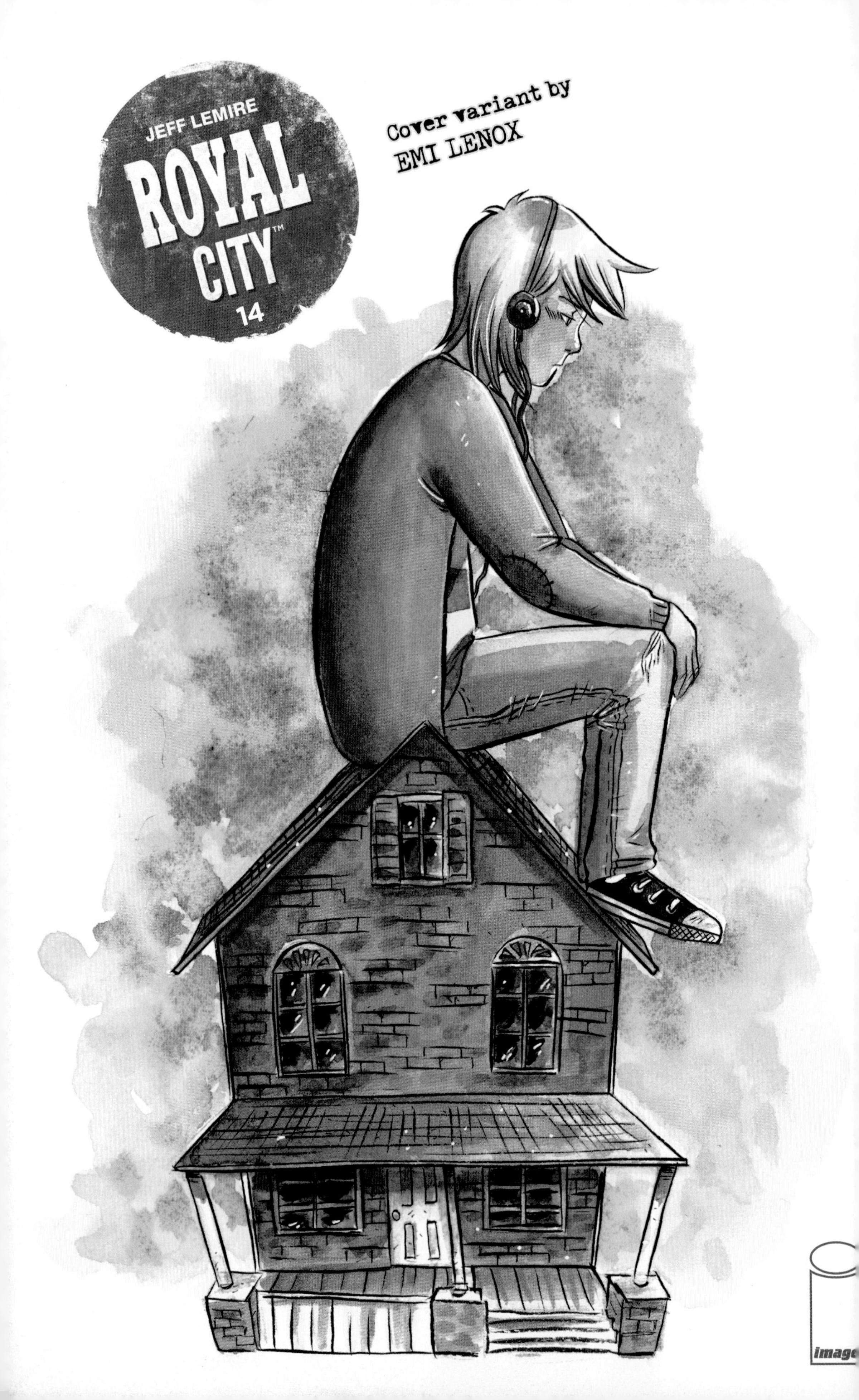
JEFF LEMIRE
ROYAL
CITY™
14
Cover variant by
EMI LENOX

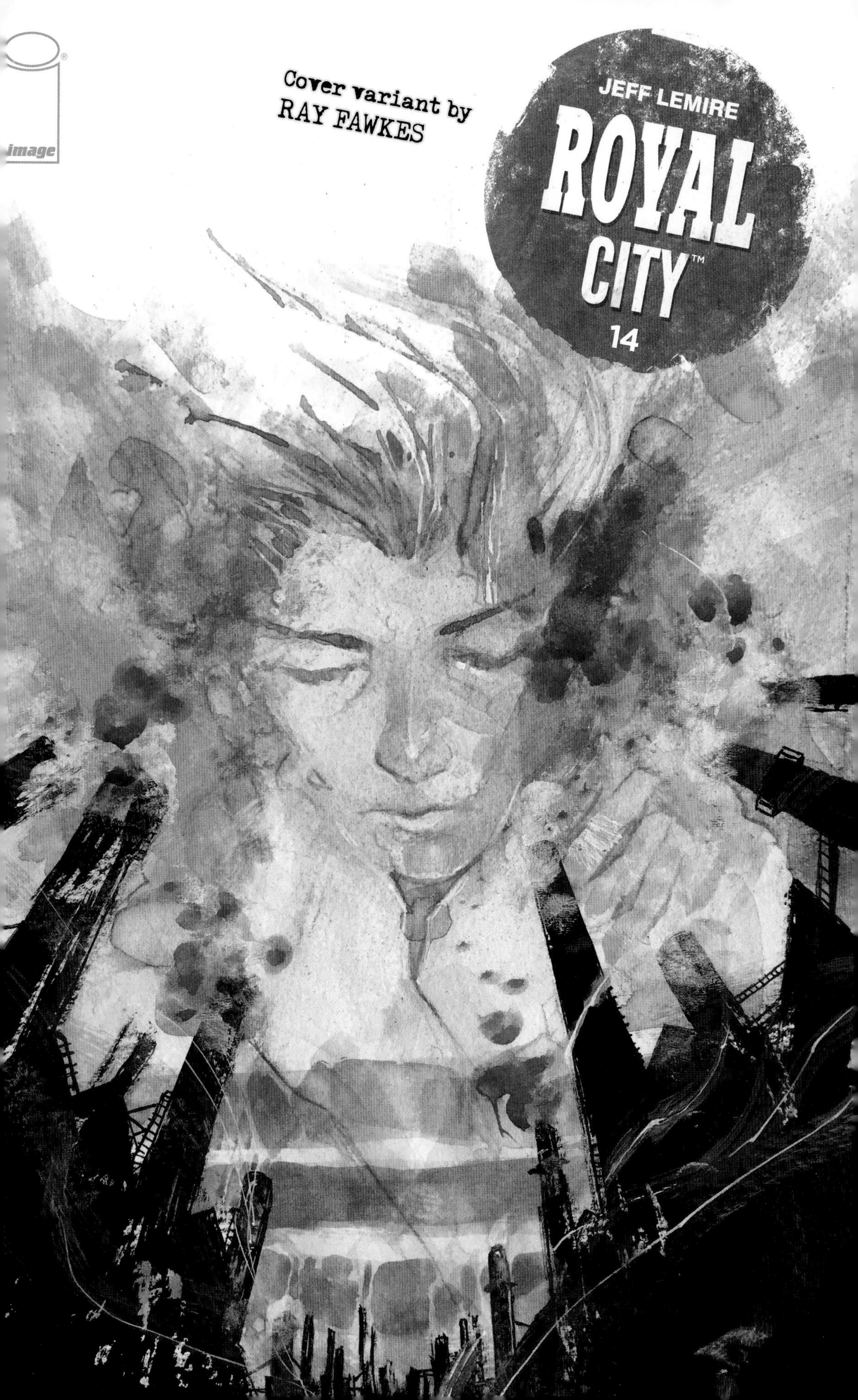

image
Cover variant by
RAY FAWKES
JEFF LEMIRE
ROYAL
CITY™
14

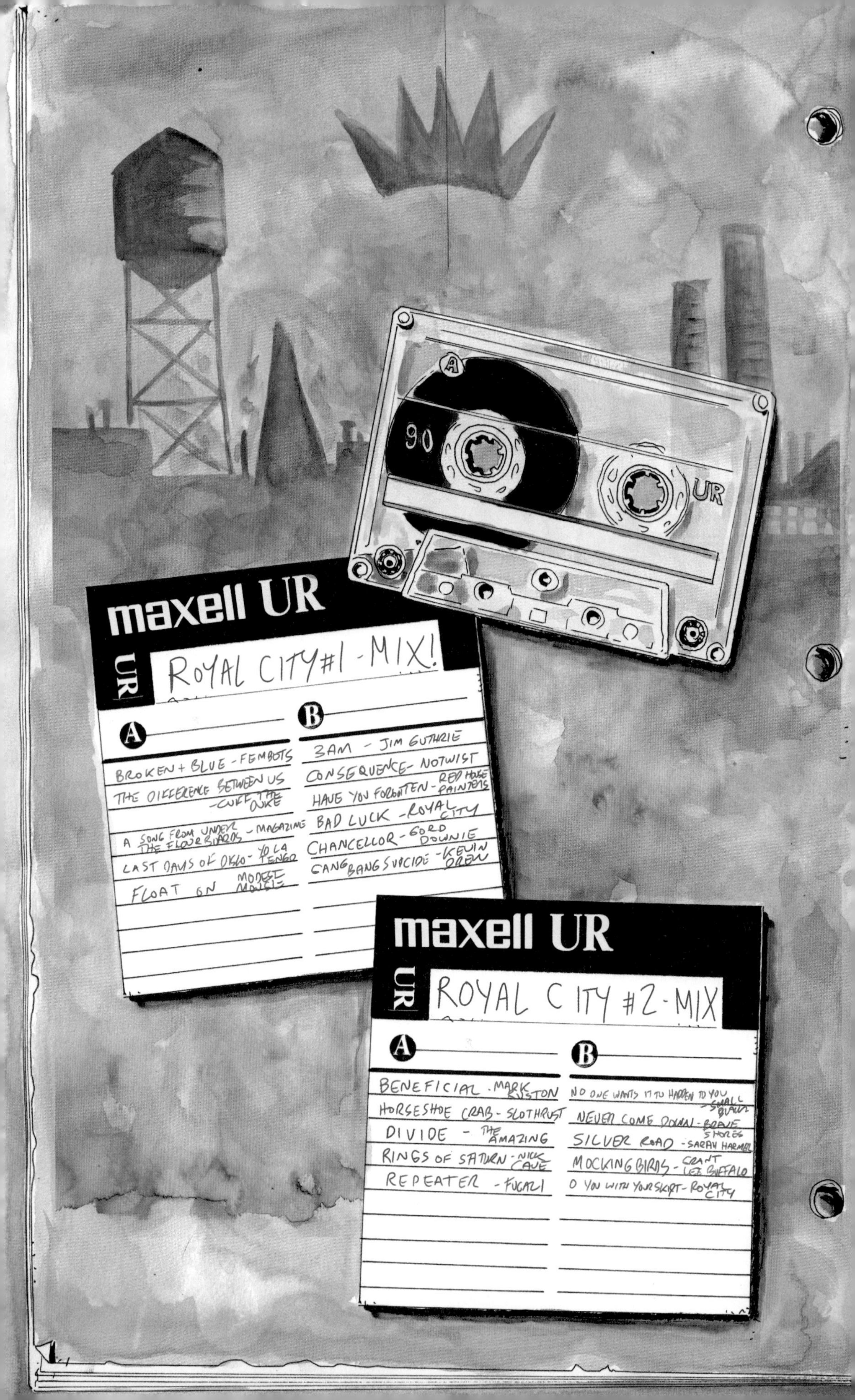
90
UR
maxell UR
ROYAL CITY #1 - MIX!
A
BROKEN + BLUE - FEMBOTS
THE DIFFERENCE BETWEEN US - CUFF THE DUKE
A SONG FROM UNDER THE FLOORBOARDS - MAGAZINE
LAST DAYS OF DISCO - YO LA TENGO
FLOAT ON MODEST MOUSE
B
3AM - JIM GUTHRIE
CONSEQUENCE - NOTWIST
HAVE YOU FORGOTTEN - RED HOUSE PAINTERS
BAD LUCK - ROYAL CITY
CHANCELLOR - GORD DOWNIE
GANG BANG SUICIDE - KEVIN DREW
maxell UR
ROYAL CITY #2 - MIX
A
BENEFICIAL - MARK KUSTON
HORSESHOE CRAB - SLOTHRUST
DIVIDE - THE AMAZING
RINGS OF SATURN - NICK CAVE
REPEATER - FUGAZI
B
NO ONE WANTS IT TO HAPPEN TO YOU - SMALL BLACK
NEVER COME DOWN - BRAVE SHORES
SILVER ROAD - SARAH HARMER
MOCKINGBIRDS - GRANT LEE BUFFALO
O YOU WITH YOUR SKIRT - ROYAL CITY

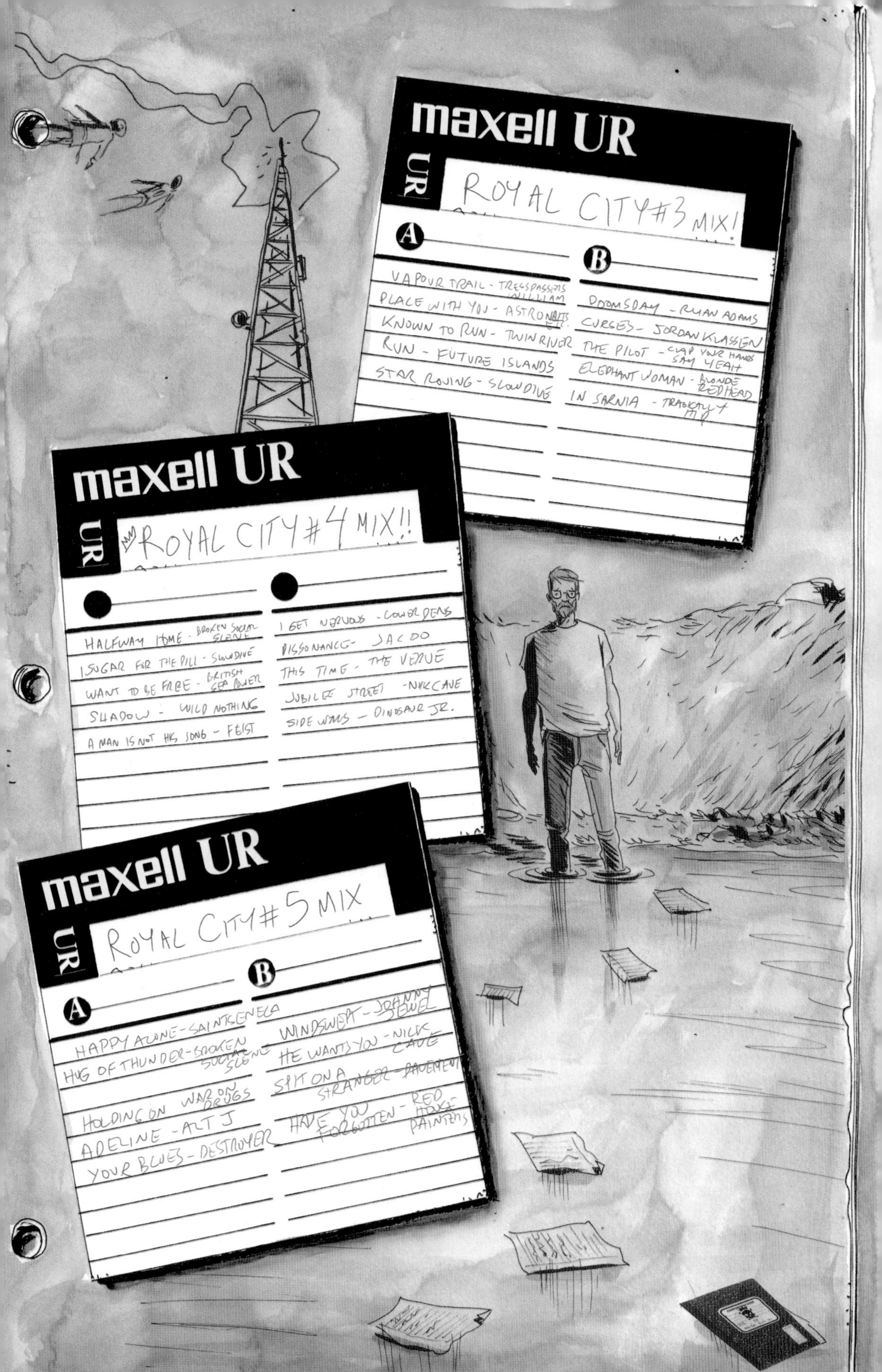
maxell UR
ROYAL CITY #3 MIX!
VAPOUR TRAIL - TRESSPASSERS WILLIAM
PLACE WITH YOU - ASTRONAUTS ETC.
KNOWN TO RUN - TWIN RIVER
RUN - FUTURE ISLANDS
STAR ROVING - SLOWDIVE
DOOMSDAY - RYAN ADAMS
CURSES - JORDAN KLASSEN
THE PILOT - CLAP YOUR HANDS SAY YEAH
ELEPHANT WOMAN - BLONDE REDHEAD
IN SARNIA - TRAGICALLY HIP
maxell UR
ROYAL CITY #4 MIX!!
HALFWAY HOME - BROKEN SOCIAL SCENE
SUGAR FOR THE PILL - SLOWDIVE
WANT TO BE FREE - BRITISH SEA POWER
SHADOW - WILD NOTHING
A MAN IS NOT HIS SONG - FEIST
I GET NERVOUS - COWERDENS
DISSONANCE - JACCO
THIS TIME - THE VERVE
JUBILEE STREET - NICK CAVE
SIDEWAYS - DINOSAUR JR.
maxell UR
ROYAL CITY #5 MIX
HAPPY ALONE - SAINTSENECA
HUG OF THUNDER - BROKEN SOCIAL SCENE
HOLDING ON WAR ON DRUGS
ADELINE - ALT J
YOUR BLUES - DESTROYER
WINDSWEPT - JOHNNY JEWEL
HE WANTS YOU - NICK CAVE
SPIT ON A STRANGER - PAVEMENT
HAVE YOU FORGOTTEN - RED HOUSE PAINTERS

HTTPS://OPEN.SPOTIFY.COM/USER/ROYALCITYCOMIC

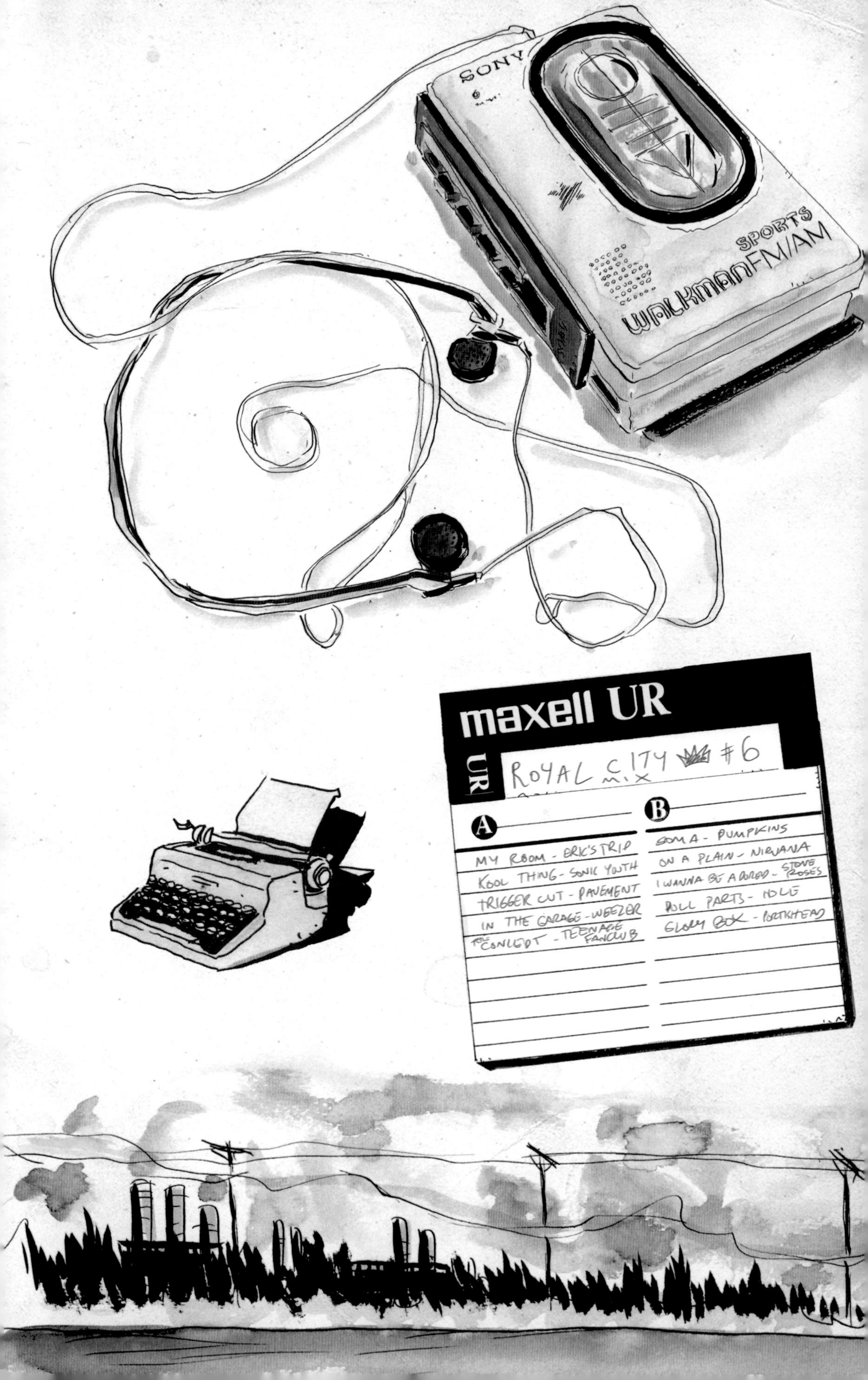
SONY
SPORTS
WALKMAN FM/AM
maxell UR
UR
ROYAL CITY MIX #6
A
MY ROOM - ERIC'S TRIP
KOOL THING - SONIC YOUTH
TRIGGER CUT - PAVEMENT
IN THE GARAGE - WEEZER
THE CONCEPT - TEENAGE FANCLUB
B
SOMA - PUMPKINS
ON A PLAIN - NIRVANA
I WANNA BE ADORED - STONE ROSES
DOLL PARTS - HOLE
GLORY BOX - PORTISHEAD

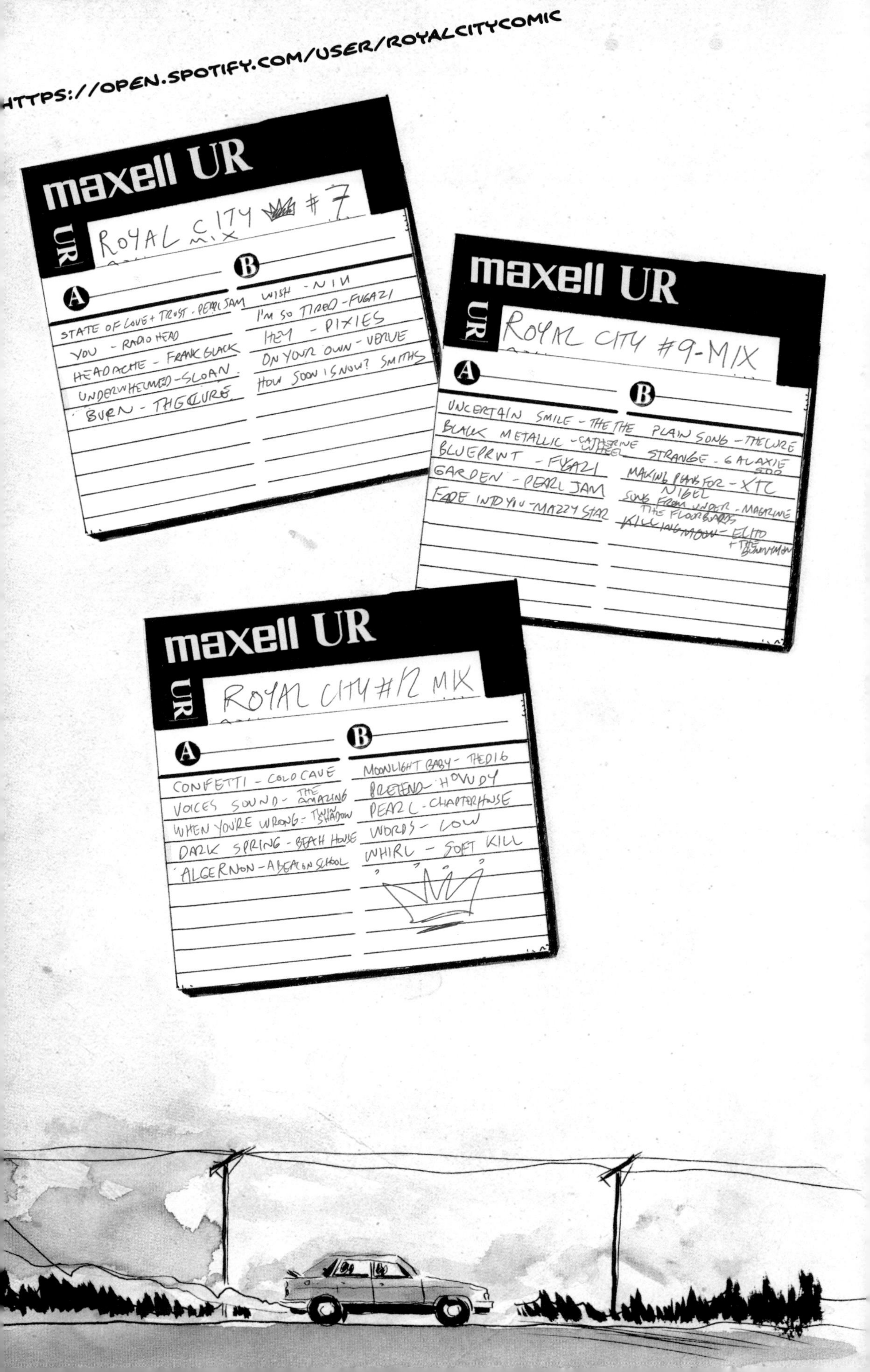
HTTPS://OPEN.SPOTIFY.COM/USER/ROYALCITYCOMIC
maxell UR
ROYAL CITY #7 MIX
A
STATE OF LOVE + TRUST - PEARL JAM
YOU - RADIOHEAD
HEADACHE - FRANK BLACK
UNDERWHELMED - SLOAN
BURN - THE CURE
B
WISH - NIN
I'M SO TIRED - FUGAZI
HEY - PIXIES
ON YOUR OWN - VERVE
HOW SOON IS NOW? SMITHS
maxell UR
ROYAL CITY #9-MIX
A
UNCERTAIN SMILE - THE THE
BLACK METALLIC - CATHERINE WHEEL
BLUEPRINT - FUGAZI
GARDEN - PEARL JAM
FADE INTO YOU - MAZZY STAR
B
PLAIN SONG - THE CURE
STRANGE - GALAXIE 500
MAKING PLANS FOR NIGEL - XTC
SONG FROM UNDER THE FLOORBOARDS - MAGAZINE
KILLING MOON - ECHO + THE BUNNYMEN
maxell UR
ROYAL CITY #12 MIX
A
CONFETTI - COLD CAVE
VOICES SOUND - THE AMAZING
WHEN YOU'RE WRONG - TWIN SHADOW
DARK SPRING - BEACH HOUSE
ALGERNON - A BEACON SCHOOL
B
MOONLIGHT BABY - THE DIG
PRETEND - HOVVDY
PEARL - CHAPTERHOUSE
WORDS - LOW
WHIRL - SOFT KILL

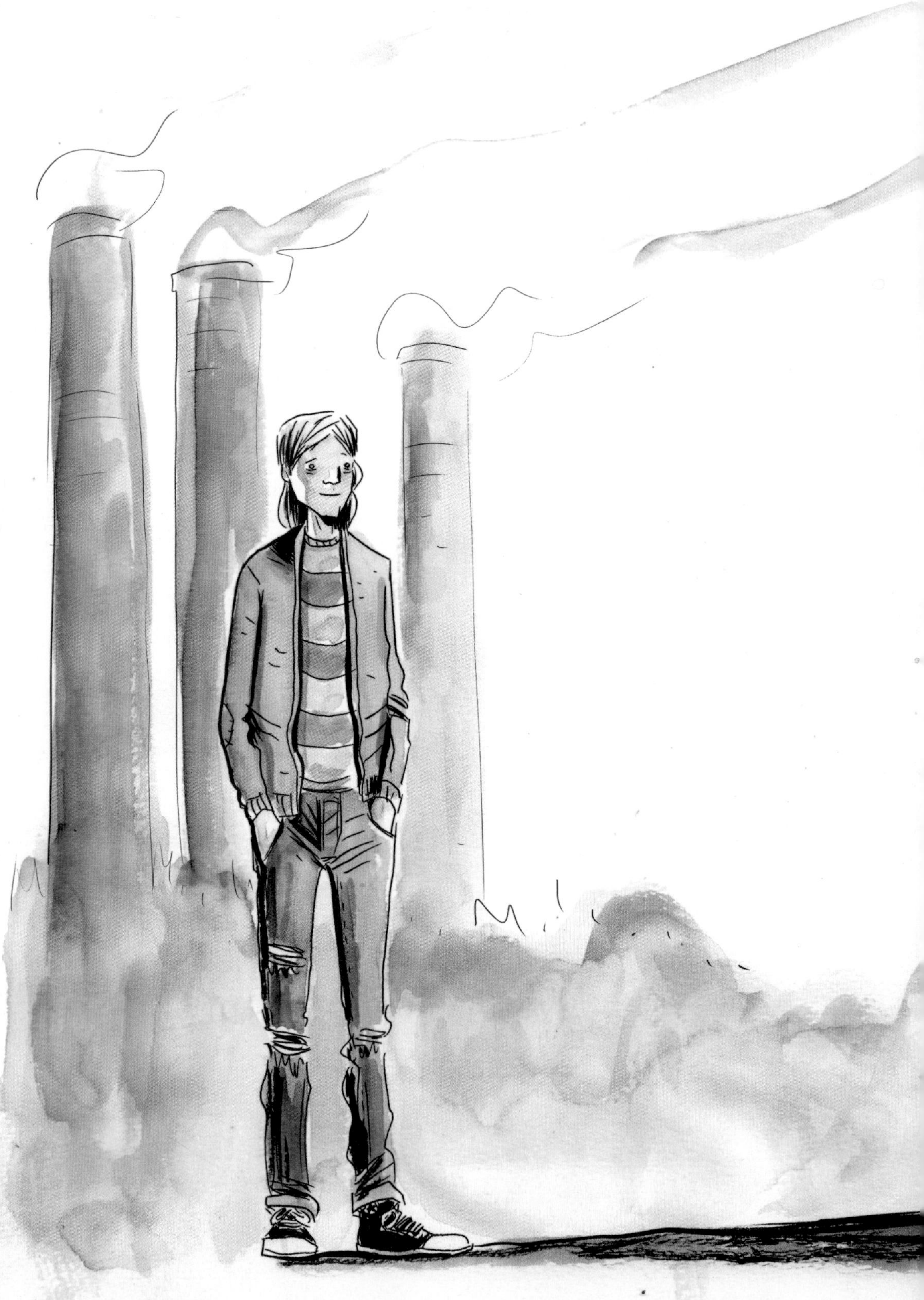